Latin America in International Politics

Latin America in International Politics

Politics

Challenging US Hegemony

Joseph S. Tulchin

LYNNE
RIENNER
PUBLISHERS

BOULDER
LONDON

Paperback published in the United States of America in 2018 by
Lynne Rienner Publishers, Inc.
1800 30th Street, Boulder, Colorado 80301
www.rienner.com

and in the United Kingdom by
Lynne Rienner Publishers, Inc.
3 Henrietta Street, Covent Garden, London WC2E 8LU

ISBN: 978-1-62637-728-8 (pb : alk. paper)

The Library of Congress catalogued the hardcover edition of this book as follows:
Names: Tulchin, Joseph S., 1939– author.
Title: Latin America in international politics: challenging US hegemony /
 by Joseph S. Tulchin.
Description: Lynne Rienner Publishers, Inc., Boulder, Colorado, 2016. |
 Includes bibliographical references.
Identifiers: LCCN 2015032480 | ISBN 9781626374485 (hc : alk. paper)
Subjects: LCSH: Latin America—Foreign relations. | Hegemony—United States.
 | Latin America—Foreign relations—United States. | United
 States—Foreign relations—Latin America.
Classification: LCC F1415 .T85 2016 | DDC 327.8073—dc23
 LC record available at http://lccn.loc.gov/2015032480

British Cataloguing in Publication Data
A Cataloguing in Publication record for the hardcover edition of this book
is available from the British Library.

Printed and bound in the United States of America

The paper used in this publication meets the requirements
of the American National Standard for Permanence of
Paper for Printed Library Materials Z39.48-1992.

5 4 3 2 1

For Sallyann,
without whose encouragement
this book would not have been completed

Contents

1

How Latin America
Sees the World

This project actually began fifty years ago when, as a graduate student, I audited a course on hemispheric relations taught by Ernest R. May. As an undergraduate, I had done some work on the Venezuelan boundary dispute with Great Britain in the nineteenth century and had come to Harvard to study diplomatic history with May. May was not a specialist on Latin America; he offered to teach the course just once as part of an effort to expand Harvard College's offerings on Latin America. He put himself through a crash course on Latin American history and fit what he learned into his own framework of how to understand international relations. In that course and in our many conversations afterward, May left me with two ideas about inter-American relations that have affected my reading and writing on the subject over the years. He also instilled in me a powerful interest in international relations theory, not typical of historians at that time. May saw theory as a source of ideas that might be fruitful and urged students of international affairs to be eclectic in using theory to explain events rather than tie themselves to a single approach into which empirical events had to be squeezed.

The first idea he left me with was that nations and national leaders might have differing perspectives on the world and that these differences, irrespective of whether they were right or wrong, affected the way policy is formulated and the way decisions are made. Furthermore, May made it clear that it was the historian's obligation to understand these differences because they could lead to very different decisions concerning the same reality. Underlying this idea is the premise that all nations understand that they are part of a larger community of nations. Although this may seem a

1

trivial observation, it is a matter of some weight to a student of Latin American history. There are clear examples in the nineteenth century—Paraguay and Guatemala are two of several—in which the country's leaders deliberately turned their nation's back to the world. There are more frequent examples—Argentina during the reign of Juan Manuel de Rosas is one—of a government simply refusing to have anything to do with another government making demands, as did the French in the River Plate in the 1830s. In none of these cases was the leader completely successful, and in all of them we can find evidence that there was at least some discussion of the wider world around them as they made the decision to isolate themselves. May's insistence that the Latin American perspective on world affairs was as valid as the US perspective was a radical proposition among mainstream students of international affairs. Surveys of US–Latin American affairs at that time by historians and by political scientists privileged the US perspective.[1] Even today, there are positivists who would find his view troubling. Some proponents of rational choice theory dismiss alternate or deviant views as less rational. May was not comfortable with that form of certitude on the part of the analyst.

In his preparation for the course, May was much influenced by Felix Gilbert, who explored the US founding fathers' understanding of their new nation's role in the world community at the time of independence.[2] May noted that he had not found any similar synthesis for any country in Latin America, which he took as evidence that the United States and the nations of Latin America were born with markedly different views of their role in the international community and what role foreign policy should play in their struggle for national stability.[3] At the same time, there were similarities, as leaders north and south were eager students of what was happening in the Western world and believed they could use this knowledge to protect their new nations' interests. North and south, they considered themselves realists who believed that nations and groups had interests that they would try to protect. At the same time, all of them talked explicitly about values they believed set them apart from other nations and in one way or another justified their rational interests.

The difference in perspective has bedeviled relations between the United States and the nations of Latin America in the two centuries and more since independence. Today, in an effort to explain this difference, Latin American critics on the left and the right have argued that the realist-idealist dichotomy in IR theory was in itself prejudicial to Latin America and an element of hegemonic control over weaker countries.[3] But the historian of hemispheric affairs knows that at independence, the United States exercised no hegemony over Latin America and it was as weak and as vulnerable as any country in the hemisphere in the early years of national independence. For that reason, it is necessary to study the difference in perspective before hegemony got in the way at the end of the nineteenth century, while recognizing that anxiety about the United States was an element in Latin American foreign affairs at least as far back as the preparations for the Congress of Panama in 1826.

It is worth noting that there is still nothing like Gilbert's book dealing with any of the proceres of Latin American independence.[4] Nor in the abundant literature of the independence period is there much discussion of how foreign policy was formulated. This book takes as one of its objectives to provide at least an outline of how to study the evolution of Latin American foreign policies from independence to the present. In doing so, I point to a set of problems that the historian can solve using tools or insights from international relations theory.[5]

The second idea May left with me was that in making decisions all actors—individuals, groups, governments—distinguish between deeply held beliefs or long-maintained patterns, which he called axioms, underlying policy and the calculated, which he saw as a reaction to opportunity and context of the moment.[6] In his view, it was entirely plausible for a government to make a calculated decision that appeared to run counter to an axiom of policy. Later in his career, May became involved in an ambitious project to teach strategic planning in a variety of graduate faculties across the country in which this distinction was the core concept.[7] In his approach to teaching strategic planning, he combined his fascination with decisionmaking, which focuses on the role of ideas and the actions of individuals, with his concern for the effect of historical memory on individual and collective thinking.[8] Whether the conflict was between states or corporations, May argued that a nation's or an individual's nightmares shape the way evidence is weighed and factors in decisionmaking are evaluated. He pointed out that these nightmares could distort or overthrow the rational calculation of interests in a specific decisionmaking situation. As we shall see, the nightmare of US hegemony and the historical legacy of anti-Americanism affect decisionmaking in Latin America today and are an important dimension in even the most scrupulously realist evaluation of factors in foreign policy decisionmaking.

To appreciate the weight of history, ask a Mexican about how the United States took half of his nation's territory. Or ask a Bolivian about the corridor to the sea, which it lost to Chile in the nineteenth century and has not stopped trying to regain. In the same fashion, people all over the hemisphere recall the US occupation of Nicaragua in the 1920s or how the United States backed a military coup against the elected government of Guatemala in the 1950s. These examples suggest that it may be as difficult for Latin Americans to shuck off the memory of anti-imperialism in formulating policy as it is for the United States to shuck off the mantle of hegemonic pretension. The "lessons" we learn from history are not always the same as those learned by the other party to the negotiations.

For Gilbert, the emphasis on process had clear and powerful ideological implications. The founding fathers wanted to be sure to distinguish themselves from the monarchical, authoritarian regimes of Europe. They considered authoritarian rulers irresponsible or even illegitimate because they represented only their own interests, not those of the people. To make sure their policy was seen as legitimate, the founding fathers insisted that it had to be the product of a democratic process in which competing interests were heard and reconciled and for which the decisionmakers would be accountable to their constituents. None of the Latin American proceres worried much about the significance of the policy process to give their decisions greater legitimacy. Simón Bolívar always was confident that he understood the will of the people, although he never spent much time verifying his understanding. The legitimacy of the policy process is an important element in the origins of the arrogance of US leaders in thinking themselves exceptional and superior to their neighbors. In the absence of such a legitimating process, leaders in Chile, Argentina, and Brazil during the nineteenth century justified their assertions of superiority over their neighbors with similar arrogance but followed positivist guides from Europe to assert their racial and cultural superiority. Just as Theodore Roosevelt and his colleagues did in the United States, Chileans, Argentines, and Brazilians insisted they were more civilized than their neighbors and therefore superior to them. The policy process did not become an important part in legitimating government action in Latin America until the transition to democracy in the 1980s and the end of the Cold War.

The role of historical memory in the policy process is by no means a fetish of historians. For many years, academics and other intellectuals referred to collective behavior as "culture," which was often a code for inferior or less modern, just as "civilized" or "modern" were used as positivist measures of success or failure, good or bad, in the nineteenth and twentieth centuries. This changed in the 1970s when progressive analysts in a variety of academic disciplines began to use the term "culture," as in "culture studies," to defend unusual or progressive points of view. Students of language and history borrowed the concept from their anthropology colleagues to justify difference without pejorative assumptions. The concept entered the IR discussion as "strategic culture" to offer clues to understanding why specific countries behaved as they did over time. Students of strategic culture traced patterns of national behavior—what May called axioms of policy—and how those patterns affect specific decisions—the ones May called calculated policies. The principal enthusiasts during the Cold War for strategic culture as a way to study international affairs were military strategists and geopoliticians.[9] May was uncomfortable with the way strategic culture came to be used because he found it inflexible. It did not provide for the way key leaders can help create strategic culture and change it. In this book, I identify individuals who were crucial to the policy process and explain how they were able to change policy over time.[10]

Another objective is to explain how, in the two centuries after independence, the recurring and persistent conflicts between the United States and Latin America have left a painful and bitter legacy that compromises efforts to achieve community in the hemisphere, even in situations when there is a broad range of shared objective interests and values and a willingness to collaborate. The historical legacy of conflict hampers efforts among Latin American nations to create effective regionalism as much as it hinders efforts to establish collaboration between the United States and Latin America. There are several examples of this in the Barack Obama administration, when counterparts in Latin America literally are not able to hear the change in rhetoric used by the president of the United States.

To untangle these problems, someone in the United States studying relations with Latin America must ensure that the Latin American perspective is taken into account. Little has been written about Latin American foreign policy before the Cold War and almost all the writing on US–Latin American relations is from the US perspective. The few books by Latin Americans dealing with inter-American relations in the twentieth century were mostly anti-US tirades.[11] One significant exception to this—and a beacon leading my journey—is a book written by my former colleague at UNC, Federico G. Gil, in which he gave as much attention to the nations of Latin America as to the United States, although he didn't give much attention to the policy process.[12] In stressing the importance of the Latin American perspective, Gil echoed May's counsel.

The next step along my road to an appreciation of the Latin American perspective was the seminar I organized with Heraldo Muñoz and the volume we edited subsequently in the 1980s, *Latin American Nations in World Politics*.[13] Muñoz's argument that no nation is without power and that the purpose of foreign policy was to make the most of the quota of power, soft or hard, available to each nation struck me with the force of an epiphany.[14] His suggestion was particularly attractive because through my own research, I was convinced that US hegemony should never be understood as total control. Even in the egregious cases of military intervention in the Caribbean Basin in the early decades of the twentieth century that I had studied, in which US forces enjoyed total dominance, I was struck by how frequently the United States was frustrated in its efforts to manipulate people who were supposed to be their puppets and how difficult it was to impose a US agenda on locals. Power should never be considered a zero-sum category in inter-American relations.[15] Muñoz indicated another dimension to the study of hegemony: it was not there in the beginning; it never was absolute, it always left wiggle room. The key, then, is to understand the perception of hegemony in Latin America and the awareness among Latin American policymakers of what wiggle room they had. In more formal language, we ask what space in the international system Latin American leaders believed they had. How they anticipated using that space is what I call the exercise of agency, which is the key concept in understanding the Latin American drive for autonomous action in the international community.[16]

I received further education in the Latin American perspective by participating in the annual meetings of RIAL, the Latin American Association of International Relations.[17] Also during the 1980s, I had opportunities to teach courses in Latin America on inter-American relations. In that context it was impossible not to take the Latin American point of view into account. The more I studied the history of Latin American international relations, the more biographies of its leaders I read, and the more I interacted with Latin American scholars and policymakers, the more I was struck by how limited were the expressions by these leaders of their sense of what agency their nations had in the international system, at least until the end of the Cold War. Muñoz's argument about the existence of power even in the weakest of nations was not obvious to many of our colleagues. Some, of course, used RIAL as a forum to express their anger with the United States and sought to paint their countries as helpless victims of hegemonic dominance. The majority was not content with anti-Americanism as an expression of foreign policy. They wanted to understand why so many countries in the region, whether governed by military regimes or by civilian regimes, put so little effort into formulating foreign policies that would protect their nation's interests.

RIAL was the origin of an epistemological community, a group interested in understanding how the nations of Latin America could define and defend their interests and exercise agency in the international system. It was a group that valued intellectual honesty and sought active participation in a larger academic community that prized theoretical sophistication. Much more than their European and US colleagues, the Latin American members of RIAL were intensely interested in how their study of international relations could help the shared concern for democracy and development. They were as interested as I was in how to stimulate agency in Latin America. This shared concern was what led me and Muñoz to put together a conference on the foreign policies of Latin American nations with participation of many of our RIAL colleagues.

In this book, I set out looking for historical evidence of agency, published writings, or recorded government discussions that a nation had a sense of its identity in the international system and that it could exercise that identity through a vast array of instruments, including what we now call soft power and values or influence.[18] Once defined, it is easy to see that articulation of agency in Latin America varied from country to country, even in the same country over time. There are few examples of such public discussion in the nineteenth century, and I discuss these in Chapter 2. Beyond these examples, there is very little expression in Latin America until the middle of the twentieth century of axioms of foreign policy and very little self-conscious discussion in the region of policy formulation, no doubt in part because legislatures and public opinion played only minor roles in governance in most countries until the second half of the twentieth century. All of this changed at the end of the Cold War.

This is in sharp contrast to the historical experience of the United States. From independence, the United States, although preoccupied with its boundaries, saw itself enmeshed in a global power system such that the local and the global were intertwined. In Latin America, the first signs of participation in the international system were acts of desperation to call on one European power to protect them from another or by calling upon the United States to protect them from European intervention. There is extremely little evidence of newly independent nations taking a proactive stance as they set out to find their way in the international system. References to a wider community up to the end of the nineteenth century were vague proposals for bringing American states closer together, which we may consider echoes of Bolivarian dreams rather than specific proposals for foreign policy. The only exceptions to this were, on the one hand, the writings of several specialists in international law who warned that the dominant powers in Europe (they included the United States only at the very end of the nineteenth century) were developing rules for international affairs that were prejudicial to the interests of Latin American countries, and, on the other hand, the writings of students of culture and literature who commented on the European sense of civilization and how far behind their countries had fallen.

The first clear example of geopolitical thinking and the assertion of agency is the Chilean war with Bolivia and Peru in the second half of the nineteenth century. The Chileans had a very clear idea of how they wanted to be in the world. They deliberately confined their aspirations to the west coast of South America. Theirs was regional agency, geographically circumscribed, and they consciously fended off threats to their hegemony in their region. The next example, chronologically, is the Brazilian definition of its foreign policy model at the end of the empire and the beginning of the republican period. The Brazilians expressed their agency by extending their borders through diplomacy while making it perfectly plain that they did not want to compete with the United States nor meddle in European politics. They saw their hegemony as regional, as did the Chileans, but the

Brazilians were not so limited geographically in their pretensions. In the case of Mexico, there were clear expressions of agency in building a defense against the French intervention in the middle of the century and in attempting to protect themselves against US encroachment at the end of the century, so that Mexican agency in the international system was defensive and continued to be so until the end of the Cold War. When the Argentines expressed their agency at the end of the nineteenth century, it was global (or at least European) but restricted almost entirely to trade and investment, so that the Argentine's sense of agency was self-restricted to specific facets of power. They were certain they had a role to play in international affairs and it involved blocking US plans for a hemispheric community while asserting their superiority to other nations in Latin America and maximizing their exchange with Great Britain and other European countries.

These early expressions of agency in Latin America, partial and self-constrained, came at a time when Alfred Thayer Mahan, Brooks Adams, Theodore Roosevelt, and others were measuring the United States against global powers and planning how to acquire the attributes of power necessary to compete with them. In the first years of the twentieth century, Argentina and Brazil purchased battleships to add to their power, but the debate in each country focused on the competition with the other, rather than as part of a Mahan-like policy to measure themselves against the world's great powers.

The relative lack of agency for so long after independence is the single most important difference between the United States and Latin America in their approaches to the world. The relative absence of agency in Latin America and the process by which agency grows and evolves in different countries is the central thread of this book's narrative. When does self-conscious agency in international affairs appear in Latin America, and what is the catalyst for its appearance? From the beginning of the twentieth century until the end of the Cold War, US hegemonic pretensions shaped inter-American relations and complicated the expression of Latin American agency. As often as not, expressions of Latin American agency in the twentieth century were framed as strategies to avoid US bullying rather than as axiomatic principles of national interest or expressions of agency in world affairs. It is not always easy to parse anti-Americanism from agency after the early years of the twentieth century. My approach is to consider anti-Americanism as a distortion of agency. That is, where it is clear the nation's leaders confined their thinking about international affairs to how to fend off the United States, foreign policy was little more than pleasing or antagonizing the United States, with little evidence of consideration of using policy as a means to maximize the nation's interests or improving the well-being of the nation's people. I consider these cases of partial agency. This is not to say that subservience or opposition to the United States were not rational policies. It suggests that in the absence of evidence that the government sought to maximize its agency through such subservience or opposition, a nation's agency cannot be complete or fully realized through such expression. The only true exception to this is Cuba after the revolution in 1959, where there is ample evidence that the nation's leaders focused their energy on protecting themselves from the United States while seeking to use their defiance of the United States to maximize their influence in the broader international system. Whether in doing so they improved the quality of life of the Cuban people has been a subject of intense debate throughout the hemisphere for many years.

My academic interest in understanding the foreign policy process and the origins of agency in Latin America got personal and very practical when I joined the Woodrow Wilson Center in 1990. The policy process was suddenly important in Latin America because of transitions to democracy. Public opinion and state accountability were front and center. The policy process always had been important in the United States, creating a sharp contrast with Latin America where the absence of process was tied to the absence of legitimacy.[19] The transition to democracy brought with it a sense of entitlement and opened the path to agency. How this agency was to be framed was the objective of a project the Wilson Center put together with Facultad Latinoamericana de Ciencias Sociales (FLACSO) in Chile.[20]

It is no shame to confess that the group of academics in this project from all over the hemisphere shared in the general euphoria after the Cold War that there was a new world order in the offing and that it would be a rules-based community centered on the United Nations and other organizations that represented the new international civil society and the inevitable international drive toward democracy.[21] We were optimists and an important part of that optimism was the expectation that the new world order would reduce or even end US hegemony in the hemisphere and that all of the nations in the hemisphere would be treated as equals. The idea was to work directly with decisionmakers, including the military and members of the legislature and press, to explore ways nations of the region might improve the policy-making process, strengthen mutual confidence, and create a sense of community in the hemisphere. We sought ways to have nations work together for common goals, become conscious of fixing their nation's policy goals, make the policy-making process more transparent, and open discussions of how they might take advantage of the transition to democracy and the end of the Cold War to insert themselves to greater advantage into the international community. Coordinating the research of this group and working closely with officials in governments throughout the hemisphere to nudge the policy process pitched a group of academics into participatory research and made us actors in the policy process.[22]

At the outset of this collaborative project, first called "Security in the Americas" and then renamed "Creating Community in the Americas," it seemed evident that the primary challenge was to bring into higher profile the opportunity for Latin American nations to have autonomous action in the international system that had opened with the end of the Cold War. This proved to be more difficult than we had anticipated. It was surprising to us how powerful a restraint was created by the heavy legacy of history on inter-American relations. On one hand, we were dismayed to see that many decisionmakers in the United States could not understand why Latin American nations wanted to maintain armed forces. Repeatedly, in the State Department, Congress, and Southern Command, we were asked why the Latin Americans simply didn't completely disarm their authoritarian militaries and enjoy the protection provided by the United States. The ideas that sovereign states wanted their own armed forces, now under civilian control, and that US hegemony was considered anathema to Latin Americans were incomprehensible to many in the US government and continues to be difficult for many to accept to this day.

On the other hand, and equally disturbing, decisionmakers in Latin America were reluctant to dedicate themselves to formulating autonomous foreign policies because they lacked the expertise to do so and were fearful that expressions of independence would antagonize the United States. The concept of collegial action in the hemisphere was not intuitively obvious. Among Latin American intellectuals and academics, there were as many who were prepared to denounce US hegemony as there were those prepared to think about what autonomy meant for their country. Few seemed able to consider both at the same time. In addition, and destructive to regional collaboration, decisionmakers appeared more interested in devoting their energies to old boundary disputes that had been put on the back burner during the Cold War and were unwilling or unable to devote much energy to exploring what role their nations might play outside the hemisphere in the larger community of nations.

The project at the Wilson Center operated on multiple fronts. We worked with decisionmakers to build confidence between them and their colleagues in other countries to discuss differences and learn what might bring them together. By virtue of our meetings with them, we increased the permeability of the states to ideas from the academic community. We aimed at the press to facilitate communication about the policy process and increase the sense of mutual accountability between the public and their representatives. Through our publications, we consciously adapted a theoretical discussion in the academic literature in Europe and the United States to the reality in Latin America and contributed to the growing debate among scholars in the region. Although the phrase "relational networks" or the term "regimes" were not in wide use when we began our efforts, it seemed logical to us that increasing points of contact among decisionmakers and their constituents and increasing the opportunities for contacts among interested parties would improve the policy process.[23]

The transition to democracy throughout Latin America in the 1980s and 1990s together with the end of the Cold War made agency more accessible to all nations. The bipolar competition of the Cold War had restricted agency through decades in which the United States forced nations to choose between alliance and subordination or be seen as in league with the Soviet Union, just as it had kept under wraps old boundary disputes and antagonisms that created animosity between states in the region and threatened the region's stability. There was little space for agency outside of the bipolar struggle, although several countries found some measure of comfort within the movement of nonaligned nations. The most effective of these efforts to create autonomy was by Costa Rica, which, under the leadership of José Figueres Ferrer, combined fierce anticommunism, which won him respect in Washington, with equally fierce support for social democracy. After the Cold War, leaders in Costa Rica leveraged this position to advance their agency in the global system, consciously building their role in world affairs on the strategic culture of neutrality in regional disputes as a liberal, pluralist democracy.[24]

Cuba was the most fully realized example of nations that set themselves against the United States and for the Soviet Union and used that position to exercise an important role for themselves in Latin America and the world outside the hemisphere (Africa in the case of Cuba) and international organizations. A more complicated example of hostility to the United States driving foreign policy is the unique pattern followed by Argentina of voting against the United States in the United Nations on 95 percent of the opportunities presented between 1950 and 1990. This pattern was maintained across civilian and military governments, Peronist governments and Radical governments, even during governments that professed support for the United States during the Cold War.[25] The behavior has a patina of agency, although a perverse form of it; it provoked more than a patina of animosity from Washington and did not win significant approbation in the region.

After the Cold War, there were efforts by former Venezuelan president Hugo Chávez to establish an alliance against the United States, which he called ALBA, the Bolivarian Alliance for the Peoples of Our America. Chávez tried to build his agency in world affairs by courting regimes that expressed their hostility to the United States, such as Iran, Russia, and Syria. Membership in ALBA is a case of partial agency or perverted agency in that the policy was formulated with the primary objective of irritating the United States, on the assumption that such irritation would enhance national interests and their influence with other countries in the region. In the cases of Cuba and Venezuela under Chávez, it certainly is agency because it is the means by which the country establishes its position in world politics. In the case of Cuba, it is clear that opposition to the United States created space for the nation in international affairs; for Venezuela, the results are less clear. For other members of ALBA—Nicaragua, Bolivia, Ecuador, and some of the islands in the Caribbean—there is little agency generated by their membership.

The same pattern of partial agency was followed by the small nations in the Caribbean Basin and Central America throughout the twentieth century with the exception of Nicaragua after 1979. Their foreign policy was focused on the United States. Foreign policy was an instrument that ruling elites used to hold on to domestic power. I refer to these cases as "penetrated polities." The government and the opposition maintained lobbies in Washington to influence the United States in their struggle for power. Only neighboring states, and then only on occasion, figured prominently in Central American foreign policy, with Costa Rica as an important exception. Discussions of foreign policy more broadly were very rare and not conducted with reference to public opinion or as part of a policy process since democratic governance was either nonexistent or extremely imperfect. This began to change when the civil wars in several Central American countries in the 1970s and 1980s provoked a public discussion of foreign policy there for the first time.[26] In addition, the new international civil society—human rights groups, international courts, aid agencies, and multilateral groups—were an important factor in stirring interest in agency in several countries in an effort to deter the militarization of their civil conflicts that had been precipitated or exacerbated by US intervention. Today, the countries of Central America constitute a spectrum of efforts to achieve agency, from the case of Costa Rica, with a fully articulated sense of its role in the international community, to Honduras and Guatemala, where interest in agency is minimal and the countries remain penetrated polities. El Salvador, Nicaragua, and Panama for very different reasons constitute a kind of middle ground in which the process of seeking agency in international affairs and making the debate over foreign policy part of the public policy discussion are just beginning. In all of the Central American countries, there is an informal alliance between those who favor expanding the space for democratic contestation and international civil society. This alliance was crucial in pushing Guatemalan president Otto Perez Molina from office in September 2015 when his government was accused of massive corruption. These groups favor stronger ties to the international community and stronger institutional organizations to bring nations together. The fact that immigration, drug trafficking, and gang violence are international in scope makes them part of the new foreign policy debate throughout the subregion.[27]

In the Caribbean, the former Anglophone colonies parlay their political stability and respect for core values into major roles in all available international organizations. The English-speaking faction forms the largest homogeneous bloc in the Organization of American States (OAS) and wields considerable influence in the United Nations. The Dominican Republic, after a long period of instability following the overthrow of the Trujillo dictatorship, has tied itself to Central America for the purposes of building international trade and attracting foreign investment. Sadly, Haiti continues its long history as an unstable, impoverished country, despite the unflagging efforts of the international donor community.

The most obvious case of the deliberate, conscious assumption of agency in South America with the objective of maximizing national interests on a global scale while taking into account the role of the United States is Chile after the transition to democracy in 1990. As it happens, the foreign policy of the Concertación government was in the hands of an extraordinary group of academic activists almost all of whom had spent time in the United States during the dictatorship and most of whom had taken advantage of their exile to earn advanced degrees. They were all active members of RIAL. These Chilenos are the heroes of the final chapters of this book. Collectively, they provided the road map away from anti-Americanism, dependence, and a sense of victimization to awareness of how to maximize national interests in world affairs. They brought the concept of soft power into the hemispheric spotlight. Without these Chilenos, I would not have a paradigmatic case to which I could point. There are other cases of agency in the period after the Cold War, and I deal with them as well. My purpose is to cover the entire process—from independence to the present—of how different countries came to see themselves in the world and how they formulated foreign policies to defend their national interests. My method will be to juxtapose the posture of the United States against those of countries in the region at different periods of history to understand better how to manage the transition from hegemony to a community of nations exercising their agency.

Most of the nations of Latin America seized the opportunity for agency presented at the end of the Cold War only timidly or in a partial manner. Even today, many of the Latin American nations remain passive or uncertain participants in the wider international community. In the past decade Mexico has moved with confidence to play a role in the international system, although dealing with the scourge of drug trafficking, with its accompanying patterns of corruption and impunity, is a powerful constraint. Since the 1990s, Brazil has asserted a role as a major power but has been uncertain as to how that role might be exercised. Venezuela, through ALBA, has led an effort to create an anti-American regional organization, but it has very little in the way of a positive agenda and has lost influence since the death of Chávez in 2013. More promising is the movement for "post-hegemonic" regionalism (UNASUR and CELAC) with the exclusion of the United States as a form of collective agency. It is too early in the process to judge the success of this new regionalism, except to say that to create regional organizations without the United States is further evidence that anti-US feeling is still a powerful driver of foreign policy thinking in Latin America and organizations founded to spite the United States have no clear rules to guide the community.

Globalization is pushing all of the nations in the region toward more active roles in the world; all are in the world to a greater degree than at any time in their history. Globalization has empowered the expanding epistemological community concerned with international affairs. Spawned and nurtured by RIAL, there is now a second generation of students of international relations who are intensely concerned with the policy process and are fully informed about the activities of their counterparts in other countries. Mexico and Brazil are remarkable for the effusion of publications in the field, websites that carry debates on foreign policy, and ambitious projects to make government documents available to the public online.[28] Chile and Argentina have also conducted massive projects to put public documents online. More and more, Latin American scholars are participating in professional discussions of matters of common interest with colleagues in the United States and Europe.[29]

In methodological terms, my primary concern is to provide the historical narrative necessary to describe the emergence of agency in the nineteenth century and the emergence of US hegemony at the turn of the nineteenth and twentieth centuries. Thereafter, the concern is how the nations in Latin America dealt with that hegemony. Once the Cold War ended and the transition to democracy occurred in Latin America, the focus widens to include the policy process and how the new democracies used public debate of policy to empower and legitimate their agency, just as the founding fathers had done in the United States two centuries earlier. The early episodes of agency in Latin America unfold with limited public discussion and a mix of realist and idealist proposals. After the Cold War, the predominant approach is neorealist or liberal with great attention paid to soft power, along with a growing concern with how to create and participate in relational networks as the best means of defending national interests. The more developed the agency, as in Chile, the more flexible and eclectic the approach to projecting power and protecting interests. Through the historical narrative I provide the perspectives of both the United States and major nations in Latin America. Throughout I pay attention to leaders and to the decisionmaking process. Nuance and subtlety make the narrative more complex, the better to reflect a complex reality.

In the final chapter, I wrestle with the dilemma of how the nations of Latin America are coming to terms with the legacy of US hegemony in the hemisphere. The mirror image of this dilemma is how the United States deals with a new geopolitical moment in which pretensions to hegemony are counterproductive. Yet, hegemonic or otherwise, the United States will be the most powerful nation in the hemisphere for the foreseeable future and relations between it and Latin America will continue to be asymmetrical in terms of national power. Is it possible in these new conditions to think of a hemispheric community of nations? The historical narrative ends with the decision by the United States and Cuba to restore normal relations. Nothing President Barack Obama could have done would be a more powerful symbol that his government, at last, was prepared to enter the posthegemonic era. By that decision and in his speech at the VII Summit of the Americas in April 2015, he invited the nations of the hemisphere to join him in the march into the future. The response from Latin America was more a babel than applause.

Notes

1. Perhaps the paradigmatic example of this hubris is Samuel F. Bemis, *The Latin American Policy of the United States* (New York: Harcourt, Brace, 1943).

2. Felix Gilbert, *To the Farewell Address: Ideas of Early American Foreign Policy* (Princeton: Princeton University Press, 1961).

3. Marxist and neo-Marxist writers take this view as does Carlos Escudé, *Realismo periférico* (Buenos Aires: Planeta, 1992); and *Foreign Policy Theory in Menem's Argentina* (Gainesville: University Press of Florida, 1997). Escudé refers to the academic debate as Anglo-American IR theory. He has harsh words for rational choice theory.

4. This is beginning to change. Mexican academics, with the full cooperation of the Foreign Ministry, are beginning to publish online a mammoth collection of documents and studies based on those documents. Scholars in Argentina, Brazil, and Chile

over the past decade have produced revisionist histories of the early national period that deal with foreign relations. Together with growing academic interest in international relations, this should lead soon to the production of such a synthesis. I deal with this growing interest in foreign affairs in Chapter 7.

5. One recent example of an attempt to do this is Max Paul Friedman and Tom Long, "Soft Balancing in the Americas: Latin American Opposition to U.S Intervention," *International Security*, Summer 2015, which explores late nineteenth century efforts to avoid US hegemony within a theoretical framework.

6. Ernest R. May, "The Nature of Foreign Policy: The Calculated Versus the Axiomatic," *Daedalus* 91.4 (1962): 653–668. Others draw the distinction between strategy and tactics; some have used the concept of strategic culture to get at the distinction between deeply felt and long-held values or long-term goals and reactions to the moment as drivers of decision making and policy. More recently, in Latin America, people refer to *políticas de estado* to suggest policies formed on the basis of wide consensus, above the interests of a single party or government.

7. I participated in such a course in the business school of the University of North Carolina at Chapel Hill. Other faculties in which the course was taught were law, arts and sciences, environmental studies, and fine arts. My colleague Otis L. Graham Jr. summarized our experience in Otis L. Graham Jr., "The Uses and Misuses of History: Roles in Policymaking," *Public Historian* 5.2 (1983).

8. For example, Ernest R. May, *"Lessons" of the Past: The Use and Misuse of History in American Foreign Policy* (London: Oxford University Press, 1973); and Richard E. Neustadt and Ernest R. May, *Thinking in Time: The Uses of History for Decision Makers* (New York: Free Press, 1986). The influence May had on his Kennedy School colleague Graham T. Allison is obvious in *The Essence of Decision* (New York: Little, Brown, 1971), which he reissued in a second edition, with Philip Zelikow, using tapes from the Kennedy decisionmaking sessions not available for the first ed. May explored the format in an earlier book on executive decisionmaking, *The Ultimate Decision* (New York: George Braziller, 1960).

9. Yosef Lipid and F. V. Kratochwil, eds., *The Return of Culture and Identity to IR Theory* (Boulder, CO: Lynne Rienner, 1996); C. S. Gray, "Strategic Culture as Context: The First Generation of Theory Strikes Back," *Review of International Studies* 25.1 (1999); S. Pore, "What Is the Context?," *Review of International Studies* 29.2 (2003); J. S. Lantis, "Strategic Culture and National Security Policy," *International Studies Review* 4.3 (2003). For an example of how the US Southern Command used strategic culture as a way to understand the foreign policy of Latin American nations, see the various publications of Florida International University, Strategic Culture, available online at http://www.arc.fiu.edu. Critics of strategic culture consider it a sloppy way to build dense analysis without real historical or anthropological research.

10. José Figueres and the Baron of Rio Branco are two such leaders who are discussed in Chapters 3 and 4.

11. See, as an example, Eduardo Galeano, *Las venas abiertas de America Latina* (Buenos Aires: Siglo XXI, 1971); an English edition appeared in 1973. Curiously, in an interview just before his death in 2015, Galeano disavowed his book (*New York Times*, April 14, 2015, A17). For a more general analysis of anti-Americanism in Latin America, see Stephen Haseler, *The Varieties of Anti-Americanism: Reflex and Response* (Washington, DC: Ethics and Public Policy Center, 1985); Mariano Aguirre and Ana Montes, eds., *De Bolivar al Frente Sandinista: Antología del pensamiento anti-imperialista latinoamericana* (Madrid: Ediciones de la Torre, 1979).

12. Federico G. Gil, *Latin American–United States Relations* (New York: Harcourt Brace, 1971). Gil sidestepped the question of hegemony because he did not want to get involved with its mirror image, the sense of victimization in Latin America. As

indicated, the interest among Latin American scholars in the history of international affairs has grown significantly in the past two decades.

13. Heraldo Muñoz and Joseph S. Tulchin, eds., *Latin American Nations in World Politics* (Boulder, CO: Westview Press, 1984); there are Spanish and Portuguese editions of this volume as well as a second edition. I met Muñoz through Gil and published his article on strategic interdependence while I was editor of *Latin American Research Review*. Muñoz went on to become foreign minister of Chile under President Michele Bachelet in 2014.

14. Muñoz began with a critique of dependency theory as distorting foreign policy in "Cambio y continuidad en el debate sobre dependencia," *Estudios Internacionales* 11.44 (1978): 88–138. His argument on power as greater than zero is in "The Strategic Dependency of the Centers and the Economic Importance of the Latin American Periphery," *Latin American Research Review* 16.3 (1981): 3–29.

15. Joseph S.Tulchin, *The Aftermath of War* (New York: NYU Press, 1971).

16. Agency is a concept used across a wide range of social science disciplines. My use has its origins in psychology, where it refers to an individual's sense of his or her capacity for action. It assumes that action takes place within the constraints of an institution, a group, or a system. It implies consciousness and will. It makes no assumptions as to power or capacity.

17. RIAL played a vital role in bringing international relations theory to Latin America. Several key players did their graduate work in the United States and then brought their learning home with them. This collective effort was an important part of the transition from the Cold War to a new period of inter-American relations and I deal with it again in Chapters 4, 5, and 6.

18. The concept of soft power was introduced by Joseph S. Nye Jr. and Robert O. Keohane, *World Politics in Transition* (New York: Little, Brown, 1977).

19. The absence of legitimacy and process during the military dictatorships of the 1970s and 1980s and the semi-authoritarian regimes of Central America throughout the twentieth century are treated in subsequent chapters.

20. The codirector of the project was Augusto Varas, later replaced with Francisco Rojas. During the Chilean dictatorship, Varas earned his doctorate in the United States in sociology from Washington University in St. Louis. Others who worked with us were Rut Diamint, (Argentina), Cristina Eguizabal (El Salvador), Raul Benitez (Mexico), Lilian Bobea (Dominican Republic), and Tomas Guedes da Costa (Brazil). Others who collaborated over the years were Luis Bitencourt, Ricardo Sennes, Ricardo Cordova, Luis Guillermo Solís, and Carlos Basombrio.

21. This euphoria is described in detail in Chapter 6.

22. The products of this project were a series of bulletins, more than a dozen books, and nearly a hundred meetings among decisionmakers and academics. All of the publications, including reports on the meetings, are on the Wilson Center website (http://www.wilsoncenter.org).

23. The first offshoot from this project was one directed by Rut Diamint that focused on communication between the military and the press and on the broader question of civil control over the military, "La cuestión cívico-militar en las nuevas democracias latinoamericanas." It produced a number of publications listed in the bibliography. Our interest in the policy process spawned another project at the Wilson Center that encouraged graduate studies programs in public policy at several universities. See Joan Dassin, Joseph S. Tulchin, and Amelia Brown, eds., "Training a New Generation of Leaders, Woodrow Wilson Center Reports on the Americas #3" (Washington, DC: Wilson Center, n.d.)

24. The strategic culture of Costa Rica is discussed in greater detail in Chapter 6.

25. Daniel Klickoff, "La historia de la experiencia de Argentina en las Naciones

Unidas," study prepared for Minister Guido di Tella, Ministerio de Relaciones Exteriores, 1994, manuscript in the possession of the author .

26. Exceptions are the cases of Nicaragua in the Sandino episode in the 1920s and Guatemala in the 1950s.

27. These issues have come to be called "intermestic" because they are at once local and international.

28. These studies are cited in detail in Chapters 6 and 7. Guadalupe González González in Mexico, Luis Maira in Chile and Mexico, and José Augusto Guilhon Albuquerque in Brazil are just a few of the major players in this new development. Maira was the prime mover in refounding RIAL in 2014 as the Council on International Relations of Latin America and the Caribbean.

29. Jorge I. Domínguez and Ana Covarrubias, eds., *Routledge Handbook of Latin America in the World* (New York: Routledge, 2015) is just one outstanding example of the fruitful exchange among scholars in the region.

2

From Empire
to Independence

Although it may appear to be an oversimplification, it is nevertheless true that the United States and the new nations in Latin America began their independent existence with markedly different approaches to the world around them. There were some similarities, but the differences tell the tale and provide the foundation for an understanding of the 200 years of hemispheric relations with such different attitudes and approaches to international affairs.

It is easier to begin with the similarities. All of the nations in the hemisphere began as colonies. At one time or another after the first voyages of discovery in the fifteenth and early sixteenth centuries, the British, Danes, Dutch, French, Portuguese, and Spanish established colonies in what the Europeans referred to as the New World. Some of the colonies were ephemeral or of little moment in the history of the region; others were significant for considerable periods of time. The big three—the United Kingdom, Spain, and Portugal—were the principal imperial powers over the longest period of time and left their stamp on the territories they occupied.

From the very beginning of the imperial adventures, the three major powers had different ambitions and very different degrees of success in establishing their control over the territory they claimed. The Spanish were the most ambitious and extended their control over the largest territory. They also dealt with the largest and most organized indigenous population. Both in the north, in the area around Mexico, and in the south, in the region around the Andean high plateau of Bolivia and Peru, the Spanish dealt with and conquered major civilizations with hierarchical governments and active trade networks that covered huge distances. They concentrated their efforts on the areas in Mexico and the altiplano, where they came upon mineral resources of great value. In these mining regions, they established their control over land and labor they deemed essential in exploiting the resources they wanted to turn into imperial income.

The British, in contrast, had to deal with relatively small communities of indigenous people, some of whom were semi-nomadic and had formed relatively thin connections among tribes or nations, as they called themselves. When the British in the eighteenth century and the Americans in the nineteenth century encountered organized resistance from settled groups, such as the Cherokee Nation, they chose to expel—or extirpate, as Thomas Jefferson put it—them rather than subjugate them within the colonial or national territory. The interest of the Americans as colonists or as citizens of their new country was to settle territory. The labor-intensive economic activity on the cotton and rice plantations or the tobacco farms was handled by slave labor imported from Africa or, in a small minority of the cases and only up to the eighteenth century, by indentured laborers imported from Great Britain.

In the Spanish colonies, the land itself and the agricultural production of that land was considered less important than mining, although the administrative structure the Spanish created could deal with both. From the imperial perspective, agriculture in the colonies was important primarily as the food supply necessary to keep the mining operations going, to feed the small urban populations in the ports and administrative centers and maintain the indigenous population. The export of agricultural commodities, such as cacao in Venezuela or coffee in Central America, or other surpluses that might be exported—always with the exception of sugar in the Caribbean Basin and Brazil—was given less priority than mineral exports, especially gold and silver.

By the eighteenth century the relative lack of administrative attention given to agriculture produced a thriving contraband trade of such magnitude in the River Plate and Venezuela that the majority of the agricultural surplus was exported illegally. Even the money crop of cacao in Venezuela, considered an important source of profit for the monopoly trading company in Cadiz and licensed by the Crown, was exported as contraband, depriving the trading company of its profit and the Crown of its share of the revenue. The contraband trade in the eighteenth century had the unanticipated consequence of putting the local merchants in touch with traders from countries other than Spain, specifically the British and their banker friends both in Venezuela and in the River Plate.

Here the contrast with the northern settlements is clear and of lasting significance. There were no mining establishments of major value in the north, and the agricultural surplus production in the first two centuries of colonization was not crucial to the British treasury and never fell completely under imperial administrative control. Furthermore, the British colonizing adventure was not accompanied by an established church that complemented the imperial mandate. To the contrary, several of the earliest settlements in North America were founded by religious dissidents seeking to get out from under the established church and urging religious tolerance as a part of settlement culture.

These factors contributed to the relative importance in the northern colonies of local rule and of a widespread sense of empowerment among creoles, who believed that they were able and entitled to make their own rules and enforce them, in the organization of their economic activity and in how they chose to structure their communities. It is true that local government, especially in the form of the *cabildo* or town council, became central to economic and political activity in the Spanish colonies in the eighteenth century, but local government in the Spanish colonies differed from its counterpart in the British colonies in the degree to which the imperial power recognized and accepted local institutions under creole control. Spanish administrative authority was spread over an enormous territory, but in the vast areas distant from mines, ports, or administrative centers, that control was thin.

More important, and central to the movements for independence, local governments in the north were knit together with government administration within larger territorial units and across units. This enabled British creoles to derive power from those linkages, whereas in the south the growth of power in cabildos came in spite of Spanish efforts to control them, especially in the eighteenth century; for the most part, cabildos could not extend their power over larger administrative jurisdictions, nor was there effective networking among viceroyalties or intendencies. The relative isolation of the cabildos in Spanish America complicated the effort after the wars for independence to establish coherent nation-states with clear boundaries and legitimate authorities.

By the middle of the eighteenth century, there was a considerable population of settlers throughout the hemisphere who considered themselves part of new countries and committed their lives and their property to making a go of it in the new world. As control over daily life became more localized in these areas, the mother country tried to tighten its administrative grip through a set of administrative reforms in the second half of the eighteenth century. These reform efforts enjoyed partial success, but they never overcame the centrifugal force of local power brokers and never brought agricultural exports under imperial control. The British tried to extract more tax revenue from the colonists in America, and that proved to be extremely problematic.

Perhaps the biggest strategic mistake the British made in their effort to control colonial territories in the Western Hemisphere was to get the colonists involved in the dynastic wars that were so much a part of the European experience. This proved to be the single most powerful influence on the British colonists' view of the world and made it clear to them that being part of the British Empire could be a terrible disadvantage. The personal experience of George Washington, a large landowner in Virginia and a powerful politician in the colony, is a model for the evolution of thinking in the colonies as to what their worldview should be as they moved inexorably toward independence. As befit his status, Washington was the chief of a local militia. As such, he held the rank of colonel in the British army. When the British and French went to war in 1754 as part of the Seven Years' War, they extended the hostilities to the Western Hemisphere and each tried to expand their holdings in North America at the expense of the other and their allies among the Indian tribes. Washington led his troops into what became Ohio and Pennsylvania and participated in a number of engagements, all of which he considered a waste of time, money, and blood. In letters to his wife, Martha, he complained that this was not a conflict in which the people of Virginia had a part. It was the idle, avaricious royals in Europe who treated the colonies as if they were puppets, pawns, or property and not people with legitimate interests of their own.[1]

Washington took two lessons from this experience, which he shared with an entire generation of leaders. The first was that real danger comes from those who do not share your interests but are physically closest to you—the lesson of propinquity. The second was that the leaders of European monarchies could not be trusted because they had at heart only the interest of the monarchy, which, perforce, did not take into account the interests of their subjects. Worse, these rulers were not accountable to their subjects and did not tell them the truth—the lesson of authoritarian perfidy.[2] It was not until 1754 that there appeared a discussion of a possible community that would be larger than any of the colonies and encompass them. This Albany Plan passed from public attention as the danger presented in the war receded.

Washington shared with his generation a sense that all people had interests and that it was legitimate to defend those interests. This was a rational approach to political action and a realist's perspective on public affairs. How competing or conflicting interests might be accommodated in a larger community was central to James Madison's concerns in writing the *Federalist Papers*. His coauthor, Alexander Hamilton, was even more of a realist and saw that the colonies were valuable in the European balance of power and should use this fact as a lever to maximize the new nation's interests. In his Farewell Address, Washington discussed this issue and encouraged his compatriots to deal with other nations but to be wary. He warned them to avoid "entangling alliances." Interests might be strategic; alliances should be ephemeral, calculated, or tactical. In drafting what was his political testament, Washington asked Madison and Hamilton to edit the draft.

The debate over foreign policy continued through the war for independence from Great Britain and after. The earliest stages of the debate produced two results that highlight the contemporaneous differences with Latin America. First, the concern for accountability and the sense of disagreement among the new nation's leaders led to a focus on process. Policy should be the result of a transparent discussion—an accommodation of interests in Madison's terms—and should be reported to the people and their representatives. It was important that foreign policy not be improvised. The second feature of the early debate that resonates to the current day is that it blended two very different perspectives on the international community, what scholars call the idealist or liberal and the realist perspectives, into a powerful sense of exceptionalism, which carried heavy overtones of religious conviction. The notion that the United States was a great experiment and should share its new vision of the world with others was extremely important and continued to have its expression in US foreign policy.[3] This idealism was present in the argument over how the new nation should make its way in the global community: either by emphasizing its isolation from the corrupting influences of Europe or by insisting on its unique role in world affairs. Washington's Farewell Address indicates that this debate was far from settled when he left office, and his advice was designed to take both perspectives into account.

North and south, the sense of belonging to a larger community produced different modes of organization in the struggle for independence, different modes of diplomatic action, different international strategies, and different international goals. These differences, despite the fact that north and south, founding fathers or proceres were aware of the discussions in Europe, especially those surrounding the English and French Revolutions and the Enlightenment. Ideas about international affairs, such as alliances, treaties, power, and the like, were European in origin and available to the literate in South and North America. At the end of the eighteenth century, there was an intense surge of activity in Spain to bring Enlightenment thinking to its colonies.[4] The difference between the colonies was not in their knowledge of the world; it was in how they used that knowledge and applied it to their experience.

There is no experience in Latin America parallel to Washington's campaign in the French and Indian War, although the European dynastic struggles certainly had territorial consequences in the Caribbean. In South

America, conflicts between the Portuguese and Spanish affected frontiers between them, as in Uruguay and the Jesuit missions of Paraguay. Several leaders of the independence movements in Latin America had European experience, but none brought home anything like Washington's sense of alienation from European struggles. Still, they were rationalists and realists in matters of politics, with differing admixtures of idealism, generally focused on the French Revolution. In the River Plate, creoles were caught up in the imperial struggle between Portugal and Spain for control of the Banda Oriental (Uruguay), the frontier between them. This experience emboldened creoles who lived in Uruguay and pushed José Gervasio Artigas and his fellows along the road to independence from both, an evolution the British were only too happy to facilitate. The Argentines also experienced a short-lived invasion by British troops, which they beat back with local militia. Although there are similarities between these two cases and Washington's experience, neither of them led to a cohort using their experience to formulate a sense of how a new nation with its own view of the world might be formed out of the conflicts.

The majority of direct involvement of Spanish colonists in the dynastic struggles in Europe took place in the Caribbean Basin, especially in the ports of Havana, Santo Domingo, and Cartagena. The British ended up with control of Jamaica, and the French took over the island of Hispaniola. Pirates also bombarded ports, and it is clear that the British were behind some of these adventures, although territorial control does not appear to have been their objective. They were after spoils. None of this left an enduring mark on the internationalism of the process.

The leaders of the independence movements in Latin America began their efforts with a clear understanding of the US experience. Several of them, such as Francisco Miranda, used the US model and support from people in the United States to launch their efforts to create separate nations independent of Spanish imperial control. Simón Bolívar used foreign support, and leaders in Argentina and Chile framed their efforts in the context of their understanding of the international system through discussions of how to secure material and diplomatic aid from European powers. Aside from these short-term appeals for support, what we might call the foreign policy of the independence movements was framed more in terms of the universalist notion of a brotherhood of humanity, taken from the French Revolution, rather than a more specific sense of how they and their local supporters might create a place in the international system. The independence movements began by declaring their allegiance to the Crown as opposed to Spain, taking advantage of the Napoleonic invasion of Spain as their excuse to define their own, local systems of governance.[5]

By 1810, all of the major cities in Latin America had created governments independent of Spanish control. It was hoped that the legitimacy of the cabildo would serve as the basis for new states. The independence struggles, however, soon demonstrated that the early notions of community would not stand and that power would be more local than they had anticipated. Only the movement led by José Artigas in Uruguay achieved a territorial settlement at the end of the armed struggle that matched the goals of the movement at its outset.[6] Perhaps more significant, no putative nation in Latin America succeeded in signing a formal treaty with any other country, in Europe or America, to buttress their armed struggle. The contrast with the United States in this facet of how to deal with the outside world is stark. The United States, while considering itself weak and vulnerable, succeeded in inserting itself to its strategic advantage into the balance of power politics of Europe. No independence movement in South America, also feeling itself weak and vulnerable, came close to this goal.

The struggles for independence in Latin America also differed from the experience in the United States in the concern for the rights and participation of nonwhite elements in the population, whether indigenous or African American. Although the results varied from region to region, in all of Latin America the rights of these marginal populations were broader as a result of the struggle for independence than they were in the United States, where the slavery of African Americans was institutionalized in the new nation and became the principal issue that divided states in a civil war later. The indigenous and African descendants in Latin America, except for the Caribbean sugar islands and Brazil, while never equal to the creole and peninsular elites, were at least not part of an enslaved minority without rights. They were included in the ongoing debate over citizenship, which was seen as one of the principal goals of independence. In this, as in many things, the Latin American precursors were much more influenced than their North American colleagues by the universalist concepts of the French Revolution, such as the rights of man, and these principles shaped their thinking about citizenship, rights, and modernity.[7] It also provided a framework for thinking about international community. For people who believed in the brotherhood of man, it followed that there would be or should be a collective or brotherhood of nations, nations of freed people and citizens. In the United States, race and racism played an important part of the discussion of expansion, community, and hegemony.[8]

Aside from Bolívar's amphictyonic meeting in Panama, 1826, there is very little evidence of agency in the foreign relations of the first generation after independence. In striking contrast with the United States, there was little sense that formulating foreign policy should be done in a transparent manner that would be accountable to the citizens for whom it was to be formulated. In this, the leaders of the Latin American independence movements did not seek to avoid the trap of authoritarian policy formulation.

Yet for the most part, they were realists in foreign policy and had an excellent grasp of international affairs. From Gran Colombia to the River Plate, everyone seemed to have a friend at Baring Brothers, the British bank that was most energetic in making loans to the new republics. Some of the leaders showed an awareness of how international trade and investment would help stabilize the new countries.

Of course, one of the reasons it is hard to find a coherent foreign policy among the new nations is that their territorial limits were mercurial throughout the independence period. Gran Colombia ended up as three separate countries—Venezuela, Colombia, and Ecuador. Argentina did not establish its borders until it had suffered military defeat in its efforts to incorporate the areas now known as Bolivia, Paraguay, and Uruguay. Peru shared a similar experience, as it attempted to incorporate Bolivia and parts of northern Chile without success. The border between Chile and Peru was the focus of an armed conflict at the end of the nineteenth century, the War of the Pacific. Although Chile won that war decisively and took the chunks of Peru it coveted, the border was not finally settled until the International Court of Justice determined the maritime boundary between them in January 2014.[9]

During the years in which Argentina lost nearly half of the territory it aspired to, the United States was acquiring the Louisiana Territory and Florida and had settled its northern boundary with Canada. A few years later, the United States went to war with Mexico and took half of that country's territory.[10] These adventures were part of a debate over whether to incorporate new territory into the union or conduct relations with states that shared core values with the United States. It was a debate that began with typical civility and wisdom between Jefferson and Madison, both in retirement, in the 1820s. Madison was leery of taking in new territories, especially those formerly in the Spanish Empire. He did not believe that the republican mode of government was suitable to such large geographical units.[11] Carrying the thinking of the *Federalist Papers* into the new age, he did not see how legitimate interests could be negotiated and reconciled in a unit that had become too large. He did, however, agree with Jefferson that the United States had something to offer the rest of the Americas. Jefferson hoped for the day when there would be a league of republics in the hemisphere. Madison agreed and anticipated that "The Eagle of Liberty would carry freedom in its talons to the new countries in the [hemisphere.]"[12]

On the other side of the border, Bolívar also envisioned a union of republics, a community among all of the newly independent nations of South America. Exactly what he had in mind is still a matter of debate.[13] He saw the United States as aggressive and did not like its expansionist drives. Nor did he appreciate the preening confidence that the United States considered itself God's gift to the rest of humanity. Still, he realized that cooperation with the United States was necessary. There was some debate between him and his second-in-command, Francisco de Paula Santander, over whether to invite the United States to the community conference in Panama in 1826. Bolívar thought it might offend the British to include its former colony; Santander considered it vital to include any country that might help the new nations defend themselves against possible attack by the Spanish. Bolívar shared with the founding fathers a distrust of tyrannical governments not accountable to their people, although in practice he had no patience for accounting to the people he governed. He said that so long as Mexico and Brazil remained monarchies, they could not join the federation, although they were to be considered equals to the members of the federation of republics. Although there were no practical results of the congress of Panama, it remains—and the Bolivarian dream remains—a powerful concept to many in Latin America. It is referenced at virtually all community meetings, including the meeting of the new regional organization, CELAC (Community of Latin American and Caribbean States), in Havana in January 2014.

Discussion and debate over the years as to what sort of community might bring the new nations of the hemisphere together never had the power in the north that it did in the south and wasn't used as a prop for policy objectives in US dealings with Latin America.[14] How strange, then, that the first serious effort to create an inter-American institution or organization, with an office and mandate to do things, begins with a US initiative in the 1880s to create a customs union in the hemisphere, the Pan American Union.

If the Amphictyonic Congress of Panama marks the end of the independence period in Latin America—an ending on a sad note because of its meager outcome—the end in the United States is President James Monroe's State of the Union to Congress in 1823, known as the Monroe Doctrine. It marks the end of the independence period because it refers specifically to Washington's Farewell Address, and it better reflects the foreign policy of the eighteenth century rather than the nineteenth. It proposes no action, positive or negative, and offers no support to the nations that felt themselves threatened by European powers. That defensive posture was as far as domestic politics in the United States would allow the executive to go.[15] It is therefore an irony of history that Monroe's message became the symbol of US aggressive pretension toward Latin America. So powerful is the symbol that Secretary of State John Kerry felt it necessary to declare in his speech to the Organization of American States (OAS) in December 2013 that the Monroe Doctrine no longer was the policy of the United

States. None of the Latin American representatives in the audience believed him. The history of inter-American relations in the nearly 200 years after Monroe's message explains their skepticism.

Notes

1. Felix Gilbert, *To the Farewell Address: Ideas of Early American Foreign Policy* (Princeton, NJ: Princeton University Press, 1961), chapter 4. A recent biography of Washington emphasizes this experience; Robert Middlekauff, *Washington's Revolution: The Making of America's First Leader* (New York: Knopf, 2015).

2. It is worth noting that this distrust of authoritarian, unaccountable rulers did not prevent dealing with such rulers in the next 200 years if it served some greater, short-term strategic interest. For example, Theodore Roosevelt had no trouble dealing with the unelected leaders of the Panamanian independence movement because he considered it necessary to clear the way to construct the Panama Canal. Later, several administrations put their democratic concerns behind them to collaborate with authoritarian rulers to maintain stability in the Caribbean Basin. In World War II, the war effort was the overriding concern. Afterward, anticommunism trumped any concerns for democratic values, whether it was dealing with Anastasio Somoza DeBayle in Nicaragua or the Argentine generals who were "disappearing" their own people in staggering numbers.

3. On the role of ideology and identity in foreign policy, see Michael H. Hunt, *Ideology and US Foreign Policy*, 2nd ed (New Haven, CT: Yale University Press, 2009); Walter L. Hixson, *The Myth of American Diplomacy: National Identity and US Foreign Policy* (New Haven, CT: Yale University Press, 2008). The debate among students of the subject is summarized in Michael Hogan and Thomas Paterson, eds., *Explaining the History of American Foreign Relations*, 2nd ed (New York: Cambridge University Press, 2004). On the religious elements of US exceptionalism, see Andrew Preston, *Sword of the Spirit, Shield of Faith: Religion in American War and Diplomacy* (New York: Anchor, 2012). Even agnostics like Jefferson and Madison saw the hand of some deity in US exceptionalism.

4. Robert J. Shafer, *The Economic Societies in the Spanish World, 1763–1825* (Syracuse, NY: Syracuse University Press, 1956).

5. John C. Chasteen, *Americanos* (New York: Oxford University Press, 2008).

6. Chasteen describes this episode in *Heroes on Horseback* (Albuquerque: University of New Mexico Press, 1995).

7. James A. Wood, *The Society of Equality: Popular Republicanism and Democracy in Santiago de Chile, 1818–1851* (Albuquerque: University of New Mexico Press, 2011); Hilda Sabato, ed., *Ciudadanía política y formación de las naciones* (Mexico: Fondo de Cultura Económica, 2002); Hilda Sábato, "On Political Citizenship in Nineteenth-Century Latin America," *American Historical Review*, 106.4 (2004): 1290–1315; Peter Guardino, *Peasants, Politics, and the Formation of Mexico's National State: Guerrero, 1800–1857* (Stanford, CA: Stanford University Press, 1996); Sarah Chambers, *From Subjects to Citizens: Honor, Gender and Politics in Arequipa, Peru, 1780–1854* (State College: Pennsylvania State University Press, 1999); Florencia Mallon, *Peasant and Nation: The Making of Postcolonial Mexico and Peru* (Berkeley: University of California Press, 1994).

8. Among many, see Eric T. L. Love, *Race over Empire: Racism and US Imperialism, 1865–1900* (Chapel Hill: University of North Carolina Press, 2004); Jonathan Rosenberg, *How Far the Promised Land? World Affairs and the American Civil Rights*

Movement from the First World War to Vietnam (Princeton, NJ: Princeton University Press, 2005); and Paul A. Kramer, *The Blood of Government: Race, Empire, the United States and the Philippines* (Chapel Hill: University of North Carolina Press, 2006).

9. The border between Bolivia and Chile, unsettled by the same war, is still in consideration by the International Court of Justice.

10. R. A. Billington, *Western Expansion* (New York: Macmillan, 1949).

11. Both Madison and Bolívar looked to the Greeks as a model, but drew very different conclusions.

12. Jefferson-Madison correspondence, Jefferson to Madison, November 19, 1823, in James Morton Smith, ed., *The Republic of Letters: The Corrspondence between Thomas Jefferson and James Madison, 1776–1826*, 3 vols (New York: Norton, 1995). See also, Monroe to Madison, August 2, 1824, and Wilkinson to Jefferson, March 21, 1824.

13. German A. de la Reza, "The Formative Platform of the Congress of Panama (1810–1826): The Pan-American Conjecture Revisted," *Revista brasileira de politica internacional* 56.1 (2013); Francisco Cuevas Cancino, *Bolívar el ideal panamericano del libertador* (Mexico: Fondo de Cultura, 1951).

14. Arthur P. Whitaker, *The Western Hemisphere Idea* (Ithaca, NY: Cornell University Press, 1954).

15. E. R. May, *The Monroe Doctrine* (Cambridge, MA: Harvard University Press, 1975) is a complete study of how domestic politics and foreign policy came together in the preparation of the message to Congress. The most exhaustive history of the Monroe Doctrine is Dexter Perkins, *Hands Off! A History of the Monroe Doctrine* (Cambridge, MA: Harvard University Press, 1927).

3

Consolidating Nation-States

The dominant narrative of the nineteenth century in inter-American relations focuses on the triumphant expansion of the United States—the closing of the frontier—and the conscious, determined assertion of its influence in and over the rest of the hemisphere—the rise of US hegemony. According to the Latin American version of this narrative, the United States imposed its hegemony on Latin America. The nations of the region were pushed into a subordinate position from which they only could complain about US arrogance and do what they could to fend off or reduce US dominance. In this narrative, the Monroe Doctrine is taken, erroneously, as the first major statement of US imperialism.

Although there is much in this narrative that is correct, it misses three crucial points necessary to understand the ongoing difficulty of Latin American governments to exercise their agency in world affairs in the twenty-first century. The first is the European origins of the quest to shape a rules-based international community. The concepts central to the emerging international system, power and civilization, were Eurocentric. Power as a feature of the nation-state was measured in economic and military terms, although there was an unspecified dimension called culture. Taken together, these measures were an indicator of the level of a nation's civilization. When used to refer to less civilized countries or peoples, this word became code for inferiority. Civilization was understood as a linear, progressive phenomenon centered in Western Europe. Countries could be arrayed along a hierarchy according to their level of civilization, which for the most part was determined by their power. It was assumed by the most civilized that they would fix the rules that guided interstate behavior, that the members of the community would compete with one another for dominance and, through the competition for trade and territory, spread civilization throughout the world. The phrase often used was that the more civilized nations would "bring civilization to" the less civilized. By the end of the nineteenth century, the United States aimed at becoming one of the members of the special rule-making club of the most civilized nations called the great powers, and formulated its foreign policy to achieve that goal. Although none of the nations in Latin America expressed such pretensions or ambitions as openly, Brazil and Argentina hinted that they deserved such status or would soon achieve it. They closely watched one another and were openly scornful of US assertions and arrogant pretensions, considering themselves every bit as civilized as the United States.

The second way in which the dominant narrative is misleading is that all of the nations in the hemisphere were equally cognizant of the dominant mores in the international system. All understood what was meant by the term "power"—economic and military capacity—and none rejected the concepts of modernity and civilization as the principal indicators of progress and power. All of the nations measured themselves by these indicators and recognized that they fell short of the standards set in Europe. At the same time, they were profoundly uncomfortable that the United States, like the nations in Europe, openly expressed its superiority over nations with less power, and they constantly sought ways to discredit the habit of more powerful nations to assert control or exert influence over the less powerful. In the twentieth century, when the United States asserted its hegemony in a more aggressive manner, the Latin Americans focused their collective efforts on making nonintervention one of the key rules in the hemispheric community. Privately, Latin Americans commented on how superior they were to their neighbors. The concept of civilization as a yardstick to measure progress and achievement was as important to them as it was to the United States, and race played an important role in their thinking.

The third way the dominant narrative is wrong is that the Monroe Doctrine was a defensive document that looked back to Washington's Farewell Address, not forward to domination or hegemony over other nations. Nothing in the original text nor any action by the United States based on the policy was remotely imperialistic. Certainly, at the end of the century and the beginning of the twentieth century, the doctrine was used to justify US imperialism. But it was not thus in its origins, and understanding the transition from defensive posture to hegemonic pretension is crucial to an understanding of hemispheric relations.

Throughout the course of the nineteenth century, the United States and Latin America drew further apart in their approach to international affairs. Most of the nations of Latin America were inhibited from expressing agency in international affairs because of their internal instability and the conflicts over boundaries with their immediate neighbors. That internal preoccupation and the inability to focus on national interests or imagine a national identity beyond immediate threats made it hard to establish institutions that could encourage investment, domestic or foreign, or that might be seen as responsible for creating and maintaining rules of the game that all participants might respect.[1] The earliest expressions of agency, in Chile and Argentina, came after national consolidation. By contrast, in the United States, despite the trauma of the Civil War and slavery, the state was a powerful handmaiden to economic activity and the territorial expansion across the North American landmass. Politics and public policy were close allies of US expansion and helped consolidate the nation's sense of itself and of its role in world affairs.

What distinguishes the Latin American assertions of superiority, for the most part, is that they were directed against their immediate neighbors—their equivalent of the propinquity principle. With few exceptions, Latin Americans did not attempt to project their power far from their own borders. While the United States certainly focused attention on its immediate neighbors, it did not rule out the possibility that it might exert influence in faraway places. From independence onward, US leaders deliberately framed their geopolitical thinking within a global context. The rest of the Western Hemisphere, despite reiterated protestations of brotherhood and shared values, was a minor player for the United States and remained, as it had been in the eyes of Monroe and his secretary of state, John Quincy Adams, little more than a potential threat because of its instability and weakness. The central focus of US policy toward Latin America continued to be keeping more powerful players out of the region.

By the end of the century, the United States asserted its primacy throughout the hemisphere and insisted that its prerogatives be taken as seriously as any of the (civilized) European powers. Aside from occasional and more modest assertions by Argentina and Brazil, none of the other nations in the hemisphere in the period leading up to World War I envisioned itself as a member of the great powers club. Chile framed its geopolitical aspirations within a subregional context. Brazil and Argentina measured their geopolitical power against one another, not against any European reference, although they used European benchmarks. The exception to this self-effacement was the exuberance expressed by Argentines during their centennial in 1910, that they would soon overtake the United States and join the club. The war in Europe ended any realistic expectation that such a transformation would occur, although the pretensions remained.

As the nineteenth century unfolded, the nations in the Western Hemisphere turned their energies to consolidating their independence and achieving stability of governance. At the same time, they were trying to define the boundaries that set them apart from neighbors, as were the leaders of the United States. All the nations, north and south, were painfully aware of their weakness and their vulnerability to outside threat, especially from one or another of the imperial, authoritarian powers in Europe.[2] The contrast between North and South lay in the sense in the United States that, though weak, they had some power in the international system and never shied away from exercising their agency. Their strategy to neutralize the threat of authoritarian perfidy was to play European powers off against one another, as they had during the struggle for independence. They dealt with the threat of propinquity by endless negotiations to secure their borders and by exporting population to the frontiers of the nation. They took advantage of Spanish weakness to take Florida by treaty. They used a demographic tide to take control over the area of Texas, and, in the resulting war with Mexico, stretched the national territory along the Rio Grande and then to the Pacific. They used an effective state growing confident of its territorial reach to subsidize with concessions to private capital, including foreign capital, the construction of an infrastructure that would ensure control over the continental landmass they had been coveting since the Louisiana Purchase. Over the century after independence, successive governments hewed to a geopolitical plan interrupted only by the Civil War.

In their own defensive crouch, several nations in Latin America reached out in the decades after independence for protection from more powerful states because they saw themselves as powerless.[3] They were bedeviled by the threat of propinquity and flailed around in attempts to secure their borders, with nearly constant lack of success. For the most part, the repeated failures were a function of persistent state weakness and the inability to achieve an internal consensus. In such a context, the Bolivarian dream of community and unity remained an aspiration beyond their grasp. Gran Colombia broke up into three parts; the Andean confederation shattered; Uruguay established its independence of both Brazil and Argentina; the Central American Union broke into five pieces.[4]

Only Brazil was successful in using the tactic, so successful in the United States, of sending population to the hinterland to establish settlements and using these phalanxes of Brazilian presence to consolidate political control at the periphery. The Mexicans tried to counter migration from the United States into Texas by bringing in migrants from the Canary Islands, but their numbers were a fraction of the human wave from the north that soon dominated Texas. In the second half of the century, the Argentines made immigration a national policy—to govern is to populate (*gobernar es poblar*)—and offered incentives to groups in Europe in an effort to fill the national space.[5] Brazil, without as much public fanfare, attracted a large number of immigrants in the same period, from the end of the nineteenth century until the end of World War II, over four million, and has continued to receive significant numbers of immigrants, mainly from Asia. At the beginning of the twentieth century, Argentina hit the highest level of foreign born of any country in the hemisphere—30 percent. At the same point in history, the United States hit its highest level of foreign born at just under 15 percent.[6]

As Chile and Argentina consolidated their internal stability in the middle of the nineteenth century, they began to think strategically about their national territory. In addition to encouraging immigration, the Argentines used a strategy similar to the United States in offering concessions to foreign capital (almost entirely British) to construct the railroad network. But the crucial difference between the two strategies is that the United States used the railroad as a means of extending and asserting national sovereignty over peripheral territory, whereas the Argentines used it to exploit more effectively territory already under national control. The Argentine railroad network extended like the fingers of an outstretched hand onto the fertile pampa from the port of Buenos Aires, so it could be drained of its agricultural production more efficiently. Infrastructure connection between the fingers did not come until a national road network stretched across the pampa in the 1930s. In the same fashion, the Brazilians, Chileans, and Peruvians used foreign capital to construct railroads to link specific population centers or, in the Brazilian and Peruvian cases, link remote enclaves of commodity resources with commercial centers. None of these investments came close to imitating the geostrategic thinking behind the public policies that facilitated construction of the infrastructure created in the United States during the nineteenth century.[7]

The leaders of the Latin American countries read the same books and were aware of the dominant thinking among European thinkers and geopoliticians, just as their fathers and grandfathers had been aware of events leading up to the American and French Revolutions. For the most part they were captivated by the central notions of civilization and racial purity and what they called "liberal ideas."[8] In cultural terms, Europe was considered a paragon of art and literature, and most of the elites aspired to educate their children in Europe, buy their furniture and art in Europe, and learn at least one European language in addition to Spanish or Portuguese. In the case of Argentina, while there was the conviction that Europe was the cultural center, there was strong respect for the education model in the United States, which Domingo F. Sarmiento tried to import.[9] He was joined by Juan Bautista Alberdi and others in the desire to imitate the US constitutional model. An entire generation of constitutional experts worked to extol the benefits of the US model while adapting it to their own political preferences, especially with reference to the powers of individual states in a federated system of government.[10] Throughout the region, there was an acute awareness of being part of a larger community of nations and that there were rules of behavior that governed the community that they wished to adopt. But there was very little sense that they could play a role in setting those rules; in the few cases in which proposals were made to change the rules, they were designed to protect Latin America from more powerful players in the community.

Both the Chileans and the Argentines, once they had achieved some semblance of stability and a state that could act on behalf of national interests, undertook military campaigns to push the indigenous population on their southern frontier further to the south. In the absence of major commodity resources in their southern regions, the Chileans invested heavily in ranching on the Argentine side of the Andes and were more successful than the Argentines in exploiting the Argentine Patagonia. It was not until the 1920s that Argentina established full control over the region on its southern flank. The border between the countries in the south remained unsettled and nearly led to a war in 1978. The final border dispute between the two, over a small stretch high in the Andes, was not resolved until the middle of the 1990s.

Commodities and their export together with demographic pressures led to conflict at various points in South America on the regional level beginning in the middle of the nineteenth century. On the eastern side of the Andes, the Argentines and Brazilians were in conflict over the best way to exercise control over Paraguay, which was locked away in an isolationist island under a megalomaniacal dictator, Francisco Solano López. In 1865, the two consolidating powers joined forces and brought Uruguay into the effort to take over Paraguay in a war that lasted from 1865 to 1870. Paraguay was dismembered and left as a buffer between the two ambitious neighbors. On the western side of the Andes, the Chileans were much better organized than their neighbors to the north, Peru and Bolivia, and began an aggressive push strongly supported by foreign capital into the sparsely populated area between them in which had been found nitrates, for which there seemed to be an insatiable market in Europe. That, too, led to a war, in 1879, which Chile won decisively and then took big chunks of territory from the defeated countries.

In Central America, there was virtually no discussion of how any of the successor states might or should assume an active role in world affairs. There was some discussion of creating a union among them that might play such a role. That talk ended very quickly and the project to create a Central American Union collapsed.[11] For the rest of the nineteenth century, attention in the Central American countries was focused on the struggle between local or regional factions of the dominant economic and social elites for control of the central government.

In each Central American case, a dominant oligarchy emerged centered on the production and export of coffee or bananas. A liberal state was created that sought to maximize the oligarchy's comparative advantage in the international market, including granting special protection and privileges to international investors who offered to build the infrastructure necessary to facilitate the export trade. Honduras was the extreme case of the concessionary state in this early period; all of the countries in the region to some extent accorded special privileges to foreign investors that had the effect of reducing the autonomy of the national state, giving rise to the phrase "banana republic." In the creation of their liberal state, the oligarchy used the European models of progress and civilization to subjugate the indigenous population within its borders, reducing the rights of the Indians and mestizos to even lower levels than they had been under imperial rule. There was a clear sense in each country that they should be in the world and of it, at least as far as participating in the international market was concerned; but there was nothing that we might call a national foreign policy that could guide participation in world affairs. It is obvious that there was no sense of policy process nor any effort to make the state accountable to its constituents except to the faction that controlled it. In other words, there was virtually no sense of agency.

During this middle period in the history of Latin America, the Bolivarian dream had few advocates. It was as if everyone had enough to worry about with the struggle for internal stability and what was happening on their borders. Though never dominant in the politics of the region, there were persistent conversations as to what might tie the peoples of the hemisphere together. These thinkers and writers, known as *Americanistas*, existed in virtually every country. In the two generations after independence, this drive for community was provoked by real military or naval threats from Spain. Americanismo was especially strong in Chile, where the Spanish actually blockaded and then bombarded the port of Valparaiso. In the broader context of external aggression against Latin American nations, the Spanish annexed the Dominican Republic (Santo Domingo); William Walker marauded through Central America in a process that came to be known as filibustering; the French, English, and Spanish invaded Mexico and the French left behind an Austrian prince as emperor; Cuba engaged in a series of wars for independence, provoking Spanish military reprisals; and Spain occupied the Chincha Islands of Peru. This last invasion in particular met with fierce opposition from the Chilean government, which expressed solidarity with Peru in the form of proclamations, donations, and voluntary regiments traveling to Peru. In 1865, Chilean disapproval of Spanish actions culminated in a declaration of war against Spain.[12] This early stage in thinking about Chile's role in affairs outside its border was important in the creation of a national identity and in forging the nationalism that was the base from which Chilean expansion was launched in the war against Peru and Bolivia from 1879 to 1883.[13] Americanismo in Chile petered out when the Spanish withdrew from the region, but it had contributed to thinking about the "new" Chile, which was now seen in a position to express its interests in the region. Foreign affairs had become a subject for public debate and part of the governing elite's sense of national policy.

In the middle of the century, a new idea was introduced in which the Latin "race" was given a privileged place. The first expression came from several Latin Americans who saw France as the center of the civilized world and thought it a good idea to associate themselves with this force. Several published their poems or essays in French journals. A few years later, the French picked up the idea as an excuse for their intervention in Mexico, and the notion of linking elements of the Latin race appealed to the royalists in Mexico who welcomed the Habsburg monarchs to the Mexican throne. Brazilian intellectuals liked the idea of being linked to France, but they never expressed any solidarity with the rest of the nations in the hemisphere. The Argentines never saw themselves as particularly Latin, although they did associate the concept of civilization with Europe more generally and considered themselves the most European of the Latin American nations.[14]

In the United States, the Western Hemisphere idea never died, but it did not prosper. The country's leaders were preoccupied with the internal split over slavery and the civil war that threatened the country's very existence. During that war, both sides followed the realist prescriptions of the founding fathers and reached out to European powers for support. In terms of trade, cotton in the South trumped wheat in the North. But, British investments were concentrated in the North, and the lobby in England that pushed foreign policy toward a neutral or pro-North position was the opposition to slavery. Only after the war would leaders in the United States begin to think of the nation's role in the hemisphere. There was talk of annexing Cuba; there was talk of annexing Hispaniola. Nothing came of either. The first serious effort to build a hemispheric community in which the United States would play a major role was the effort by Secretary of State James G. Blaine to get a customs union going through the mechanism of a Pan American Conference. In his first, brief tenure as secretary of state, Blaine was concerned about the conflict between Chile and Peru, the boundary dispute between Chile and Argentina, and the threat of conflict between Mexico and Guatemala. In all of these, he feared European intervention. He saw British power behind Chile and French capital behind the Peruvians and instructed US ambassadors in those two countries to use their good offices to settle the conflict without benefit to the Europeans.[15]

The Guatemalan minister in Washington appealed to Blaine to intervene "as the natural protector of the integrity of the Central American territory" and Blaine asked the Mexicans not to push Guatemala.[16]

The project was delayed when Blaine resigned following President James A. Garfield's assassination and Blaine's successor, Frederick Frelinghuysen, pulled back from what he considered Blaine's aggressive anti-British policy. When he was appointed secretary of state in 1889, under President Benjamin Harrison, Blaine returned to the idea of a Pan American Conference, but now he was interested mainly in a customs union to give the United States greater advantage in the growing markets of Latin America. The notion of expanding trade into foreign markets was fast becoming an obsession in the United States, although most of the attention was devoted to Asia, not Latin America. Blaine spoke frequently about the shared history and culture of the nations in the hemisphere and showed himself to be aware of the Bolivarian dream.[17]

In the final quarter of the nineteenth century we get the first real examples of geopolitical thinking and the earliest stirrings of agency among the major countries in Latin America, always as a reflection of the European drive for progress and civilization. The Brazilians, in monarchy and in republic, called it Order and Progress; the Mexicans under Porfirio Díaz called it Peace, Order and Progress. Domingo F. Sarmiento, who later became president of Argentina, wrote a book, *Civilization and Barbarism*, in which he called on his fellow Argentines to adopt the values and habits of the Europeans and North Americans. A few years later, the Argentines created a Progress Club (El Club de Progreso) in which they discussed everything from how to attract foreign investment to buying a battleship to counter Brazil's growing power.[18]

The Chileans first converted progress into an ideology of civilization to justify their economic expansion into the desert that stretched across the northern provinces of Chile, the southern region of Peru, and the western region of Bolivia. It was an expanse rich in nitrates, the demand for which in Europe was growing at a steep rate. The British wanted to pay for the new mines; so did the Americans. The Chileans were more than willing to accommodate eager investors and tried for a short while to interest Peruvians in some joint ventures. When the Peruvians proved too slow and too disorganized, the Chileans decided to take the territory by force. In the first instance, the Chileans had to justify the war at home, so they advertised the campaign as a civic war in which all citizens had a role to play—an incipient policy process. This made a new virtue of democracy of the people. The next step was to contrast this civic-republican effort with the tyranny and tribal chaos in Peru and Bolivia. As the Chileans saw it, faced with the threat of tyranny and lawlessness, the democratic people of Chile were obligated to go to war. But when Peru did not give up, even when Chilean troops occupied the nitrate zone, Chile needed justification for invading the rest of Peruvian territory; sacking the capital, Lima; and seizing whatever riches they could get their hands on. In this effort, the Catholic Church was quick to call the conflict a "holy" and "just" war. The sins of the enemy were not those of individuals, it was the Peruvian government's failure in "the respect for international law, political integrity, morality and honor of public men and compliance towards religion and justice."[19]

As the war went on and Chilean armies invaded more Peruvian territory, there evolved a civilizing discourse to justify their decision to take so much territory from Peru and Bolivia. Part of the justification was their insistence on their racial superiority. They were white; the Peruvians and Bolivians were a mongrel race. But it was also their promise of order and commercial security in the occupied territories. International business in the nitrate zone—and the onward march of civilization—would be protected and advanced. To give content to this boast, the Chileans pushed through a radical transformation of their public administration so that they could demonstrate their capacity to fulfill this role. This finally was the justification for aggression by the strong against the weak.[20]

Chilean foreign policy was geographically circumscribed by its desire for expansion in the nineteenth century and, in the twentieth century, by its obsession with protecting that expansion, virtually turning its geopolitical back on the rest of the world to guard its northern frontier.[21] This self-restricting policy was maintained by civilian and military governments alike. It is one of the major successes of the transition to democracy after 1989 that the nation's foreign policy gradually shook off the constraints of its territorial conquests in the nineteenth century and began to understand its national interests in a wider framework.[22]

In the case of Argentina, the nation's pretensions were global, not regional, and commercial, not territorial. By the last decade of the nineteenth century, the Argentine economic model of exporting commodities to insatiable European markets while receiving vast quantities of European investment in return was a resounding success. From 1880 to 1910, Argentina grew at a faster rate than any other country in the world, even the United States. The country's leaders were convinced of the nation's inevitable greatness. That greatness would be based on the critical importance of its agricultural goods to the well-being of Europe, especially Great Britain. That importance would only increase because of the international division of labor and, they believed, would be what determined Argentine power and influence in world affairs. For the majority of Argentines, the world was ruled by reason, and the international division of labor was a rational model that guaranteed Argentine international power and respect.

There were dissenters within the governing elite. A few commentators advocated taking advantage of the huge windfall from the sale of commodities to diversify the economy and pay more attention to productivity on the pampa.[23] One economist pointed to the potential for a nation that exported primary products becoming dependent on centers of capital and manufactured goods.[24] The majority laughed off the thought that the export boom would ever come to an end or that the laws of classical economics would be ignored or weakened. They believed the boom would carry Argentina into the club of the great powers. They also laughed off the notion that concentrating their exports on one customer would create a vulnerability that later would be called dependence. The commercial link between Argentina and Great Britain was extraordinary from a historical perspective. From 1880 to 1940, Argentina sent 35 percent of its exports to Great Britain. In return, the British sent to Argentina 40 percent of their foreign direct investment in the same period.[25] These data boosted the confidence of Argentine leaders, who did not want to change the country's model for growth and prosperity.

One dissident within the elite, Estanislao Zeballos, had read the European geopoliticians and studied the history of the United States. He urged his fellows first to secure the national territory by clearing the indigenous and the Chileans from Patagonia in the south and then, to demonstrate Argentine superiority over the Brazilians, by modernizing the military and purchasing the military equipment, which was so much a part of European definitions of power. For about a decade, there was an arms race between Brazil and Argentina centered on the purchase of large vessels of war, the dreadnought. That arms race ended abruptly with the outbreak of war in Europe in 1914, as the producers of the arms directed all of their resources to the war effort. Brazil and Argentina sold their battleships, new or still under construction, to one or another of the belligerents in Europe. Zeballos was twice foreign minister and both times was thrown out of the cabinet for what his peers considered an overly belligerent posture toward Brazil and Chile.

Zeballos was an admirer of Alfred Thayer Mahan and Theodore Roosevelt, key members of the US elite who called for a powerful navy to facilitate the projection of national power. For them, the navy was a vital adjunct of international trade. Zeballos was more concerned to intimidate or compete with Argentina's immediate neighbors than were Mahan and Roosevelt. But like them, he was a racist and a social Darwinian. When Roosevelt left the presidency, Zeballos gave him an honorary degree at the University of Buenos Aires. In a speech, Zeballos said that the Monroe Doctrine was no longer necessary in Argentina "now that our civilization has been attained."[26] He was a prodigiously productive writer throughout his career and, at the end of his life, gave a series of lectures at Williams College that explained with great clarity the thinking of an Argentine who would have emulated Mahan had he been able to persuade his peers to go along with his vision of the world.[27]

The Argentine leadership was skeptical of Zeballos's reading of the European power index. The majority view was that wheat and meat trumped military might and that the value of those commodities was such that Argentina could be assured of a constant supply of energy and industrial goods that they could not or would not bother to produce. Race was also an element in establishing their place on the hierarchy of civilized nations. Most Argentines believed that they were superior to the Brazilians because of their pure European blood, compared to the corrupted, mixed blood of so many Brazilians. Britain simply had to send Argentina coal because it needed the foodstuffs Argentina exported. Even when petroleum was discovered in Patagonia in 1905, the first reaction by the Argentine government was that it was not necessary to exploit the resource since they always could get as much energy as they needed through international exchange. That view dominated policymaking until the beginning of the war when British military needs ended coal shipments to Argentina; literally, the lights in Buenos Aires went out in August 1914. Geopolitics trumped the international division of labor and strategic commodities such as oil became more important than wheat and beef.

Ignoring this wartime experience, the international division of labor suited Argentines' conception of their pathway to greatness and agency, so that at the end of the war, the Argentine congress rejected legislation designed to expand petroleum exploration and exploitation as part of a plan to diversify the economy, on the grounds that the international division of labor was bound to return as the classical economic orthodoxy that drove trade policy in Europe.[28] It never happened. Argentine agency in the midst of their extraordinary period of growth did not go beyond their role as a key player in the international economy. They expressed their satisfaction with the division of labor that facilitated the export of their products to European markets—the restrictions on their products in the US market was an irritation but not an obstacle to their growth and development—and the free movement of capital to build their infrastructure and supply the industrial products they wanted. That model collapsed completely during World War I and, like Humpty Dumpty, never quite got put back together again.

Given this view, Argentines were determined to deny any effort to create an American community of nations. The initiative sponsored by the United States in 1889 was especially noxious as the United States was a competitor of Argentina in the agricultural commodities business and because the United States always had been arrogant and so forth. As with

Brazil, the United States was inferior to Argentina in its racial makeup because of the heavy portion of Africans in its population. The Argentine delegates to the first Pan American Conference in 1889–90 succeeded in blocking any meaningful action by the group and even emasculated the new organization created during the meeting.[29]

The Brazilian case combines elements of the Argentine and Chilean cases, and in some ways points ahead to the debate of the twentieth century. Brazil was an outgrowth of the Portuguese monarchy. The first chief of state, Pedro I, sailed in 1807, from Lisbon to South America, at the age of nine with his parents, João VI and Dona Carlota Joaquina, the king and queen of Portugual, who were fleeing Napoleon's invasion. It was João's idea to rule his empire from Brazil, Portugal's prized colony. When João sailed back to Portugal in an effort to reclaim his throne, he left Pedro behind to deal with the messy local politics. Pedro became emperor in 1822 and abdicated in 1831 in favor of his six-year-old son. Brazil was ruled by a series of unstable regencies until Pedro was declared of age in 1840 and was named emperor as Pedro II in 1841. Pedro II ruled Brazil until 1889 when he was deposed and spent the last two years of his life in Paris.

Great Britain was the principal foreign influence in Brazil, even providing the naval escort for the royal court on its journey from Lisbon. The British were central to Brazil's international trade and to the growing investment in the new commodity, coffee, that was so important to Brazil's development. As the abolition movement in Britain grew in strength, the relationship became quite complicated. The British were instrumental in orchestrating the transition to the emperor's son, Dom Pedro II, who took power in 1840 and ruled until Brazil became a republic in 1889. They also played a major role in the end of slavery in 1888.

The elites in Brazil in the nineteenth century were jealous of the new nation's prerogatives. They were solidly behind the attack on Paraguay and Argentina that guaranteed Brazil's access to the River Plate in the war from 1865 to 1870. They supported the demographic policies that opened land in the interior of the country to settlement by subsidized groups known as *bandeirantes* and to the extension of state control. Most important, they cooperated with the emperor in transforming the Brazilian state by modernizing public-sector administration, including a professional foreign service.[30] There was a broad consensus that the other nations in South America were chaotic, disorganized, and racially inferior.[31] Beyond that, the elite was split between those who favored Europe, such as Eduardo Prado, and those who saw the United States as a model and potential friend, such as Joaquim Nabuco.[32] Nabuco had the last word in that he opposed slavery, yet he was a fierce defender of Brazilian territorial sovereignty and considered the Monroe Doctrine and the US hegemonic pretension that came with it as the best method of maintaining that sovereignty. Nabuco spawned the creation of a professional foreign service and construction of the palace in Rio that gave the ministry its name, Itamaraty. He nurtured his protégé, José Paranhos, Viscount of Rio Branco, who brought together the complex elements of foreign policy that combined what he called an approximation to the United States and aggressive but nonviolent expansion into the Amazon Basin to acquire territory from Brazil's neighbors—by treaty, by arbitration, by occupation, and by demand.[33]

While Rio Branco was foreign minister, he adopted an aloof posture toward the rest of South America, but he made it clear that he saw Brazil as the most important country in the region. The core of Brazilian foreign policy in the twentieth century would be to have that hegemony recognized without causing friction with the United States. In that effort, the evolution of Brazilian hegemony would be profoundly affected by the evolution of US efforts to project its own hegemony in the hemisphere, which is the subject of the next chapter.

There were other expressions of resistance to US pretensions. In addition to the numerous complaints by various governments against meddling in their affairs by the United States or its representatives, many intellectuals in the region found US aggressiveness objectionable and sought to make a virtue of their own culture. The most famous literary expression of this was *Ariel*, an essay by Uruguayan José Enrique Rodó, in which he castigated the United States as a Caliban to Latin America's more civilized Ariel. The region's ultramontane Catholics derided US society as mongrel and considered as lunatics those authors who trumpeted the US mission to bring its values to the rest of the hemisphere. The Nicaraguan poet Rubén Darío wrote harsh criticisms of the United States, placing Latin America as a civilized, peace-loving alternative to US materialism and militarism. Even admirers of US political practices and its economic energy were disdainful of its cultural achievements.

Carlos Calvo (1842–1902), an Argentine jurist and academic, took a more positive approach to containing US hegemony as well as the pretensions of the European powers. He wrote books and articles that called for an American international law that would protect the sovereignty of the region's states against interventionist aggression by more powerful states even in defense of the interests of their citizens. He formulated a set of propositions, known in the region as the Calvo Doctrine (an obvious reference to the Monroe Doctrine), in which he opposed the intervention of states in the internal affairs of other states, specifically rejecting the proposition then common in Europe that it was legitimate to protect the private interests of investors or traders with military power. Specifically, the Europeans considered it legitimate for a creditor to collect debts by force if a debtor refused to pay. Calvo called for a mode of dispute resolution that would use the international court, then in its infancy in The Hague, and would protect the sovereignty of those states that were accused of violating the rights of private capital from overseas.[34] Although influential throughout the region, Calvo's arguments never found their way into Argentine foreign policy until the twentieth century, when they were presented by the Argentine government as formal proposals to the third and fourth Pan-American Conferences (Rio in 1906, Buenos Aires in 1910) and again at the sixth conference in Havana in 1928.

Calvo's writings anticipated by nearly two decades the declaration of the US secretary of state Warren Olney in 1895 in reference to the British effort to force a resolution of a boundary dispute between the colony of British Guiana and neighboring Venezuela, that the United States "was practically sovereign in this hemisphere." Robert Gascoyne-Cecil, Lord Salisbury, the British foreign secretary, was scornful of the Olney position, but his objections were never followed by specific action. The boundary in question was settled at the time, but remains in dispute between Venezuela and the now-independent nation of Guyana.[35] Olney's message to Salisbury was only the first expression of US hegemony in the hemisphere, the content or nature of which was to be worked out in the first years of the new century. Olney, like Madison and Monroe before him, never specified what that hegemony might entail.

Calvo also anticipated the wave of US interventions in the Caribbean Basin, but his doctrine, without institutional support or some regional organization to enforce it, was powerless to stop them. Nevertheless, nonintervention, as it came to be called, was an idea whose time would come. It remains the most compelling link that holds together Latin American nations in a form of community. Even when there are disagreements as to territory, economic interests, and core values, the nations of the hemisphere can agree that they oppose intervention in the internal affairs of a sovereign state. That is part of the legacy of US hegemony in the twentieth century.

Notes

1. A good introduction to a comparison between the United States and Latin America during this formative period is the work of John H. Coatsworth and Douglass North. See, for example, John H. Coatsworth, "Structures, Endowments, Institutions and Growth in Latin American Economic History," *Latin American Research Review* 40.3 (2005) and "Inequality, Institutions and Economic Growth in Latin America," *Journal of Latin American Studies* 40 (2008); and Douglass North, William Summerhill, and Barry R. Weingast, "Order, Disorder and Economic Change: Latin America versus

North America," in Bruce Bueno de Mesquita and Hilton L. Root, eds., *Governing for Prosperity* (New Haven, CT: Yale University Press, 2000).

2. Here, the concept of evolving citizenship is important. See Sarah Chambers, *From Subjects to Citizens: Honor, Gender, and Politics in Arequipa, Peru* (University Park: Penn State University Press, 1999) and Hilda Sabato, *The Many and the Few: Political Participation in Republican Buenos Aires* (Stanford, CA: Stanford University Press, 2001).

3. The pervasive and enduring nature of this attitude is significant and makes the rebuttal by Muñoz all the more important. (See Heraldo Muñoz, "The Strategic Dependency of the Centers and the Economic Importance of the Latin American Periphery," *Latin American Research Review* 16.3 (1981): 3–29.) For Muñoz, it was not how much power a nation had but how it exploited the quota of power it had to maximize its own national interests.

4. On the creation of national identities in Latin American in the nineteenth century, see John Charles Chasteen and Sara Castro-Klaren, eds., *Beyond Imagined Communities: Reading and Writing the Nation in Nineteenth-Century Latin America* (Washington, DC: Woodrow Wilson Center Press, 2003).

5. The nation's leaders, for the most part, descendants of Spaniards, believed there were "good" immigrants and "bad" immigrants and offered incentives in the 1850s and 1860s to Swiss farmers, Germans, some French, and a group of Irish sheepherders, but got few takers. Over time the so-called alluvial wave that populated the pampas was composed mainly of Spanish and Italians, with a smaller percentage of Eastern European Jews and refugees of the Ottoman Empire. On Sarmiento's views of education and the other dimensions of his influence in Argentina and Latin America, see Tulio Halperin Donghi, Ivan Jaksic, Gwen Kirkpatrick, et. al, *Sarmiento: Author of a Nation?* (Berkeley: University of California Press, 1994).

6. Today, when immigration is a major policy issue in the United States and in Europe, and xenophobia and diversity are polarizing issues in many countries, the level of foreign born in the United States is just under 13 percent, increased from a low of 4.7 percent in 1970. Argentina today is at 4.5 percent and Brazil is 2.4 percent. By comparison, Australia is at 27 percent; New Zealand, 24 percent; and Canada, 20 percent. The highest level of foreign born in Europe is Sweden at 10.6 percent.

7. When Walt W. Rostow was an adviser to President Lyndon Johnson in the 1960s, he suggested using the Alliance for Progress as the mechanism for building strategic infrastructure in Latin America, but nothing came of it.

8. Simon Collier, *Chile: The Making of a Republic, 1830–1865* (New York: Cambridge University Press, 2003); James A. Wood, *The Society of Equality: Popular Republicanism and Democracy in Santiago de Chile, 1818–1851* (Albuquerque: University of New Mexico Press, 2011).

9. Laura Malosetti Costa, *Los primeros modernos. Arte y sociedad en Buenos Aires fines del sigle XIX* (Buenos Aires: Fondo de Cultura, 2001). On Sarmiento and other travelers, see David Viñas, *De Sarmiento a Dios: Viajeros argentinos a los Estados Unidos* (Buenos Aires: Sudamericana, 1998).

10. Eduardo Zimmermann, "Translations of the 'American Model' in Nineteenth Century Argentina: Constitutional Culture as a Global Legal Entanglement," in Thomas Duve, ed., *Entanglements in Legal History: Conceptual Approaches to Legal History* (Frankfurt: Max Planck Institute, 2014).

11. John D. Martz, "Justo Rufino Barrios and Central American Union," University of Florida Monographs No. 21 (September 1962).

12. The Chilean case is described in Gabriel Cid, *La Guerra contra la Confederación. Imaginario nacionalista y memoria colectiva en el siglo XIX chilena* (Santiago: Ediciones Universidad Diego Portales, 2011); Ricardo Lopez Muñoz, "El

americanismo en Chile ante la expansión política y militar europea sobre Hispanoamérica (1861–1871)" Ph.d dissertation, Santiago: University of Chile, 2011.

13. Gabriel Cid, "En defensa de la 'Patria Grande': Guerra e imaginario en el Chile de los 1860s. Ponencia presentada en el seminario Arma Virumque: Estado, nación y guerra en América Latina, 1810–1895, Centro de Estudios Bicentenario-Perú/Cooperación Regional Francesa para los Países Andinos, Lima, July 4, 2012. The definitive work on Chilean nationalism in the War of the Pacific is Carmen McEvoy, *Guerreros civilizadores: Política, sociedad y cultura en Chile durante la Guerra del Pacífico* (Santiago: Ediciones Universidad Diego Portales, 2011). This book is particularly useful in understanding Chilean imperialism in that war and will be discussed in detail later in this chapter.

14. Leslie Bethell, "Brazil and 'Latin America,'" *Journal of Latin American Studies* 42 (2010): 457–485.

15. Herbert Millington, *American Diplomacy in the War of the Pacific* (New York: Columbia University Press, 1948); V. G. Kiernan, "Foreign Intervention in the War of the Pacific," *Hispanic American Historical Review* 35 (1955).

16. Quoted in Russell H. Bastert, "A New Approach to the Origins of Blaine's Pan American Policy," *Hispanic American Historical Review* 39 (1959).

17. Benjamin A. Coates, "The Pan-American Lobbyist: William Elroy Curtis and U.S. Empire, 1884–1899," *Diplomatic History* 38.1 (2014).

18. D. F. Sarmiento, *Facundo: Civilization and Barbarism* (Berkeley: University of California Press, 2003).

19. McEvoy, *Guerreros civilizadores*, p. 180. The clergy in Peru disagreed on this point with their brethren in Chile.

20. Robert N. Burr, *By Reason or Force* (Berkeley: University of California Press, 1965). While Burr mentions the rhetoric of the civilizing mission that Chile adopted, he emphasizes the realpolitik behind its actions. He also notices the Chilean advances in efficiency and public administration. Burr and McEvoy complement one another. This is language virtually identical to that used by Theodore Roosevelt twenty years later justifying facilitating Panamanian independence from Colombia for the benefit of civilization and progress. This language shows full assimilation of the European concepts of civilization and the hierarchy of superiority including the crucial variables of race, modernity, economic power, and military prowess.

21. McEvoy, *Guererros civiliadores*, explores in detail the Chilean obsession with superiority over the Peruvians and Bolivians and how their greater degree of civilization legitimated their military conquest of territory that had been Peruvian or Bolivian. Burr, *By Reason or Force*, explains the geopolitics of Chilean expansion and the origins of Chilean regionalism.

22. Chilean military training until the beginning of the twenty-first century persisted in focusing on threat scenarios that anticipated invasions from Peru or Bolivia. In this strategic framework, peacekeeping with the United Nations was an inappropriate activity.

23. Alejandro Bunge, *El desarrollo en la Argentina* (Buenos Aires: Banco de la Nación, 1924).

24. Emilio Lahitte, *Informes y estudios I* (Buenos Aires: Sociedad Rural Argentina, 1914). Bunge began his studies during the war and continued to publish his views in the *Revista de Economía Argentina* throughout the 1920s. His protégé, Raúl Prebisch, began his career in the Banco de la Nación in the 1920s and carried on the lonely tradition of heterodox economists in Argentina through the 1930s and 1940s.

25. By comparison, today Argentina's three top trading partners are Brazil (20 percent), European Union (17 percent), and China (7.5 percent); its FDI is diversified in a similar manner.

26. Estanislao Zeballos, "Theodore Roosevelt y la política internacional americana," *Revista de derecho, historia y letras* (December 1913).

27. Roberto Etchepareborda, "Zeballos y la política exterior argentina," *Estrategia y Política* (Buenos Aires: Pleamar, 1980). Estanislao Zeballos, *La conferencias en Williamstown* (Buenos Aires: Talleres Gráficos de la Penetenciaría Nacional, 1927); Alfred Thayer Mahan, *The Influence of Sea Power upon History, 1770–1783* (New York: Little, Brown, 1890).

28. It is interesting to note that the Left, as represented by socialist Juan B. Justo, anticipated that classical economics would solve the Argentine problem. The communists, who began to operate in Argentina after the war, had a different view of the international economic system, and by the Great Depression, the Left had begun to look for alternate modes of international organization.

29. Thomas F. McGann, *Argentina, the United States and the Inter-American System, 1880–1914* (Cambridge, MA: Harvard University Press, 1957).

30. On abolition of the slave trade, see Leslie Bethell, *The Abolition of the Brazilian Slave Trade* (Cambridge: Cambridge University Press, 1970); on the war with Paraguay, Pelham H. Box, *The Origins of the Paraguayan War* (Champaign: University of Illinois Press, 1930); and Efraim Cardozo, *El imperio del Brasil y el Rio de la Plata* (Buenos Aires: Librería del Plata, 1961). On the imperial bureaucracy, Jose Murilo de Carvalho, "Political Elites and State Building: The Case of Nineteenth Century Brazil," *Comparative Studies in Society and History* 24.3 (1982): 378–399.

31. Race remained an important question in Latin American foreign policy into the twentieth century, when writers in several countries made a virtue of race mixing rather than insist on racial purity and whiteness as a measure of civilization.

32. Eduardo Prado, *A Ilusão Americana* (São Paulo: Brasiliense, 1958), is an excellent example of an anti-US diatribe. On the other side, see Leslie Bethell, "O Brasil entre a Europa, os Estados Unidos e a América Latina no pensamento de Joaquim Nabuco," *Novos estudos* 88 (2010): 73–87.

33. José Maria da Silva Paranhos Junior, given his title by Pedro II just before the end of the empire.

34. Liliana Obregon, "Should There Be an American International Law?," in Rene Uruena, ed., *Derecho Internacional* (Bogotá: Universidad de los Andes, 2012). John Bassett Moore (*Collected Papers of John Bassett Moore* [New Haven, CT: Yale University Press, 1944]) may be considered a US response to the European tradition of international law as well as to Calvo's efforts to curb the enthusiasm for intervention to protect private interests.

35. The dispute became heated in 2015, when ExxonMobil, with a concession from the government of Guyana, announced the discovery of oil in the Essequibo Basin. The government of Venezuela claimed that the territory was theirs and was part of a military defense zone. The Guyanese government moved to have the dispute arbitrated by the United Nations or the OAS.

4

The Rise of
US Hegemony

While the assertion of Secretary of State Warren Olney in his 1895 note to the British foreign minister, Lord Salisbury, that the United States "was practically sovereign in this hemisphere" certainly was a boast, it reflected a vein of thinking in the United States at the time that although it might not be true, it certainly should be and probably would be in time. Exactly what that predominance meant and how it should be exercised were to be worked out over time. In addition, the implications of such anticipated hegemony and what it would mean for US relations with Europe and other powers had to be worked out.[1]

In looking back on the period of US interventionism, there was remarkably little thought given, at least until after World War I, to these issues. There was no plan concerning Latin America among the policymakers and intellectuals who led and encouraged the United States to move toward world power status. There was no consensus among the country's leaders as to what hegemony in the Western Hemisphere actually meant.[2] In part, this was because geopolitical debate in the United States at the time was not focused on Latin America; it was part of a broader drive for recognition as a world power. If we take the proposals of Alfred Thayer Mahan, the expert in naval power, as a proxy for long-term policy planning in the United States at this time, we can see that the thinking was global, not hemispheric, and, following European models, it explicitly used trade and military capacity as metrics for measuring power.[3] Mahan's policy plan was to identify strategic points and markets to which the United States would naturally seek access as part of its economic growth. The State Department spent more time struggling for an open door for trade in Asia than it did worrying about the possibility of European incursions in the Western Hemisphere. At that point in the discussion, access and control were not taken to be zero-sum contests. It was generally assumed that where the United States might trade, as in China or Argentina, others might as well. For Mahan, it was crucial for the United States to develop a modern two-ocean navy, what is referred to as a "blue-water" navy. Along with the military capacity, the country was to seek places where ships could refuel and be provisioned, known as coaling stations.

It was in this context that the United States got into a dispute with Spain over how to deal with the insurgency in Cuba. It was no accident that when the dispute reached the point at which the US government decided to take action, the fleet was available to move against Manila as well as Havana.[4] In doing so, it was responding to a powerful push from public opinion and solid backing from Congress. The public's intense involvement gave the government confidence in the legitimacy of its aggression against Spain, but it proved a terrible distraction in making peace. The jingoist press succeeded in firing up the public's demand for war, but it was profoundly ambivalent about acquiring territory as part of the peace process. President William McKinley was reluctant to take control over the Philippines and did so only because he was convinced he couldn't give the islands back to Spain and couldn't turn them over to another power. In Cuba, at least, there was a local revolutionary group to which power could be delivered even if strings were attached to their independence.[5]

This chapter begins with the independence of Panama from Colombia and encompasses the two world wars to describe the manner in which the United States established its hegemony over the hemisphere. There was a variety of anti-imperial urges and frequent expressions of hostility from Latin Americans to this imposition of hegemony, but there was no strategic opposition; no formal, official complaint or protest by one state against another; nor the organization of a movement against hegemonic pretensions. Hipólito Yrigoyen, the president of Argentina from 1916 to 1922 and again from 1928 to 1930, frequently asserted his opposition to US hegemony through the declaration of his moral foreign policy, which he called *principismo*. He expressed his solidarity with the government of Mexico when the United States sent troops across the border in pursuit of Pancho Villa. When he dispatched an Argentine naval vessel to Nicaragua to take possessions of the poet Rubén Darío, a fierce critic of US imperialism, who at his death had been Nicaraguan consul in Buenos Aires and a correspondent for the Argentine paper *La Nación*, he ordered the vessel to stop in Santo Domingo and salute the Dominican flag so he could take public exception to the US occupation. Beyond these gestures, he did nothing to win support for his position among the nations of the region, except to instruct the Argentine representative to the Pan American Conference in Havana in 1928 to join other representatives in condemning US interventions.[6]

Although anti-Americanism took many forms, it could cohere politically only in defense of national sovereignty as a barrier to intervention. There were frequent calls for a hemispheric policy of nonintervention, based mainly on the Calvo Doctrine, but there was no sense of community in Latin America to present a collective alternative to US hegemony. The only official expressions of opposition to US hegemony occurred at the periodic meetings of the Pan American Union, which itself was a creature of the United States. So powerful did the Latin American consensus with regard to nonintervention become that a majority managed to convince the government of Franklin D. Roosevelt to accept it as a principle of their hemispheric community in a vote at the Pan American Conference of 1936 in Buenos Aires.[7]

The imposition of hegemony was a gradual process. It began at the turn of the twentieth century with two episodes in which the United States asserted its primacy in advancing global progress and civilization in the hemisphere and its right to enforce the rules of the international community within its area of influence.[8] In the war with Spain the United States gained control over the Windward and Mona Passages, two of the three entry points to the Caribbean Basin to which Mahan had drawn attention. An isthmian canal was a logical complement to this progress. Even before the war with Spain had concluded, Theodore Roosevelt had opened negotiations with the government of Colombia to secure the land necessary to build a canal across the province of Panama. As the Colombian legislature debated the treaty their executive had negotiated with the United States, Roosevelt lost patience. In a tirade, he condemned the Colombians as a "bunch of monkeys" and vowed that the interests of civilization would not be compromised by such backward, insolvent people. Agents of the US government proceeded to organize an opposition movement in Panama, got that group to declare independence from Colombia, and pushed them to sign a treaty to allow building of a canal. The United States recognized the new republic with unseemly speed and sent warships to deny the Colombian navy access to the territory, thereby preventing the Colombian government from bringing the rebellious province under control.[9]

Building the canal across Panama was a critical piece in the Mahan strategy to project US power in the Atlantic and the Pacific. In addition to its obvious military benefits to the United States, the canal played a crucial role in the economic development of the country, a role that lasted until the end of World War II. As the strategic importance of the canal declined after the war, it became easier to return the canal to Panamanian control, which came after a period of violent protests in Panama in the 1960s and 1970s.[10]

Virtually at the same time as the drama in Panama was playing out, there was a sequence of events in the Caribbean Basin that set the logic of US hegemony until the beginning of the Cold War.[11] It involved persuasion and the imposition of national will over the weaker country, with the use of force as a last option. The process began in Venezuela, where the government of Cipriano Castro failed to make payment on some of its sovereign bonds. In keeping with the gunboat diplomacy then customary, the bondholders elected a committee to represent them and asked the German government to protect their rights, precisely the sequence that Carlos Calvo had argued against in his call for a Latin American international law. Far from denouncing the intervention, contemporary public commentary in Argentina, Brazil, and Chile was sympathetic to the interests of the offended bondholders. The exception was a note by an Argentine Foreign Ministry official, Luis M. Drago, to US secretary of state Elihu Root extending Calvo's argument to object to use of force in collecting debts.[12]

The German foreign office reported its planned penetration of the Caribbean to the State Department and asked the United States to recognize the validity of their action. Theodore Roosevelt gave his approval. Within days, however, he repented having sanctioned an armed incursion by a European government in the name of European bondholders into the Western Hemisphere. Where was the Monroe Doctrine? Worse, when the Germans landed at the Venezuelan port of La Guaira to collect customs duties on behalf of the bondholders, they privileged the bondholders from countries that contributed to the naval incursion. The International Court affirmed this discriminatory treatment, effectively ignoring the Calvo Doctrine.[13]

While debate over the Venezuelan episode proceeded, another incident occurred, this one in the Dominican Republic. The bondholders' committee in this case asked the Italian government to send a naval force to Santo Domingo to collect the money owed them. When the Italians consulted the US Department of State, the answer was an immediate refusal. But Roosevelt believed something had to be done to ensure observance of the rules of the game. Moreover, there were significant US interests in Santo Domingo so the European bondholders were seen as competing with US entrepreneurs operating as the Santo Domingo Improvement Company, who were trying to advance the economic development of the country.[14] Roosevelt decided that the United States should enforce the rules on behalf of the "other civilized nations." The United States dispatched a naval force to collect duties at the port of Santo Domingo and pay off all the bondholders equally (pari passu) without privileging the nation(s) that had taken the initiative. Once the debt was repaid, the customs collectors left Santo Domingo. They returned in a few years with lots of company.

By the end of 1903, Roosevelt was ready to make his new policy public. He chose the same mechanism as had Monroe eighty years earlier, making it part of his message to Congress in December. As a result of the timing and content of the message, it has become known as the Roosevelt Corollary to the Monroe Doctrine. Although the corollary was clear in indicating that the United States would become the policeman in the Caribbean on behalf of the civilized nations of the world, it gave no indication as to what sort of behavior would require the action of the policeman, other than nonpayment of bonds, which had precipitated the crises in Venezuela and the Dominican Republic. What would happen if the customs collectors did their job and left, only to find that the country fell into the same pattern of nonpayment? Should the customs collectors remain permanently? Should the misbehaving government be removed and a better one installed?

Answering these questions proved messy. By the time it entered World War I, the United States had sent troops into Costa Rica, Nicaragua, Honduras, Mexico, the Dominican Republic, and Haiti in an effort to work out the implications of its hegemony. Roosevelt began with the goal of keeping Europe out of the hemisphere. After a few episodes, the goal of US policy became the elimination of the bad behavior. William Howard Taft, Roosevelt's successor as president, thought the premise of the corollary too broad and had the State Department focus on more narrow goals, such as rewriting constitutions, so that governments might be less unstable, or by writing legislation for the governments in the region that would require them to pay their debts. This approach led to sending advisers to various countries to help their rulers obey their own rules or write better ones more in tune with the practice of the dominant powers. It was no accident that these advisers also provided access to New York bankers who helped the governments balance their books and borrow money in the United States, which at least would eliminate the problem of European creditors threatening to collect debts through the use of force. Taft's secretary of state, Philander Knox, proposed "to make American capital the instrumentality to secure financial stability, and hence prosperity and peace, to the more backward Republics in the neighborhood of the Panama Canal."[15] This was dollar diplomacy.

When Woodrow Wilson became president in March 2013, he and his secretary of state, William Jennings Bryan, considered Taft's approach too partial to bankers and corporations, which only increased the chances for corruption, and that dollar diplomacy did not get at the underlying problem, which was bad government. Wilson wanted to improve the quality of democracy so that the governments would be accountable—not only to their people but to the rest of the international community as well. Under Bryan and his successor, Robert Lansing, the State Department sent political advisers to several countries in the region. The Wilsonian approach proved to be a slippery slope in that it was based on the premise that the elites and common people would welcome Wilson's idea of good governance. In a series of crises in Mexico in 1913, then Haiti in 1914, and the Dominican Republic in 1915, the United States intervened with armed force in an effort to end bloodshed and restore legitimate government.

In the Mexican case, the United States tried to end a civil war. In 1910, what appeared to be a fairly popular revolution ousted longtime dictator Porfirio Díaz. The leader of the revolution, Francisco I. Madero, was in turn ousted and killed by henchmen of Victoriano Huerta. That led to armed uprisings by three different leaders in three different regions of the country. In a fairly short period, the most powerful of the three, Venustiano Carranza, gathered his forces for an attack on the capital city in 1914. At this juncture, Wilson attempted to mediate among the warring factions and restore some order. Carranza would have nothing to do with US aid or advice. While he was considering his options, US troops on shore leave in Veracruz were detained by Carranza's forces. Wilson demanded their release. When that was done, he demanded that the Mexicans salute the US flag on the naval vessels in the harbor. When Carranza refused, Wilson ordered marines to land in Veracruz, thinking they would help restore order. When they were fired on, Wilson was appalled. He could not understand why Carranza or the other revolutionary leaders, Emiliano Zapata and Pancho Villa, did not realize that the United States was on the side of democracy. In discussing Wilson's policy in Mexico with the British foreign secretary, the US ambassador in London is reported to have said that the president wanted to "shoot men into self government."[16] While these exact words may be apocryphal, they convey a clear idea of the Wilsonian belief in the virtues of bringing democracy to a people who may not want it and in overcoming the objections of a people on whom good governance is imposed by military force.

In the other two cases, Haiti and the Dominican Republic, Wilson discovered that intervention to create a legitimate, democratic government where such government did not exist was complicated. There was no welcoming committee to embrace the US representatives. In both cases, intervention began by landing a small number of troops to restore order where a sitting president had been murdered and rioting had ensued and to turn authority over to a legitimate ruler. When no such ruler could be found, Wilson sent more troops and some political advisers. He anticipated that the political class would sit down with the US advisers and peacefully agree on procedures to restore order and stability. That did not happen. The leaders of the countries in the Caribbean Basin had no intention of listening to US advice or following orders issued from Washington unless they felt it in their interests to do so.[17]

The political actors and their armed cohorts quickly learned to use the US centurions in their midst as an additional political actor and play off the US representatives to gain advantage against their competitors for power. In short order, all of the factions sent representatives of their own to Washington to plead their case and convince the US government that they, not their opponents, should benefit from the presence of US power to take control of the government. Within two years in both Haiti and the Dominican Republic, the United States had sent hundreds of advisers who took over the government, the customs house, the treasury, the police, and finally, even the school system. To prepare for the withdrawal of US troops after decades of frustration and a powerful sense of having failed, the United States together with the group they considered most responsible in each of the countries created a new police force to maintain order. This was the ultimate extension of the Wilsonian logic of creating democracy in a country where none had existed before. In each case—and in Cuba and Nicaragua where similar policies were followed in the 1920s and 1930s—when US troops left, the new police force took power and placed its chief in office as president. That officer—Rafael Trujillo in the Dominican Republic, Anastasio Somoza García in Nicaragua, Fulgencio Batista in Cuba— quickly consolidated personal power and ruled as a dictator for many years, until killed or overthrown. In Haiti, the result was essentially the same, although the dictator, François Duvalier, did not emerge directly from the new police force.

Over time, it became clear to a succession of administrations in Washington that the Wilsonian dream of creating democracy where none had existed could not be achieved no matter how much or for how long US power might be applied. In the State Department it became preferable to keep in power a government that was less than democratic to avoid the slippery slope of intervention in an attempt to create a democracy by means of overwhelming force. In intervention, total power or dominance did not mean total control. In the absence of external threats to US security, though less desirable, stability was an acceptable alternative to instability and much preferred to total, endless intervention. The result was a triangular pattern of politics throughout the Caribbean Basin in which local politics was penetrated by US influence. In these penetrated polities, contestation for power was played out less through elections or the institutions of constitutional government, rather than through the use or threat of force and influence in Washington. In such a situation, the government in question had little sense of its place in the wider global community. Its foreign policy was to please the United States and secure such influence in Washington that would ensure its continuation in power. As US hegemony evolved, it became common to refer to Central America as the "backyard" of the United States. Even after the Cold War, the idea remained current that military doctrine would be based on geographical proximity and that powerful countries should expect "to police [their] own backyards."[18]

Over the course of the twentieth century, the United States meddled in the affairs of every country in the Caribbean Basin, most frequently with advice and encouragement or by providing experts who could clean up the nation's accounts, help write a coherent bank contract with a US bank, organize the collection of customs, or write a constitution and oversee elections.[19] In general, this interference was a diplomatic effort to maintain stability and some semblance of democratic governance in places the United States considered underdeveloped, weak, and even inferior.[20] When diplomacy failed, the United States intervened with troops or through the use of proxies in virtually every case, some more than once. The reason given by Washington was that instability threatened to precipitate armed conflict and endanger the lives of civilians or, worse, open the way to intervention by a hostile power—that is, a power hostile to the United States.[21]

The exercise of hegemony became more complicated if there was a division of opinion among actors in the United States, as there was with regard to Costa Rica in 1919, Nicaragua in 1927, Honduras in 1962, El Salvador in 1985, or Honduras in 2009. When such a disagreement became public, the effectiveness of US power was vitiated. In none of these cases, covering nearly a century, was there a serious external threat, direct or indirect, to the security of the United States, although on several occasions, one group or another invoked the Monroe Doctrine to justify its position. In every case, it is clear that no one in the penetrated polity followed US instructions except to gain power and that exerting US influence over a regime which had been placed in power by US influence was problematic and always the occasion for mutual manipulation. There always was some wiggle room within US hegemony.

From the Latin American perspective, the threat of US hegemony had some short-term benefits by eliminating the threat of European gunboat diplomacy. It also pushed the small states along the road of political modernization by imposing certain rules of political behavior. There were elections, political parties were formed or at least factions took the names of parties, and in some cases constitutions or sets of laws were promulgated. None of this would have satisfied a Wilsonian reformer who wanted to see the development of democratic governance, but it did win the grudging approval of many people in the larger countries of South America and Europe. Until after World War I, US hegemonic pretension had the effect of splitting Latin America into two geographic camps in which the southern group considered itself immune from such pretensions. How penetrated politics functioned can be conveyed through a historical vignette in

Nicaragua, one that could be repeated in different countries and was in fact repeated in an almost identical way a century later in Honduras.[22]

On a warm spring day in 1909, with the cherry blossoms still very much in evidence, Chandler P. Anderson left his office to walk over to the State Department, just to the west of the White House in Washington. He was on a mission for a client, Emiliano Chamorro Vargas, a prominent landowner from León, a self-proclaimed general, and a leader of the Conservative Party in Nicaragua. Anderson's goal was to get the State Department to look with favor on Chamorro's efforts to oust the long-time ruler José Santos Zelaya. Chamorro's plan was to threaten to use force and have himself elected as Primer Designado. Then, with the help of the State Department, he would convince Zelaya to step down so that he would be replaced by the Primer Designado, Chamorro, as the constitution stipulated.

Anderson was a specialist in international law. A graduate of Yale University and the Yale Law School, he had extensive experience in treaty making and arbitration and was on a first-name basis with the State Department hierarchy—and continued to be so with every administration until Franklin Roosevelt. For the next twenty years, he shifted back and forth from his private practice to service in the government, beginning just one year after this episode when Secretary Knox appointed him to the post of counselor of the department. During this period, most of the key people making Latin American policy were Harvard or Yale men, such as Leland "Summy" Harrison and Frank Polk, or sidekicks in the international law field, such as Robert "Bert" Lansing. The only outsider who joined the department in the 1920s was Dana G. Munro, a Princeton man.

Anderson got the State Department to do its part. It threatened to withdraw its recognition from Zelaya and encouraged him to step down. Zelaya objected and refused to budge, a reminder that hegemony does not mean the weaker party is without power or without room in which to manipulate; nor does it mean that the whim and will of the hegemon will be obeyed or respected at every turn. Zelaya bowed to the pressure eventually, mainly because Chamorro had hired a bunch of mercenaries who landed at Bluefields on the Caribbean coast. The State Department ordered the navy to prevent forces loyal to the government from disembarking at the port and would not to recognize Zelaya's puppet, José Madriz. But Chamorro didn't get his way immediately, even though Anderson had done his job well. It took Chamorro nearly three years to get his fractious conservatives united behind his candidacy.

Nearly twenty years later, Chamorro was back in the same situation. He wanted to oust the president, Juan Bautista Sacasa, and have himself named president. So he called on Anderson to go to work. But this time it was not as easy. Anderson told Secretary of State Charles Evans Hughes that Chamorro was pro–United States and his opponent favored British investments. Hughes was not moved. His successor, Frank Kellogg, was more susceptible because he feared subversion by the Communist International coming from Mexico into Central America. Anderson spent hours with Kellogg and all the appropriate officials, especially Harrison and the new man in the Latin American Division, Sumner Welles (also from Harvard). Again, Anderson earned his fee, and this time Chamorro had his ducks in a row. But his success was short-lived. The world had changed, and so had Nicaragua. The very success of the Anderson-Chamorro gambit in mobilizing US influence in Nicaraguan politics helped drive rebellion leader Augusto Sandino into the hills.[23]

The issue of asymmetry of power between the United States and the rest of the nations in the hemisphere, especially the smaller nations of Central America, affects our understanding of hemispheric relations. Countries operating within the confining framework of US hegemony and that deliberately used the United States as an actor in their domestic contestation for power cannot pretend to have an autonomous foreign policy. In those cases, there is reciprocal, if asymmetrical, manipulation and the maneuvering by the smaller power is evidence of its limited autonomy. Where that occurs, we want to have evidence of a conscious effort of agency. What are the conditions under which a group in power in a particular country thinks of the country they control as having agency in the world community? In most of the small nations of the Caribbean Basin through the twentieth century, foreign policy generally meant maintaining approval by the US State Department and using other nations as cards to play in a weak hand. In South America, where the asymmetry of power was less marked and where the hegemonic pretension of the United States was much lower, the capacity for agency was correspondingly greater.

The small but real degree of autonomy and the capacity for agency among the states of the Caribbean Basin becomes clearer when we consider the response of the nations in South America to the gradual advance of US hegemony. Obviously, both Venezuela and Colombia had felt the edge of US pretension and the effects of its power at the beginning of the century. Leaders throughout South America were outraged at the arrogance of US statements explaining its interventions. At the same time, many writers and leaders agreed that the behavior of Caribbean nations was bad—uncivilized—and that something had to be done about it so that the international system would function properly. The most commonly stated view was that *their* nation was simply more civilized and would not commit such transgressions or ever be subject to such correction by an outside power. The fact of the matter is that the United States did not consider intervening in the internal affairs of nations in South America after the two episodes involving Colombia and Venezuela at the beginning of the century until it entered World War I.

When World War I started in Europe, the nations in the Western Hemisphere declared their neutrality. Some Argentines had misgivings because they favored Great Britain, but the dominant view was that the international division of labor would guarantee their trade, including the supply of strategic goods imported from Europe. They were wrong. Within six months, the British had diverted all shipping to war purposes and commandeered all available supplies of coal for the navy. The German submarine campaign was annoying and economically hurtful, but no nation in Latin America suffered losses anywhere close in magnitude to those suffered by the United States. The international lawyers in the hemisphere were pretty much of an opinion that the combatants should not be allowed to disregard their rights, but there was no concerted effort among them to enforce that view. The closest to such an effort was a request by Peru that the Latin American emissaries in Washington should join together to protect neutral rights. The Pan American Union created a neutrality committee to study the subject, but the US declaration of war ended the effort while it was still inconclusive.

As ships were sunk and other violations of international law were committed, notes were presented to the British and the Germans, responses were received, and the process was repeated every time accepted peacetime practice was violated. The Argentines threatened to declare war on Germany in 1915 for the sinking of the *Toro* and the Germans apologized. When a similar episode occurred in 1917, involving the Peruvian vessel *Lorton*, the Peruvians demanded an apology, but the Germans procrastinated and promised only to study the incident. When the United States declared war, the Peruvians followed suit, declaring the need for "American solidarity," and reiterated Peru's commitment to the principles of international law.[24] The Brazilians, who also lost ships to German torpedoes, followed suit. The Brazilians also sent units of their navy to join the British at Gibraltar, sent medical personnel to help the French, and added air force members who were incorporated into the RAF. Uruguay's president Baltasar Brum applauded the US position and called for an "American union of action." He noted that "Although in the past its [the US] policy may have been unjust and harsh with some of the Latin countries, that fact should not now constitute an obstacle to a closer friendship . . . It must be recognized that nations as well as men enjoy the right of evolution toward goodness."[25] An Argentine, Lucio M. Moreno Quintana, who worked for the new president, Hipólito Yrigoyen, thought that Brum had gone overboard and considered instead the utility of a league of Latin American nations that would defend the region against the United States.[26] At the same time, however, former foreign minister Luis María Drago, who had a decade earlier complained to the US secretary of state that the US was violating the Calvo Doctrine against intervention, stated, "The war between Germany and America is a struggle of democracy versus absolutism and no American nation can remain neutral without denying its past and compromising its future."[27] When the United States declared war, Yrigoyen's ambassador to Washington, Rómulo Naón, noted that his government recognized "the justice of that decision" and went on to say that all of the nations in the hemisphere were affected by the war in the same way.[28] In Mexico, the revolutionary leaders toyed with German emissaries hoping to unsettle the United States and make the Wilson administration more mindful of Mexican sovereignty. Both parties manipulated the other and caused considerable concern in Washington. On balance, the majority opinion in Latin America was that there were core values in the hemisphere and that they were on the side of the United States, although several preferred to keep out of the war and others did not want to be pushed into the war by the United States.

As the war went on, both sides became increasingly desperate. The British were running out of money and fuel for their fleet and turned to the private sector in the United States for support. The Germans had a more complicated situation. They had to stop supplies reaching the British, if they could, and that meant increasingly provoking the US government. As part of Wilson's preparations to enter the war, he began to line up friends in Latin America to be sympathetic to the position the United States was taking against violations of neutral rights. When the United States finally entered the conflict, Brazil joined in addition to the dependent states in the Caribbean Basin. Peru jumped in a bit later. In prosecuting the war, the United States extended its strategic requirements geographically to include South America for the first time by working to cripple German trade with Latin America and weaken German trade capacity after the war. The principal instrument in this effort was the blacklist, an extension of belligerency to nations that considered themselves neutral. This was especially sensitive in Argentina and Chile, where German trade was significant and where there were numerous citizens of German descent. The enormous expansion of the wartime bureaucracy in the United States and its international projection was a source of tension with the nations of South America. They resisted, but they could not stifle the US urge to extend its reach. The reach of US hegemony was extended—imperfect, but extended.

In more general terms, the war was a shock to the Latin American economic systems, especially the commodity exporters. Although none suffered as rude a shock as the Argentines had in 1914, when the lights went

out in the capital, Buenos Aires, because the British had stopped all shipments of coal, all the countries in the region experienced a diminution in
their economic activity and a radical diminution in their ability to influence the price of the commodities they exported. Nor could they secure the
capital goods they required to keep their small domestic manufacturing industries in operation. Little was done to increase domestic manufacturing
because everyone believed that after the war the international system
would return to the patterns that had been set in the last half of the nineteenth century and the first decade of the twentieth. They were wrong and
suffered the consequences in the 1920s. What seemed a rational decision
in 1918 proved to be misguided once the time frame had shifted. The Great
Depression was a greater shock and moved most of the countries to attempt some form of import substitution as a means of self-preservation.[29]
As in the trade competition before the war, creating an industrial base was
a national decision. It was not until after World War II that talk of a regional approach to development became part of the policy debate.

Yrigoyen and Argentina represent a special case. Yrigoyen was the
first president elected under the new Sáenz Peña reform law, and he led his
Radical Party to power for the first time at the national level. His foreign
policy, which he called *principismo*, was a combination of moral values—
or soft power—plus open criticism of the United States. But he always operated in isolation. Despite his strong opposition to US intervention in
Mexico, Nicaragua, and the Dominican Republic, he proposed in 1920 in
response to an attempted coup in Bolivia that the nations of Latin America
recognize only governments elected in a democratic and constitutional
manner, which sounded very much like Woodrow Wilson's nonrecognition
policy. Yrigoyen's proposal provoked howls of protest from law professors
and commentators but only studied silence from governments throughout
the region.

Argentina did not enter the war and therefore was not invited to participate in the peace conference that followed. Yrigoyen instructed the Argentine ambassador to the United States to protest their exclusion from the
conference and sent a representative to the first meeting of the League of
Nations in Geneva in 1921, with instructions to submit to the assembly a
proposal to democratize the League by eliminating any distinctions in the
memberships of former belligerents and those nations that had not participated in the war. When that proposal was tabled, the representative, former
foreign minister Honorio Pueyrredón, was ordered to leave Geneva and return home.[30] Yrigoyen was applying Calvo's principle of pari passu, that
all sovereign nations should be treated as equals and that having fought in
the war should not give any nation a privileged position in the new world

organization. It was an idea whose time had not yet come. Brazil, which had entered the war and thought that it was important enough to be given a seat on the Security Council, withdrew when it did not receive that honor. There was no attempt to bring the Latin American nations together in a bloc to reform the new organization; to the contrary, individual nations, such as Peru and Bolivia, tried to get the new organization involved in solving local or subregional border disputes. The League was not up to the task.

While the rejection of the League of Nations by the US Congress appeared to signal a strong turn away from involvement in world affairs and a turning inward or isolationism, the United States never reduced its international activities in the period after the war. Trade, investment overseas, participation in international meetings—all of these continued. The United States took its seat at international meetings as one of the world's leaders. With regard to the hemisphere, the aftermath of war meant two important shifts in US policy. First and foremost, it ended realistic fears of military interposition or imperial control by a country outside the hemisphere. This meant that successive administrations in Washington became increasingly skeptical about US interventions in the region generated by a belief in the assumptions of the Monroe Doctrine and the Roosevelt Corollary and began to wind down the several occupations that had begun under Wilson. Second, the war had made plain not only that the international division of labor was suspended but also that security was more than military might or national economic capacity; it included access to strategic goods, specifically fuel, communications, and financial assets. The lack of the first very nearly brought the British to their knees in 1915. The lack of control over the second had made US prosecution of the war more difficult. The failure to control the third had undermined the war effort of the central powers. The core of US strategic planning during the war was to ensure access to adequate supplies of petroleum, establish networks of international communication under US control, and make sure that financial instability in Latin America or elsewhere would not threaten the nation's security. This was a global policy and continued after the war. The open door had been expanded beyond trade to include a broader definition of strategic assets than Mahan had imagined. Within the hemisphere, the United States was not sure it wanted the door to be open.[31]

In its dealings with Latin America, this meant providing focused and energetic diplomatic support for private companies in the sectors of energy, communications, and finance. In some cases, it might mean encouraging a private company to enter a specific market considered of strategic importance. The goal was to make sure that no foreign power held monopoly control over strategic resources. National petroleum companies or telephone companies were not favored, but they were much less troubling than Dutch oil companies, British cable companies, or French telephone companies. The war had demonstrated that in times of crisis, those companies would follow the flag to the detriment of US interests and that local or host nations did not have the power or the will to bring them under control.

The Argentines certainly understood this, as the British had stopped shipping coal to them during the war, even though they wanted Argentine foodstuffs. Beginning with Yrigoyen, Argentine governments began to provide financing to the national petroleum company and passed legislation that sought to guarantee that foreign-owned companies would bow to national (local) demands in times of emergency. Argentine strategic thinking was similar to the United States, but its capacity to carry out policies was less robust. When Marcelo T. de Alvear succeeded Yrigoyen in 1922, the government curtailed financing for the national petroleum company, YPF. For the most part, the other countries in South America were content to allow their energy to be supplied by foreign companies and their communications to be provided by multinationals and to allow foreign banks to play a significant role in their markets. This began to change after the Depression made free trade an illusion.

In political terms, while US governments in the 1920s never were shy about indicating their preference for political stability, they were reluctant to intervene militarily in the internal affairs of nations in the region and began the process of winding down the military occupations in which the United States was involved. The State Department even went so far as to draft a policy memorandum in 1928 explaining why intervention was to be avoided in the future.[32] Revolutions, however, were considered destabilizing and, with very few exceptions, were opposed with every means short of military intervention.[33]

Mexico, of course, was a special case. In the period after World War I, the Mexican government struggled to restore state capacity while attempting to create a bilateral relationship with the United States that would provide Mexico with some sense of its autonomy as a sovereign nation. For the two decades between the world wars, the twin goals of Mexican foreign policy were to use nations outside the hemisphere as levers in their relations with the United States while simultaneously seeking to establish their defense against US aggression, especially in defense of its economic interests.[34] Successive administrations sought to control the same strategic assets within their own borders as the United States attempted to control throughout the hemisphere. Oil turned out to be the major cause of tension between the countries in this period. Ironically, after the crisis precipitated by nationalization of the foreign-owned oil properties in 1938 during the administration of Lázaro Cárdenas, the intense bilateral negotiations to ease the crisis actually produced a constructive strategic partnership that accomplished the principal goals of both nations.[35]

Withdrawal from intervention was always messy in part because it was difficult for the vice-regents in Washington to be confident that they were leaving behind a stable government. At first, in the Dominican Republic, Cuba, and Nicaragua, the goal was to establish a democratic regime to take over. By the end of the 1930s, it was clear that democracy was too vague an objective and the goal of policy was to leave behind stable governments that might aspire to democracy in the future. One of the classic cases of creating a stable nondemocracy was the Nicaragua of Anastasio Somoza García (1936–1956).

While the Wilsonian dream of creating democracy to establish stability to protect US interests was shown repeatedly to be unattainable, US influence in many of the penetrated polities in Central America (though not all) enhanced the formation of a modern state. That may have been the principal accomplishment of the Somoza clan. They remained in power because they were able to negotiate with an evolving merchant elite and provide the framework for that elite's success. The existence of a functioning state was one of the factors in creating a viable opposition to the successors of Anastasio Somoza García in the 1970s.[36]

In the interwar decades, anti-Americanism spread throughout the hemisphere, although it took various forms that were not necessarily compatible with one another.[37] One of the major shifts in how Latin Americans thought about themselves was in how they understood race and race relations. All of the countries of the region had been swept up in the racial orthodoxy of European superiority in the nineteenth century. Even those countries, such as Mexico and Brazil, where non-Europeans were the majority and people of mixed ethnicity (mestizos or mulattos) constituted the largest single portion of the population, the images of civilization and modernity were closely linked to the purity of European race. This changed radically in the period following World War I. The expressions of race mixture helped strengthen national identity, an identity that could legitimately stand autonomously from European or US influences that treated Latin America in a colonial manner. In this sense, all of these movements represent elements in the creation of national agency in a broader world.

In Mexico, there was a strong movement to recognize the worth of the indigenous population and make a virtue of race mixing. José Vasconcelos referred to the benefits of miscegenation in Mexico as the creation of a new cosmic race.[38] In the Andes, Víctor Raúl Haya de la Torre began a political movement, the American Popular Revolutionary Alliance (APRA), that celebrated the worth of the indigenous population and the virtues of miscegenation. The Venezuelan intellectual Arturo Uslar Pietri, like José Carlos Mariátegui in Peru and Haya de la Torre, took *mestizaje* as a sign of national identity and an element in the creation of a progressive, inclusive movement, the Partido Acción Democrática (Democratic Action Party), which he hoped could deal with the nation's new petroleum riches. He was linked politically with Rómulo Gallegos and Rómulo Betancourt.[39] In Brazil, the anthropologist Gilberto Freyre celebrated a New World in the tropics that had resulted from the mixing of African and European races, while his compatriot, Oswald de Andrade, chastised what he called Brazil's colonial urge to devour European culture and urged expression of a modern, Brazilian culture.[40] In Cuba, the sociologist Fernando Ortiz Fernández spoke of a syncretic culture, one that was produced by the blending of people from different races, a new, dynamic culture that was stronger than any of the original component parts.

While race discrimination continued in every country and non-Europeans in the population—whether of African descent, indigenous, or mixed ancestry—continued at the bottom of the socioeconomic ladder, by 1930, race mixture and indigenous culture had become a source of national pride and cultural strength in many countries.[41] It also served—and continues to serve—as a force legitimating nationalism and nationalistic policies in a manner more politically palatable and more inclusive than the romantic notions of nationhood that had predominated in the region in the nineteenth and early part of the twentieth century, which had been blatant efforts to fit the history of Latin American nations into some sort of mythical European framework. Over time, *indigenismo* served as a centripetal force, bringing countries in the region together and separating them collectively from the United States, where the separation of the races continued well into the second half of the twentieth century.

The new emphasis on nativism was generally linked to progressive anti-imperialist movements based on Marxist visions of the international system.[42] It also served and continues to serve to justify nativist postures with reference to natural resources—"This lithium is ours!" as Bolivian president Evo Morales put it in 2010—and to policies of social inclusion, especially in the Andes. After the Cold War, it would be used also to protect the rights of citizens who had migrated to other countries in the region. Mexico began to defend the rights of Mexicans in the United States only after the Cold War; Bolivians began to protest the treatment of Bolivians in Argentina, and Peruvians have used protests about treatment of Peruvians in Chile as an instrument of foreign policy to build support for nationalist policies demanding the reopening of the territorial and maritime issues arising from the War of the Pacific. In each case, the people whose rights were alleged to be threatened were indigenous or mestizo in societies dominated by more European or whiter political elites.

Other strains of anti-Americanism in the period had the opposite effect—they exerted centrifugal force, pulling nations in the region apart, especially in their dealings with the United States. For example, the ultra-montane Catholics in Argentina and Chile considered themselves superior to the heathens in the United States. They also claimed that they were of purer European stock than the Americans or any other Latin Americans. This added a racial element to the economic drive toward self-sufficiency in the 1930s, and served to justify the tilt toward forms of fascism in Argentina, Brazil, Chile, and Uruguay.[43] This was not a theme that attracted many in the region outside of the Southern Cone. More widespread was a movement among intellectuals called *Arielismo*—after the essay by Uruguayan José E. Rodó—in which Latin Americans considered themselves superior to the United States because they were spiritual and the North Americans were crude and materialistic. The critique of US imperialism was something that linked progressives with the most conservative groups in several countries.

The most significant and most widely held argument of anti-Americanism was the opposition to intervention by one state in the internal affairs of another. Ironically, the most frequently used forum to express their hostility was the series of hemispheric meetings, called by the Pan American Union in Washington, which represented the effort by the United States to institutionalize its hegemony. In these meetings the representatives of the nations in the hemisphere debated among themselves in support of or opposition to the rules that governed their community. The nations of South America were scornful of the puppet governments in Central America and the Caribbean, but they were not able to formulate rules to exclude the puppets without themselves undermining the principle of nonintervention, which was the glue that held them all together (to the degree that they held together at all). Nonintervention continues to be a force in regional cohesion up to the present.

The Great Depression had a powerful impact on all the nations in Latin America. First, international trade imploded and put all exporters of primary products at a disadvantage, part of a cyclical rise and fall of commodity prices that would continue to haunt most nations of the hemisphere into the current century. Second, international flows of capital virtually disappeared and led to a staggering number of defaults of both sovereign debt and private debt. Third, the capital goods that the primary product producers imported to satisfy internal demand became scarce and increasingly expensive. The effects certainly were traumatic, and not just in economic matters. As they looked around for solutions to the extraordinary problems they confronted, Latin American leaders saw suggestive models in the European responses to the crisis. Latin Americans were particularly impressed by the rise of strongmen and authoritarian parties in several countries. Fascism and national socialism were appealing because they appeared to simplify the decisionmaking process and made action easier by eliminating the need for consulting the electorate and dealing patiently with political parties and legislatures. Corporatism and national socialism also offered facile solutions to intractable economic problems by organizing potential political and economic actors into groups responsible directly to the state while celebrating all that was national. Even the arts were influenced by trends in Europe that celebrated a romantic notion of nationalism and looked to a mythic semi-classical past for models. Social realism in plastic art and in public art was hugely popular throughout the 1930s.[44]

The decade is significant in the evolution of autonomy in the region in part due to the work done by Raúl Prebisch and others. They searched for an economic model that would allow countries that had been inserted into the international economy as exporters of primary products to defend themselves when the international market froze and the difference in price between primary products and capital goods increased to the point that the unequal exchange threatened to bankrupt the Latin Americans or lock them into a situation in which they would be in permanent thrall to the countries that provided capital and manufactures.

Dominant theories of development since Adam Smith and David Ricardo to World War I conceived of the process as something similar to biological evolution in which countries that were less developed had to go through the same stages or processes through which the developed countries had gone. This linear progression, when linked to the evolution of political systems and social inclusion, came to be called modernization theory. Although Prebisch accepted the underlying assumption of linearity in development, he followed John Maynard Keynes in rejecting a passive approach to it and argued that the less developed countries had to accelerate or alter the path of the process by jumping ahead of the developed countries to create their own industries. This would be the role of the state, not the market or an invisible hand. With import substitution industrialization, as it was called, each country (or group of countries) would have its own steel industry and automobile industry and take control of its own natural resources. The dog-eat-dog economic model, so different from the Ricardian model of international comparative advantage in open markets that had dominated thinking before the Great Depression, created an inertial force driving decisionmaking toward national autonomy from the international market and state control of the economy. In his early policy prescriptions, Prebisch did not deal with the issue of market size or how to deal with competition among developing countries. In some cases, such as Juan Perón in Argentina and Getúlio Vargas in Brazil, the policy planning tilted toward a form of autarky. In its more extreme forms, it created semi-command economies in which the state attempted to control production and prices and provide capital for domestic investment, without creating revenue flows that would pay for such activities. These flows were expected to come from domestic demand and the international market. The former often was inadequate, and the latter could not be controlled. Over time, the inefficiencies of such economies, including staggering levels of corruption and union featherbedding, together with short-term political decisionmaking made them uncompetitive and provoked periods of uncontrolled inflation and stagnation called stagflation.

Several of Prebisch's students, who came together with the master after World War II to form the staff of the new Economic Commission for Latin America (ECLA/CEPAL) of the fledgling United Nations, were concerned that asymmetric relations and the deteriorating price disparity between primary products and capital goods were fixed features of an unfair, unequal economic structure, in which the market was a sometime thing and nothing like the neutral invisible hand envisioned by classical economists. They saw a rigid structure they wanted to change. In other words, they wanted to change the rules of the economic community of nations in which they felt obliged to participate. They also were skeptical of the capacity of command economies to sustain competitiveness and preferred to seek reforms of the dominant form of market economy. In the hands of political scientists and sociologists, this mode of thinking was synthesized as "dependency theory."[45]

This inward-looking model of economic development, import substitution industrialization (ISI), dominated thinking in the region for nearly fifty years and fell from favor only because it became clear that the gross inefficiencies of industrial production in a restricted, semi-autarkical market could not be sustained and, perversely, that it perpetuated the inequality in the international system it was designed to overcome because the industries that were created at any given time could not be improved or updated because there was no local source of capital or innovation. In addition, the progressive economists of ECLA/CEPAL were worried that in such a national market, economic decisions left in the hands of politicians whose primary concern was keeping themselves in power would lead to economic crisis over and over again. Ultimately, the underlying premise of ISI—that each nation could determine its own economic policies and protect itself from vulnerability to the international market and pressures from richer or more powerful countries—was not a sustainable position. As part of their effort to perfect the model, ECLA/CEPAL began to promote regionalism as a solution to the problem of market size. It was assumed by the Cepalinos that there would be a convergence of interests among countries that shared the experience of underdevelopment.

The final factors in the decline of ISI and the original ECLA/CEPAL model were first that the inefficiencies of many national economies produced unmanageable quantities of debt, as government printed money or sold bonds to cover the costs of their domestic programs. The sovereign debt crisis of the 1980s pushed a number of countries away from ISI and toward more open markets. Second, at the end of the 1980s, there was a surge in the development of international economic institutions and a protracted drive for more open trade, together with a technological revolution that lowered the cost of manufactured goods. The opening of global trade was accompanied by a cyclical upswing in the international price of commodities, driven by the voracious demand of China, which reversed the terms of trade that had appeared so unfavorable to commodity producers in the 1930s and so fixed. For nearly two decades after 1990, exporting primary products again looked as if it were a form of comparative advantage.

Because the decade-long crisis of the 1930s pushed the leaders of many of the nations into thinking about their autonomy within the international system and to seek ways to buffer or diminish the vulnerability they experienced in moments of international crisis, the interwar period may be considered an incubator for thinking about agency and for foreign policy experiments that were designed to increase national autonomy and to push countries into becoming proactive in protecting national interests. Whatever its shortcomings as macroeconomic policy, ISI expanded the scope of foreign policy thinking in every country in Latin America.

Argentina represented a major exception to these trends in Latin America and to Latin America's response to the war in Europe. Although World War I had been a profound shock to the Argentine system, when the war ended, there was a broad consensus that the international market would soon return to the old "normal." The market did—for a while. When the Great Depression began, Argentines again expected that they would be exempted from its worst consequences and to a considerable extent, they were. Just to be sure, the Argentine government negotiated a deal with the British that would maintain the lucrative trade between the two countries, including the flow of capital to Argentina to expand its infrastructure and its public utilities. In essence, Argentina deliberately inserted itself into Britain's informal empire, anticipating that by doing so they would prolong their period of remarkable economic growth begun at the end of the nineteenth century. They did so despite the fact that the benefits of such a relationship were enjoyed by a shrinking landed oligarchy and their banker allies, that British capital became more difficult to access as the decade unfolded, and that the United States was rapidly becoming the principal economic partner of most of the hemisphere.[46]

One of the reasons the Argentine leadership could pursue such a retrograde foreign policy was that the conservative oligarchy extended its rule of the country with the help of the military and gradually closed the political space open to dissenting voices, even the voices of such writers as Prebisch. Many of these military figures were friendly toward the totalitarian countries of Europe, and a significant portion of the political leadership was sympathetic to the political style and mode of organization of the German, Italian, and Spanish regimes. These leaders scorned liberal democracy. They expressed their preference for what they called more vigorous, masculine, or organic modes of organization. These leaders were increasingly hostile to efforts by the United States to bring the hemisphere together through the regular meetings of the Pan American Union and openly opposed all efforts by the United States toward the end of the decade to extend its security zone from the Caribbean to South America.

When hostilities began in Europe, the United States redoubled its efforts to create a common security posture in the hemisphere. Curiously, this occurred just as Roberto Ortiz was elected president in Argentina and put in José María Cantilo as his foreign minister. These men, together with Felipe Espil, the Argentine ambassador in Washington, represented a more liberal faction of the political leadership. Thinking to use their relationship with the United States as a lever against the domestic groups that sided with the Axis powers, Cantilo proposed to the US government that the hemisphere, in collective manner, create a nonbelligerency zone to keep both Americas out of the war. Deeply enmeshed in his own complex maneuverings with the British and Congress, Franklin Roosevelt declined the offer. Cantilo was ousted; Ortiz, terminally ill, took a leave of absence and was replaced by his vice president Ramón Castillo, who was openly pro-German and more friendly with the military.[47]

The 1930s saw the military rise to power (or very close to it) in several countries in addition to Argentina: Chile, Peru, Bolivia, Brazil, Venezuela, and Paraguay. In Central America, they never were far from the seat of power. The militarization of politics reduced the space for democratic governance, brought nationalism to the center of discussion, and provided an excuse for state control over the economy at a time when the international community was rushing toward such regimes everywhere.[48] Chest-beating nationalism not only produced regimes with pretensions to authoritarian control, it also produced assertions of national greatness and demands to revindicate territory considered rightfully part of the fatherland. Here, the colonial legacy of indeterminate borders came back to haunt leaders in the twentieth century. There were three major conflagrations in South America in the years before World War II: the Chaco War, between Paraguay and Bolivia, and the Leticia and Marañón border disputes between Peru and Ecuador in the first and Peru and Colombia in the second.[49] The United States was called in by participants to mediate all of these conflicts, with uneven results, and the League of Nations played a constructive role in calming (without solving) the two boundary disputes. Each conflict produced a flurry of diplomatic activity on the part of neighbors. In the absence of an institutional framework within which to seek peace—the Pan American Union was not up to the task—countries formed ad hoc groups of "friends" to bring the combatants to the bargaining table.[50] The lack of an effective architecture of hemispheric community was noted by leaders throughout the region. The United States set out to create an architecture that would serve its own national purposes.

The growing tension in Europe and Asia, together with the combative environment in the international economy, convinced leaders in the United States that pulling together the members of the hemispheric community would be a good thing. The premonition of impending trouble was one factor behind Roosevelt's acceptance of the nonintervention vote at the Buenos Aires conference in 1936.[51] In the following years, there was a series of special meetings in which the question of hemispheric security was discussed and in which a set of consultative mechanisms was established. In the meeting in Havana in 1941, concerned about European island colonies in the Caribbean, the parties agreed that there would be no transfer of territory from one European power to another as a result of the hostilities. This might be considered a restatement of the Monroe Doctrine in which all the countries of the hemisphere had a voice. Strategic planners in the United States saw the approach of the war in Europe and set staff to thinking about what to do about the Western Hemisphere. Until 1942 or 1943, military planning was driven by the historical Mahan model with some Monroe Doctrine concerns about European intervention thrown in for good measure. The concentration of US military assets was to be in the Caribbean Basin, with focus on the outer or eastern islands, and a watchful eye on the European colonies within the basin.[52]

For the first time, US geopoliticians considered the security zone to extend south from the Caribbean to include the bulge of Brazil, the closest point in the Western Hemisphere to Africa. On the one hand, this might serve as a land bridge for an invasion of the hemisphere by the Axis; on the other hand, it might serve as a jumping-off point for an Allied movement into Africa.[53] By 1942, it was clear that this new security zone should be made part of a collective effort. The United States called for a meeting in Rio to coordinate a common defense strategy for the hemisphere. As they had fifty years earlier in the first meeting of the Pan American Union, the Argentines succeeded in watering down the language of the final document so as to render it without force as a statement of collective action. It did not block the United States from unilateral action or making bilateral arrangements with countries in strategic places, such as Brazil.[54]

For the most part, the nations of Latin America tried to keep the war at arm's length, which proved difficult, if not impossible. The Germans tried to influence their behavior through threats of trade restrictions and the use of submarines as well as through careful show of their limited naval assets in the Atlantic. Once the United States formally entered the war, access to strategic materials in the hemisphere, especially metals from the countries on the west coast, was a matter of great importance. Chile struggled to maintain its neutrality against Allied pressure, arguing that the Allies could not protect the long Chilean coast from German or Japanese attack were Chile to side openly with the Allies. For nearly two years after the attacks on Pearl Harbor, US policy was to promise to protect the hemisphere and provide such economic aid as necessary to replace trade or investment lost by a declaration of war against the Axis. These promises proved empty, but that did not stop the United States from increasing the pressure on its hemispheric neighbors. The United States had sufficient leverage to force them to behave, but not sufficient resources—or will—to provide for them, a situation that would maximize the hostility generated in the region.

US hegemony in the hemisphere intensified during the war, as it had during World War I, through the energetic application of such programs as the blacklist of Germans and German firms, of financial controls over banking in the region, and effective market monopolies of strategic commodities, which gave the United States extraordinary power over the economic well-being of commodity-exporting countries such as Argentina, Chile, Peru, Bolivia, and Ecuador. Argentina escaped some of the pressure only because the British coveted their foodstuffs. Rising ill will throughout the hemisphere went along with the geographic extension of US hegemony and the penetration of its wartime programs. US agents penetrated countries throughout the hemisphere in ways never before attempted as they pushed governments to confiscate property owned by Axis nationals, confiscate firms alleged to be doing business with Axis powers, and in some cases to incarcerate people suspected of sympathizing with the Axis. This pressure created resentment, especially in the Southern Cone countries where political sympathies were divided and descendants of Germans and Italians were a significant portion of the population. After the war, these countries showed their defiance of the United States by opening their borders to a number of major Nazi leaders and officers of the German armed forces who could pay for special visas. This wartime penetration of South America presaged the nightmare of US dominance in the Cold War in the way the definition of US security kept shifting and the denigration of Latin American sovereignty seemed to have no limits.

Brazil and Mexico were two prominent exceptions to this pattern. Both had close relations with the Axis countries before the war, and Mexico toyed with the Germans as a foil against the United States during the tense negotiations over the expropriation of foreign-owned oil companies. In both cases, for very different reasons, the governments struck mutually beneficial bargains with the United States and played active roles in the war on the side of the Allies. In Brazil, the process was part of a strategic plan by the Vargas government to achieve the economic diversification necessary to create the conditions for national autonomy. In essence, Vargas negotiated with the Roosevelt administration to build the base for Brazilian industrialization. In return, Vargas allowed the United States to use Brazilian territory in preparation for an invasion of Africa, committed Brazil to sending troops to the European theater of war, and opened the Amazon to exploitation of the natural rubber that was so important to the war effort. The key to the success of these negotiations was the extraordinary personal relationship between Sumner Welles, then undersecretary of state, and Brazilian foreign minister Osvaldo Aranha.[55]

The Mexican agreement with the United States was the product of a slow process of understanding in Washington that true security in the coming war could come only with a stable, confident, and reasonably content neighbor on the southern border. Without accommodation, the US security position in the hemisphere would be untenable. Moreover, as the planning for strategic commodities became more sophisticated, it was clear that Mexican petroleum would be critical to the war effort and that a secure supply of fuel was more important than the profit of a few multinational petroleum companies. The strategic partnership between government and business had to benefit the state or it could not endure. In this case, the oil companies would get their profits somewhere else.

Postwar planning began even before the tide of hostilities had turned in favor of the Allies. This time, Roosevelt made sure that the United States would be a founding member of the new global organization, the

United Nations. New global players such as the Soviet Union and China participated in the division of the spoils. The Allies were exhausted and in desperate need of economic aid. Once again, the nations of Latin America were only marginal players in the negotiations for the postwar world. The war did not enhance relations between the United States and the rest of the hemisphere. Nations that produced strategic commodities, such as Chile and Peru, were left without adequate compensation and were much weakened by the war. In the Caribbean Basin, dictators were allowed to consolidate their control in the interests of hemispheric security. Brazil probably benefited most from the war, and that was in large measure the result of the deals that Vargas struck before the war began.

In the case of Argentina, which had resisted US pressure to join the war effort, the United States was determined that it should be made to pay the price by exclusion from the United Nations. But at the preliminary conference of hemispheric nations, at Chapultepec Castle in Mexico City in 1945, the Latin Americans joined forces to persuade the United States that regional organization was crucial and that no nation should be excluded. The United States bowed to the Latin American united front and went so far as to create within the United Nations recognition of regional organizations, presumably with the Pan American Union in mind.[56] After all, the Latin American nations together represented the largest single voting bloc in the new organization and the United States expected that they would join the effort to protect the values that had been the declared goals of the war effort. Optimists in Washington were certain that the nations in the hemisphere would happily accept US leadership (hegemony without coercion) in the era of peace and cooperation ahead. They failed completely to appreciate that in the Depression and the war, all of the Latin American nations had played increasing roles in world affairs and that their new sense of agency in world affairs would not easily be reconciled with US control.

The meeting in Mexico City was remarkable not only for the broad consensus among the Latin American nations that Argentina should not be left out of the United Nations but also for the way it served as the catalyst for Latin American support for a hemispheric community with rules and for the belief that the Pan American Union should be reformed if it was to serve as the community's organizing institution. They had tried to protect themselves from intervention by more powerful states through the League of Nations and failed. Now, they saw the United Nations as the way to protect their independence and the principles of nonintervention and legal equality of sovereign states through a UN-sanctioned international institution. They hoped they could play a greater role in making rules for their community through the United Nations. Many wanted the Pan American

Union to expand its agenda to include economic and social questions. Swept up by the triumphalist rhetoric celebrating the Allied victory, optimists in Latin America hoped the moment had come to realize the Bolivarian dream, including cooperation with the United States. Once the Cold War began in earnest, that dream became a nightmare.

Notes

1. Archibald C. Coolidge, *The United States as a World Power* (New York: Macmillan, 1908), is a typical example of self-conscious consideration of the United States' new status in the world.

2. The most comprehensive study of the US approach to imperialism is E. R. May, *American Imperialism: A Speculative Essay* (New York: Atheneum, 1968). Latin America scarcely figures in the conversations that led to action by the US government.

3. On the economic dimension of US expansion, see W. A. Williams, "Brooks Adams and American Expansion," *New England Quarterly* 25 (1952): 225–228. The thinking on the need for US expansion was strongly Darwinian. Mahan's classic work, *The Influence of Sea Power upon History, 1660–1783* (New York: Little, Brown, 1899) was first published in 1890. A more general approach to the economics of imperialism is Parker T. Moon, *Imperialism and World Politics* (New York: Macmillan, 1926).

4. On the war with Spain, see E. R. May, *Imperial Democracy* (New York: Harcourt, Brace & World, 1961); Pablo de Azcárate, *La Guerra del 98* (Madrid: Alianza Editorial, 1968); David F. Trask, *The War with Spain in 1898* (New York: Macmillan, 1981).

5. Given the central role of race in nineteenth-century discussions of imperialism and civilization, it is interesting that the anti-imperialist forces in the United States were numerically divided between progressive groups and conservatives and that both factions were unwilling to take "inferior" races into the republic; see Joseph S. Tulchin, "Edward Atkinson, the Reformer Who Would Not Succeed," *Essex Institute Historical Collections* 110.2 (April 1969): 1–21.

6. Maximiliano G. Gregorio-Cernadas, *Vestigios conceptuales del idealismo kantiano en las ideas e instituciones que confirguraron la política de seguridad external del gobierno de Alfonsin*, unpublished paper in collection of Joseph S. Tulchin, n.d.

7. This vote is often taken as the high mark of the good neighbor policy. See Bryce Wood, *The Making of the Good Neighbor Policy* (New York: Columbia University Press, 1961).

8. Following Hedley Bull, *The Anarchical Society: A Study of Order in World Politics* (New York: Columbia University Press, 1977), dominance is one state's acquisition of military, political, and economic superiority over others; its routine use of force against weaker powers; and its habitual disregard of the weaker states' right and sovereignty. Hegemony implies less control and does not necessarily imply the use of military force.

9. The Panama episode is well chronicled. Roosevelt's outburst can be found in Elting E. Morison, ed., *The Letters of Theodore Roosevelt* (Cambridge, MA: Harvard University Press, 1951).

10. Noel Maurer and Carlos Yu, *The Big Ditch: How America Took, Built, Ran, and Ultimately Gave Away the Panama Canal* (Princeton, NJ: Princeton University Press, 2011).

11. This episode and the events of the succeeding paragraphs are recounted from the US perspective in great detail by Dana G. Munro, *Intervention and Dollar Diplomacy in the Caribbean, 1900–1921* (Princeton, NJ: Princeton University Press, 1964).

12. Root accepted this thinking and the US delegates to the Rio conference of 1906 were instructed to follow the Drago line. Albert B. Hart, *The Monroe Doctrine: An Interpretation* (Boston: Little, Brown, 1916), pp. 265–268.

13. As a result of this episode, most sovereign debt contracts now carry a clause stating that all bondholders must be treated equally, pari passu. This has caused complications for restructuring defaulted bonds to the present, but that is another story.

14. Cyrus Veeser, *A World Safe for Capitalism: Dollar Diplomacy and America's Rise to Global Power* (New York: Columbia University Press, 2002).

15. Munro, *Intervention and Dollar Diplomacy in the Caribbean*, pp. 235–236.

16. The episode is in Arthur S. Link, *Wilson: The Struggle for Neutrality, 1914–1915* (Princeton, NJ: Princeton University Press, 1960). The quote is from Arthur Walworth, *Woodrow Wilson: American Prophet*, 2 vols. (New York: Longmans, 1958). This Wilsonian insistence on forcing democracy down the throats of unwilling governments was repeated nearly a century later when George W. Bush and his neo-Wilsonian advisers promised to impose democracy in Iraq by military force. They assumed that the Iraqi people would flock to the cause of democracy.

17. Wilson's ambassador to Buenos Aires, Charles H. Sherrill, tried to extend the Wilsonian vision to a Pan-American triangle of peace, in which the nations of South America, seen as consolidated, stable democracies, would work with the United States to maintain the peace. Charles Hitchcock Sherrill, *Modernizing the Monroe Doctrine* (Boston: Houghton Mifflin, 1916).

18. Greg Grandin, "The Pentagon's New Monroe Doctrine," *The Nation*, February 8, 2010; Greg Grandin, "Halfway In with Obama," *New York Times*, April 24, 2011, WK 1, 5. This idea surfaced in March 2014, when the Russians imposed their control on the Crimea. The parallels between Wilsonian experience in the Caribbean Basin and US efforts to impose democracy in Afghanistan, Iraq, or Syria a century later are too obvious to belabor.

19. There were some cases in which the United States sent financial advisers, known as money doctors, to countries outside the Caribbean. See Paul Drake, *The Money Doctors in the Andes* (Durham, NC: Duke University Press, 1989). After World War II, representatives of the World Bank and the International Monetary Fund took on these duties.

20. Michael H. Hunt, *The American Ascendancy: How The United States Gained and Wielded Global Dominance* (Chapel Hill: University of North Carolina Press, 2007); Lars Schoultz, "Latin America in the United States," in Eric Hershberg and Fred Rosen, eds., *Latin America after Neo-Liberalism: Turning the Tide in the 21st Century* (New York: Norton, 2006); Lars Schoultz, *Beneath the United States: A History of U.S. Policy toward Latin America* (Cambridge, MA: Harvard University Press, 1998); Brian Loveman, *No Higher Law: American Foreign Policy and the Western Hemisphere since 1776* (Chapel Hill: University of North Carolina Press, 2010).

21. The literature on US interventions in Central America is huge. For an introduction, see Joseph S. Tulchin, *The Aftermath of War* (New York: New York University Press, 1971); D.G. Munro, *Intervention and Dollar Diplomacy in the Caribbean*.

22. See Chapter 7. After the Cold War, states that were pushed toward democracy by international pressure as well as pressure from their own populations were called "competitive authoritarian regimes." See Steven Levitsky and Lucan A. Way, *Competitive Authoritarianism* (New York: Cambridge University Press, 2010). Levitsky and Way treat the international dimension of this phenomenon in "International Linkage

and Democratization," *Journal of Democracy* 16.3 (2005) and "Linkage versus Leverage," *Comparative Politics* 38.4 (2006).

23. All of this material is taken from the diary of Chandler P. Anderson, Library of Congress. There is a partial biography of Anderson by Benjamin T. Harrison, *Dollar Diplomat: Chandler Anderson and American Diplomacy in Mexico and Nicaragua, 1913–1928* (Pullman: Washington State University Press, 1988). On the Latin American policies of Hughes and Kellogg, see David J. Danelski and Joseph S. Tulchin, eds., *The Autobiographical Notes of Charles Evans Hughes* (Cambridge, MA: Harvard University Press, 1973); L. Ethan Ellis, *Frank B. Kellogg and American Foreign Policy* (New Brunswick, NJ: Rutgers University Press, 1961); William Kamman, *A Search for Stability: United States Diplomacy toward Nicaragua, 1925–1933* (South Bend, IN: University of Notre Dame Press, 1968).

24. Juan Bautista de Lavalle, *El Perú y la Gran Guerra* (Lima: Imprenta Americana, 1919). On Chilean neutrality, see Enrique Recuant y Figueroa, *The Neutrality of Chile* (Valparaiso, n.p., 1919).

25. Baltasar Brum, *American Solidarity* (Montevideo: Imprenta Nacional, 1920).

26. L. M. Moreno Quintana, *Política americana* (Buenos Aires: Menéndez, 1922).

27. Quoted in Percy Allen Martin, *Latin America and the War* (Baltimore: Johns Hopkins University Press, 1924), pp. 13–15. Yrigoyen expressed this idea several times during his administration and got no response.

28. Rómulo S. Naón, "The European War and Pan Americanism," *Columbia University Quarterly* 20 (1919).

29. Rosemary Thorp, *Latin America in the 1930s: The Role of the Periphery in World Crisis* (London: St. Martin's, 1984).

30. This episode is recounted in Joseph S. Tulchin, *Argentina and The United States: A Conflicted Relationship* (Boston: Twayne, 1990). For a discussion of various Latin American recognition "doctrines," see J. Irizarry y Puente, "The Doctrines of Recognition and Intervention in Latin America," *Tulane Law Review* 28.3 (1954): 313–342.

31. Tulchin, *Aftermath of War*. For a contemporary discussion of the importance of oil, see Pierre de la Tramerye, *The World Struggle for Oil* (New York: Knopf, 1924).

32. Known as the Clark Memorandum; discussed in Tulchin, *Aftermath of War*. This memo explicitly questioned the reasoning behind the Monroe Doctrine as the basis for US policy in the hemisphere.

33. Lloyd Gardner, *Safe for Democracy: The Anglo-American Response to Revolution, 1913–1923* (New York: Oxford University Press, 1984).

34. George Beelen, "The Harding Administration and Mexico: Diplomacy by Economic Persuasion," *The Americas* 41.2 (1984): 177–189. The views of Secretary Hughes are in his *Autobiographical Notes*.

35. Daniela Spenser, "Forjando una nación posrevolucionaria," in Jorge Schiavon, D. Spenser, and M. Vazques Olivera, eds., *En busca de una nación soberana* (Mexico: CIDE, 2006); Friedrich Schuler, *Mexico between Hitler and Roosevelt* (Albuquerque: University of New Mexico Press, 1998).

36. Knut Walter, *The Regime of Anastasio Somoza* (Chapel Hill: University of North Carolina Press, 1993); Michel Gobat, *Confronting the American Dream: Nicaragua under U.S. Imperial Rule* (Durham, NC: Duke University Press, 2005).

37. A. McPherson, *Yankee No! Anti-Americanism in Latin American Relations* (Cambridge, MA: Harvard University Press, 2006); Richard V. Salisbury, *Anti-Imperialism and International Competition in Central America, 1920–1929* (Wilmington, DE: Scholarly Resources Books, 1989). In a recent book, Max Paul Friedman, *Rethinking Anti-Americanism: The History of an Exceptional Concept in American Foreign Relations* (New York: Cambridge University Press, 2013) focuses on the US response

to criticism and considers it an unreasonable reaction stemming from exceptionalism and opposition to reform movements.

38. José Vasconcelos, *La raza cósmica* (Mexico: Espasa Calpe, 1925).

39. Arturo Uslar Pietri, *De una a otra Venezuela* (Caracas: Monte Avila, 1949).

40. Gilberto Freyre, *New World in the Tropics. The Culture of Modern Brazil* (New York: Knopf, 1959); Oswald de Andrade, "Manifesto antropófago," *Revista de antropófago* 1 (1928).

41. Harry Hoetink, *The Two Variants in Caribbean Race Relations* (New York: Oxford University Press, 1967).

42. For example, see José Carlos Mariátegui, *Siete ensayos de interpretación de la realidad peruana* (Lima: Biblioteca Amauta, 1928). While Mariátegui linked nativism and Marxist anti-imperialism, labor movements in the region were mostly ambivalent on the race question, and the racial makeup of the labor force was a source of internal conflict in progressive movements and organized labor in most countries until World War II.

43. Federico Finchelstein, *Transatlantic Fascism* (Durham, NC: Duke University Press, 2010).

44. On the rise of social realism and the propaganda function of art in the Depression in Argentina, see Wolfsonian Foundation of Decorative and Propaganda Arts, *Journal of Decorative and Propaganda Arts* 18 (1992). Mexico celebrated public art in the 1930s, and was fortunate to have at hand a generation of muralists whose work outlived them.

45. The classic text is Fernando Henrique Cardoso and Enzo Faletto, *Dependencia y desarrollo* (Mexico: Siglo XXI, 1969). Cardoso took his main ideas from his mentor, Raúl Prebisch, who first developed them during his period at the Central Bank of Argentina in the 1930s. Prebisch expanded on his thinking with the aid of an extraordinary group of junior colleagues including Cardoso, Celso Furtado, Osvaldo Sunkel, and Anibal Pinto. Prebisch's first article appeared in English as *The Economic Development of Latin America and its Principal Problems* (Lake Success, NY: UN Department of Economic Affairs, 1950), based on his presentation to the UN conference in Havana the previous year. That same year, economist Hans Singer published his paper covering the same subject, "The Distribution of Gains between Investing and Borrowing Countries," *American Economic Review, Papers and Proceedings* 40.2 (1950): 473–485. Today their work is known as the Singer-Prebisch thesis on the deterioration of the terms of trade between primary products and manufactured goods and the wage differentials that are part of this unequal exchange. Orthodox Marxist economists were more comfortable with command economies and distrusted capitalists; see Paul Baran, *The Political Economy of Growth* (New York: Monthly Review, 1957).

46. Joseph S. Tulchin, "Decolonizing an Informal Empire: Argentina, Great Britain and the United States, 1930–1943," *International Interactions* 1.3 (1974): 123–140.

47. Joseph S. Tulchin, "The Argentine Proposal for Non Belligerency, April 1940," *Journal of Interamerican Studies*, 11.4 (1969): 671–704.

48. Governments controlled by charismatic military figures who pushed an aggressive nationalist agenda came to be called Nasserist regimes, after the Egyptian ruler Gamal Nasser.

49. Bryce Wood, *The United States and Latin American Wars, 1932–1943* (New York: Columbia University Press, 1966); David H. Zook, *The Conduct of the Chaco War* (New York: Bookman, 1960).

50. Wood considers these efforts a sign of growing community in the hemisphere and a positive result of the good neighbor policy. Norman A. Bailey, "The Inter-American System for the Maintenance of Peace and Security in the Western Hemisphere,"

Ph.D. dissertation, Columbia University, 1962, sees it as a repetition of the Latin American use of outside powers to protect them from aggression. It is more of the latter, in my opinion; but there is evidence of a growing sense of community, even if it is only driven by advancing communication technology.

51. Carlos Marichal, ed., *México y las conferencias panamericanas, 1889–1938* (Mexico: SRE, 2002) is a pioneering exploration of Mexican archival material on this subject.

52. Stetson Conn and Byron Fairchild, *The Western Hemisphere: The Framework of Hemispheric Defense*, 2 vols. (Washington, DC: Office of the Chief of Military History, Dept. of the Army, 1960).

53. This new security zone is described in Conn and Fairchild, *The Western Hemisphere*.

54. At this meeting the Argentine representative, Enrique Ruiz Guiñazú, told Undersecretary of State Sumner Welles that he thought the Axis would win the war and that the Nazis represented the true future of political democracy. Sumner Welles, *The Time for Decision* (New York: Harper, 1944).

55. Frank D. McCann Jr., *The Brazilian-American Alliance, 1937–1945* (Princeton, NJ: Princeton University Press, 1973); Stanley Hilton, *Brazil and the Great Powers* (Austin: University of Texas Press, 1976) and *German Military Espionage and Allied Counter Espionage in Brazil* (Baton Rouge: Louisiana State University Press, 1981); John D. Wirth, *The Politics of Brazilian Development, 1930–1954* (Stanford, CA: Stanford University Press, 1970).

56. The State Department continued its campaign against Argentina for several years. The autonomy shown by Juan Perón, the nation's new leader, did not make the US government any more sympathetic to Argentina's aspirations for global agency. In less than twenty years, when the Cold War was in full force, the United States ignored Latin American pleas not to expel Cuba from the OAS.

5

Cold War
in the Hemisphere

Various dates are used to mark the beginning of the Cold War. President Harry Truman used the term in his message to Congress, March 12, 1947, asking for support to send money and arms to the Greek government to fend off threats of a communist coup. More famous is the stark statement by Winston Churchill a year earlier on March 5, 1946, in a commencement address, "The Sinews of Peace," in Westminster College in Fulton, Missouri.[1] As far as the US government was concerned, the struggle against subversion in the Western Hemisphere by agents of the Soviet Union began even earlier, with consequences for the modalities of US hegemonic pretensions during the Cold War.

The period of the Cold War was characterized by an increasingly Manichean approach by the United States to protection of its security in the hemisphere. Whereas instability in Latin America had been considered an indirect threat to the United States in the possibility of inviting intervention from outside the hemisphere, during the world war, the focus on US security had tightened to a fear of attack by belligerents. At the same time, however, the concept took root that US security also could be threatened by agents of enemies who might operate within a Latin American country and subvert that country's government in the interests of a foreign power. As the Cold War intensified, the concept of subversion assumed increasing salience in the evaluation on both sides of the relationship between Latin American nations and the United States. Who had the right or power to determine who was subversive of which government and of how that supposed subversion might become a threat to the United States? The hunt for subversives corroded the moral fiber of politics and society within the

United States during the Cold War. It damaged hemispheric relations for much longer.

The indifference to or tolerance of the Communist Party or known agents of the Communist International (Comintern) in Latin America had been a subject of concern in the US government as far back as Secretary of State Frank Kellogg's complaint about such agents operating with the forces of Augusto Sandino in Nicaragua. Kellogg was also unhappy about Mexican influence in the civil conflict in Nicaragua, confessing to Congress that it was not clear whether the government of Mexico, which called itself the Movement for National Revolution, was an independent actor or the puppet of the Soviet Union in fomenting discord in the hemisphere.[2]

There was very little follow-up on Kellogg's warnings, mainly because subversion simply was too vague and subjective for a State Department that was trying to end interventions in the region and reduce the scope of US meddling. Subversion had none of the concrete quality of a foreign warship or troops. Furthermore, the Soviet Union was not a declared enemy of the United States, so its influence or potential influence could not be fit easily into the Monroe Doctrine framework of strategic thinking. Despite the hesitation by the State Department in peacetime, during both world wars, the US government had no difficulty identifying agents of belligerent powers and attacking subversion wherever they thought it might be lurking, no matter how resistant the host government might be.

The concept of subversion during both wars became an open invitation to some officials of the US government to intervene in the internal affairs of nations throughout the hemisphere. During the Cold War, a concern for subversion was like removing all inhibitions against hegemonic penetration in terms of geography or possible cause. Subversion was in the eye of the beholder and could be denounced even before there had been actions that might be verified. As the Cold War extended its grip over US politics and strategic thinking, tensions with the nations in Latin America grew exponentially and undermined whatever community feeling of goodwill had resulted from the good neighbor policy and the common battle against the Axis.

During the Cold War, subversion took on an ideological dimension that it had lacked during the world wars. The struggle against the Soviet Union was systemic. Anticommunism became the core of US hegemonic pretensions, overpowering other factors such as concern for democratic governance, economic development, or what had been considered the core values that tied together the nations of the hemispheric community. Just as there had been debate between Thomas Jefferson and James Madison in the nineteenth century and between Wilsonians and strict constructionists before World War I, during the Cold War there was debate between those who believed that US strength was in sharing its core values—its soft power, respect for human rights, and democracy—and those who insisted that the threat of communist subversion was so dire that respect for North American values could not be used as an excuse to allow evil to triumph anywhere in the hemisphere or, for that matter, anywhere in the world. It was not enough for Latin Americans to assert that they were democratic. They had to prove that they were sufficiently anticommunist and sufficiently resolute to protect themselves—and by extension the United States—from communist subversion. There were democratic forces in the hemisphere throughout the Cold War, but almost always their voices were drowned out by those who brandished lists of subversives. There were democracy-strengthening programs in the US arsenal of weapons against communism, but almost always they were shunted aside by military training programs or programs training local police how to root out subversion.[3]

The confidence of those who insisted on the prerogatives of US hegemony in the hemisphere was buttressed by the fact that at the end of World War II, the United States had the most powerful armed forces in the world, its gross national product was half that of the world's total production, and the dollar had become the world's principal medium of exchange. What distinguishes the period of the Cold War from what came before and after is the zero-sum, Manichean calculation by the US government of its interests in the hemisphere and its imposition on the nations in the region of this rigid straitjacket of ideological calculus of security. Except for brief episodes, it made a second-order priority of all conversations about development, democratic governance, and human rights. Where subversion was seen to exist or where it was considered to be a threat, democratic governance, human rights, civil rights, and political contestation, as well as economic development and social progress, were to be sacrificed in US policymaking over and over again, precisely at the time when all of these issues were becoming more important to people in Latin America.

It is impossible to exaggerate the damage done by this myopic, ideological calculus of US national security interests to the people in the hemisphere and to relations between Latin America and the United States. The armed forces in a dozen of the countries in the region wrapped themselves in the ideology of anticommunism, created national security states, and killed tens of thousands of their own citizens to extirpate subversion. The advance of democratic governance and the rule of law was set back decades. Many in the region who had been sympathetic to the United States and had taken its core values as a model for their own countries came to see the government in Washington as the enemy of their quest for democracy, development, and social progress. In Central America, where the military did not take over the government, it was used by civilian oligarchies to war against their own populations, again on the grounds of communist subversion, creating a virtual civil war in Guatemala in which over 200,000 indigenous people were killed and precipitating civil conflict in El Salvador and Nicaragua. This was the Bolivarian dream turned into a nightmare.

The end of World War II had been a period of optimism with regard to the evolution of the hemispheric community. Many in Latin America saw the preeminence of the United States in the world as an opportunity to consolidate their own fragile democracies and work with the United States to achieve further development of their economies, which had suffered grievous deterioration. At Chapultepec and later in San Francisco at the meeting that organized the United Nations, Latin American leaders successfully inserted into the UN charter privileged recognition of regional organizations. That meant that the Pan American Union had to be strengthened and expanded. Latin Americans wanted to add economic issues to the agenda of the hemispheric system. The new United Nations would have a special Economic Commission for Latin America (ECLA), headed by Raúl Prebisch, one of their own, and they wanted their organization to deal with the same issues. Whether they saw no other option or they were truly committed to this form of hemispheric community, the vast majority of hemispheric leaders turned to the new Organization of American States (OAS) as their mechanism for achieving community and national goals. It was the only mechanism of collective pressure against the United States that they had. During the Cold War, in pursuing its anticommunist campaign, the United States emasculated the OAS and undermined its utility as an instrument of Latin American agency and rendered the OAS suspect in Latin American eyes after the Cold War had ended.

Before the Pan American Union could be reorganized, the United States insisted on a regional security treaty against communist aggression. That was accomplished in Rio de Janeiro in 1947 in a treaty known as TIAR, or the Rio Treaty. The following year, the community met in Bogotá and created the OAS, which was empowered to take up social and economic questions as well as the usual political and security matters. While they met in April 1948, the charismatic, populist leader of the Liberal Party in Colombia, Jorge Eliécer Gaitán, was assassinated. Gaitán was demanding precisely the sort of social and economic reform that the new OAS was supposed to consider to forestall violent uprisings. His murder precipitated massive riots in Bogotá, known as El Bogotazo. These riots soon led to the formation of a guerrilla group, Revolutionary Armed Forces of Colombia (FARC), which took to the jungle to seek the changes that Gaitán had sought. In the decade following the El Bogotazo, more than 250,000

Colombians were killed in what is known as La Violencia.[4] More than fifty years later, FARC continues to fight from the countryside, although in 2012 they began peace talks in Havana with the Colombian government. Those talks appeared in 2015 to be heading toward a successful conclusion. It is said that Fidel Castro was in Bogotá during this period of riots and upheaval, although there is no proof of that. Even so, the myth provides a symbolic link between the popular uprising in Bogotá and the revolution in Cuba in 1959, which was then and remains the ultimate struggle for social change and defiance of US hegemony.

The most significant episode that produced a left-leaning regime was the election in 1945 of Juan José Arévalo in Guatemala to replace the long-time dictator Jorge Ubico. Supported by a growing labor movement that channeled long-standing grievances against the foreign-owned banana companies together with a growing urban middle class, the new government promised land reform and recognition of the rights of the country's indigenous and mestizo majority. But Arévalo was a timid reformer. He was succeeded in 1950 by Jacobo Árbenz, who had led the military in 1944–1945 against those who wanted to install a new dictator to replace Ubico. As president, Árbenz brought some communists into the government and moved against the United Fruit Company, which had dominated the economy for half a century.[5] The Dwight Eisenhower administration moved aggressively against the Árbenz government and, in 1954, the Central Intelligence Agency (CIA) brought Coronel Carlos Castillo Armas out of retirement to lead a coup that overthrew Árbenz.

The Guatemala episode is memorable because it led the United States to abuse the still relatively new OAS to such an extent as to make it virtually impossible for that organization to function in an effective manner for decades. It is memorable also because it demonstrated that all progressive reformers in the region were vulnerable to attack from the right on the grounds that they were nothing but stalking horses for communist subversion or could so weaken the political system as to make it easier for the communists to take control. The episode demonstrates how intolerant the United States had become of homegrown efforts to reform unequal and unfree societies. The symbolism of the Guatemalan episode became—and continues to be—a powerful argument against trusting the United States to protect the core values of democracy and human rights.

The social democratic option had seemed at the end of the war, for the first time, to be a valid alternative to reactionary, oligarchic regimes. Given hope and example by the New Deal in the United States, reformers throughout the region came together in what came to be called the Caribbean Legion to offer a progressive agenda for the future. They were helped as well by the Spanish republicans who came to Latin America when Francisco Franco came to power. These republicans were a key element in the Popular

Front government in Chile (1938–1941), an important factor in the evolution of the Argentine labor movement, a strong buttress to the Lázaro Cárdenas regime in Mexico (1934–1940), and a voice of opposition to the Rafael Trujillo dictatorship in the Dominican Republic.[6] A bridge between the New Deal and the Caribbean Basin was built by Rexford Tugwell, one of FDR's original "Brains Trust," who was appointed governor of Puerto Rico in 1941 and worked closely with Luis Muñoz Marín, then president of the island's senate, to create viable social programs on the island. Arévalo was one of the founding members of the Caribbean Legion, along with Rómulo Betancourt, then in exile from Venezuela, and Juan Bosch, in exile from the Trujillo dictatorship in the Dominican Republic. They were joined a few years later by José Figueres Ferrer, who led an armed revolt against the military in Costa Rica and became president in 1949. All of them took as a reference point the Cuban constitution of 1940, drafted with the cognizance of Roosevelt's representatives. The efforts of these reformers were buttressed by programs in support of labor unions and social democracy coordinated by the State Department and the US Agency for International Development after World War II.[7]

In the decade following the creation of the OAS, Latin Americans never felt that the United States paid attention to their interests or needs, while it pushed them time and time again to support hemispheric defense against subversion. The violent response to the May 1958 visit of Vice President Richard M. Nixon to Venezuela, one of the countries closest to the United States and led by a social democrat who was a supporter of US soft power, provided a wake-up call to the United States. In an extraordinary joint effort of agency, the presidents of Colombia, Alberto Lleras Camargo, and Brazil, Juscelino Kubitschek, put together a framework of social progress, with a little help from some friendly academics in the United States, which they presented to the US government. By the time President Eisenhower left office in 1961, he had managed to get his bureaucracy to produce a massive economic aid program, the Social Progress Trust Fund (SPTF), which was intended to quiet Latin American grumbling that they had never received a Marshall Plan after the war. The SPTF morphed into the Inter-American Development Bank, as well as a congressional appropriation for a significant aid program, which became the Alliance for Progress in the administration of John F. Kennedy.[8]

These steps were a new effort by the United States to achieve its security goals through a combination of the democracy promotion of the Wilsonian sort with an updated version of dollar diplomacy in which the state provided most of the capital, not private banks or investors, and in which local leaders were called upon to define their nation's development goals and negotiate rules for spending the development aid. Even with these efforts at reform, the central tendency in the hemisphere in the early decades of the Cold War was toward a more suffocating, comprehensive definition of security. The debate over the Alliance for Progress included the notion that hunger and underdevelopment created social unrest and led to communism, whereas economic development would strengthen the capacity of states to withstand the pressures of subversion. The inability or unwillingness of US officials to recognize the difference between social reformers and subversive radicals, with some important exceptions, handed to the conservative oligarchies a gift that kept on giving. US leadership provided a perverse form of legitimacy for governments to reduce the political space accorded to contestation, repress organizations that demanded social justice, and shutter institutions that might enable discussion or dissension. Politics throughout the hemisphere in the first three decades of the Cold War were unstable and polarizing, with a strong tendency toward the erosion of democracy. Where the armed forces had achieved institutional status, this trend culminated in something called bureaucratic authoritarianism and the national security state, in which the armed forces and their civilian allies assumed power in the name of the nation, security, and anticommunism.[9]

The desire for economic development, not ideology, drove the worldview of most of the countries in Latin America during the Cold War. The economic collapse of the Great Depression put many of the regimes there under great stress. Political and economic contestation became more acrimonious, and episodes of social violence became more frequent. What we might consider prerevolutionary episodes occurred in El Salvador, Cuba, Honduras, Brazil, Argentina, and Peru. The military in several countries were called in to restore order and in some cases reorganize the national order. In most cases this produced right-wing authoritarian regimes, with or without military buttress. Even here, European models were studied. General Juan Carlos Onganía, who took power in Argentina in 1966, is said to have declared to his first cabinet meeting that his friend Francisco Franco (the Spanish dictator) had taught him that "things" had to be "tied down and well secured."[10]

The economic experience of the Depression and World War II had made it brutally clear that the central dilemma of less developed countries was their lack of capital. If in the nineteenth century, the international division of labor had promised a supply of capital in return for primary products, that promise had turned to dross. Following Raúl Prebisch and other critics of what came to be called "unequal exchange," leaders in the region now emphasized the need for greater control over national resources and a need for some domestic production that would reduce the vulnerability of the country to an international market over which they had little or no control. This produced a set of policies that were followed by civilian and military governments, by governments that professed progressive views or by conservative ones. The common elements of these policies were nationalism and a privileged role for the state.

One the of the most significant accomplishments of social democrats in Venezuela was creating OPEC (Organization of the Petroleum Exporting Countries), a cartel to wrest control of the international price of oil from the large multinational companies that dominated the market. The key figure in this episode was Juan Pablo Pérez Alfonso, Betancourt's minister of Mines and Hydrocarbons and a founding member of their social democratic party, Acción Democrática (Democratic Action), who got Iran, Iraq, Kuwait, and Saudi Arabia to join together in Baghdad. Founded in 1960, precisely the year Dwight Eisenhower set up the Social Progress Trust Fund, OPEC was the first successful effort by any Latin American country to influence the price of its principal export.[11] Its original goal was "the inalienable right of all countries to exercise permanent sovereignty over their natural resources in the interest of their national development." The OPEC experience led the Venezuelan government to create the national petroleum company, PDVSA, which brought Venezuela in line with Argentina, Brazil, Bolivia, and Mexico in attempting to exert national control over the extraction, production, and export of their petroleum.[12] This was a significant step in the creation of Venezuela's agency in the international system in that it extended beyond the hemisphere and provided a new lever for developing countries to take control of their economic destiny. The Betancourt government in Venezuela, combining OPEC with its democracy, enjoyed unprecedented agency in hemispheric affairs, an agency the nation maintained for decades.

There was one case of a progressive military regime, in Peru, led by General Juan Francisco Velasco Alvarado (1968–1975), which combined national development policies with an effort to improve the lot of the nation's indigenous and mestizo majority. The government's expropriation of a petroleum company owned by a subsidiary of Standard Oil (now Exxon-Mobil) got the regime in trouble with the United States. Its efforts to include rural indigenous groups in the political process created great friction within the military and the civilian elites. Velasco Alvarado was replaced by a more conservative general in 1975.[13]

Peru was not that exceptional. The military in all of the countries had their developmentalist factions, some more prominent in the policy process than others. In several countries, military leaders introduced strategic studies to the curriculum of the military academies. In South America, the military felt it had a major role to play in this effort and in justifying their forward posture in the policy debate referred to the success of General Gamal Nasser in Egypt. Some in the military referred to themselves as Nasserists, by which they meant that they would intervene in the policy process to use the state in a disciplined manner to protect national interests, particularly national resource endowments, which they believed should be used for national advantage and not simply poured onto the international marketplace. The military in Brazil did their best to remain an actor in Lusophone Africa and spent a great deal of energy maintaining their presence in the South Atlantic. They were guided by their own strategist, General Golbery do Couto e Silva, who insisted the country could maximize its agency through its geographic influence.[14] Golbery adapted traditional European geopolitical schemes to the Brazilian experience and urged the military and the government to focus on the Brazilian landmass. Brasília was one of his favorite projects. As chief of the military household of the military president in 1964, he urged a set of policies to promote national development.

Golbery spawned imitators among the military in Argentina where General Juan E. Guglialmelli founded a journal called *Estrategia*, which he edited from 1969 to his death in 1983. Guglialmelli used the journal to warn Argentines about Brazilian hegemonic pretensions in South America and joined forces with civilian politicians to encourage Argentine governments to promote infrastructure policies, such as roads, dams, and the exploitation of the country's natural energy resources to establish an appropriate rejection of Brazilian hegemony in South America.

Except for Brazil and Argentina in the 1970s, these national security states abandoned the pretense of seeking an autonomous foreign policy. Their principal purpose was the consolidation of power in open alliance with the United States and the elimination of domestic subversion, real or imagined. Democratic institutions, rarely robust in the first place, were weakened, undermined, or simply eliminated. Freedom of the press was out of the question. Development policy, if that implied diversification and social mobility, was pushed aside. The Argentines were content to toe the anticommunist, anti-Soviet line until the Jimmy Carter administration indicated its displeasure with the generals' human rights record. This drove the Argentines to display a sudden interest in economic and diplomatic relations with the Soviet Union. The Chilean dictatorship under General Augusto Pinochet combined a developmentalist approach in turning over control of exploitation of the nation's natural resources to the military and the state with a fundamentalist neoliberal (that is, conservative) free market macroeconomic policy.

On balance, the conservative approach that privileged concern for national security interests dominated discussion in the United States. When the CIA led the coup against Árbenz in Guatemala, Secretary of State John F. Dulles was persuaded to attend the scheduled meeting of the OAS in Caracas in 1954. Dulles showed up for the plenary and gave a short speech justifying the intervention in Guatemala and then left Caracas before any of the issues on the agenda of concern to the other member states could be considered. His behavior undercut the value of the OAS and stained it forever as a puppet of the United States and of little value to the United States except to cover its unilateral actions in the hemisphere with a patina of collective legitimacy. But until the end of the Cold War, no alternative to the OAS could be sustained, so it continued, limited but active, as the member states sought ways to make the organization useful. After the Cold War, Latin Americans looked to create regional organizations of their own. One early expression of regional community and for intellectual support for the reform movements in the region was the creation in 1957 of the Facultad Latinoamericana de Ciencias Sociales (FLACSO) an intergovernmental organization affiliated with UNESCO, which continues to be an expression of intellectual solidarity and Latin American identity.

Although the conservative option dominated US policy in the region, internal debate continued and the liberal or progressive alternative was not silent until, in the 1980s, it reasserted itself and the argument for democracy preservation again took prominence in US foreign policy in the region. Until then, in the years following the CIA-sponsored coup in Guatemala, the United States paid special attention to Guatemala and offered a wide variety of programs to support the military and the government. In one discussion, the State Department objected to the fact that the US police and military sent to Guatemala to train the local police in counterinsurgency were encouraging indiscriminate and brutal tactics. The State Department representative Viron "Pete" Vaky, asked, "Is it conceivable that we are so obsessed with insurgency that we are prepared to rationalize murder [and torture] as an acceptable counterinsurgency weapon?"[15] The answer in this meeting, as in many others, was "yes."[16]

Secretary of State Henry Kissinger and President Richard Nixon used the CIA to encourage the military to carry out a coup against Chilean president Salvador Allende in 1973 and appeared sympathetic to the killing and torture that followed.[17] A few years later, when the Argentine military overthrew the government of Isabel Martinez de Perón, Juan Perón's widow, the junta sent a representative to Washington to coordinate their policy with the Nixon administration. Kissinger was quoted as telling the visiting general to "get the killing done quickly." In the face of this clear signal, the ongoing debate over democracy and values still left enough space within the bureaucracy to allow activities by foreign service officers in Argentina to openly defy the generals and save lives, lots of them.[18] Imagine the confusion and anger in Buenos Aires, just two years later, with

Jimmy Carter in the White House and Patricia Derian the top official in the State Department dealing with Latin America, when the United States made it clear that human rights violations by the military regime were a serious matter and cut off military cooperation with Argentina![19]

Of all the progressives in Latin America, Figueres seems to have understood the need to win support in the United States if he was to continue in power in Costa Rica and that the categories of debate in Costa Rica would have to hew at least to some degree to the terms of US strategic concerns. This is not to suggest that he began his career as a student of international relations theory. It does suggest that Figueres, who came by his anticommunism honestly, saw stability in Costa Rica as possible only if the nation's strategic objectives were realistic in a bipolar world in which the United States dominated the Western Hemisphere. It also suggests that Figueres came to understand that the space Costa Rica could occupy in the international system—its agency—was a function of his ability to create a comfortable juxtaposition between Costa Rican interests and those of the United States. Within a decade of coming to power, Figueres formulated a foreign policy for Costa Rica that maximized its autonomy in the international system broadly by simultaneously separating itself from the stifling oligarchic pressures and dangerous instability of the other countries in the subregion while maintaining its anticommunist credentials with the United States. For this he laid the foundation for a strategic culture that emphasized a progressive agenda, democratic stability, and a Swiss-like neutrality in regional conflicts. The consistency of this strategic culture over time became the essence of Costa Rican agency through the remainder of the Cold War and to the present day, making it a country that enjoys hemispheric and global influence far beyond its size and economic power. Doing without a military is one of the central features of this agency in world affairs. This singular success warrants some discussion of how Costa Rican strategic culture was established.

To appreciate the Costa Rican drive for agency in international affairs, we must take into account several factors that are not often taken seriously by theorists of international relations. First is the concept of a nation's nightmares and how they contribute to consensus on foreign policy and the continuity of that policy over time, what is known as strategic culture. Second is the role of individual leadership in creating the basis for a nation's foreign policy. Third is the notion that agency can be achieved through a deliberate compromise of autonomy in the world community by accommodating the pressure of US hegemony in the hemisphere. The three cases of success in achieving agency in the face of US hegemony—Chile, Costa Rica, and Cuba—offer different approaches with similar outcomes. All three support the existence of a rules-based international community, in which traditional variables of a realist approach are given weight but made subordinate to other variables, such as soft power, the role of international civil society, and the need to express resistance to US hegemony. That success is crucial in understanding the evolution of opposition to US control and the capacity of nations in Latin America to achieve some form of regional identity.

The strategic culture of Costa Rica is based on the widespread belief that the nation is fundamentally different from the rest of the countries on the isthmus. Their pre-Columbian experience was different; their colonial experience under the Spanish was different, and their national history has been different. Of course, it is possible to argue that these differences are minor, even trivial, and did not prevent Costa Rica from developing a coffee-export economy that has the same essential features as the economies developed by liberal elites in the nineteenth century in the other countries of the region. Those who focus on economic structures tend to favor the basically similar argument, as do those who focus on the structure of social power, even though it is certainly true that Costa Rica does not have the same percentages of indigenous or Afro-Caribbean peoples as do the other countries. There is a hierarchy, there is an elite, and coffee along with the financial and merchant activities tied to it are central to the formation of the elite and the distribution of power.

This once dominant explanation for Costa Rica's distinctiveness is now being attacked and revised, particularly by a new generation of scholars who were drawn to Central America to study the civil violence of the 1970s and 1980s. For these scholars, the presence of Afro-Caribbean people on the Caribbean coast is an important phenomenon that has been overlooked. At the same time, a coffee economy is a coffee economy. As if that were proof, the Costa Rican elite is considered by this new generation as every bit as cohesive, every bit as exclusive as its counterparts in the other countries of Central America. The revisionists have some good points to make. Nevertheless, there remains a broad consensus within Costa Rica as to the nation's security and what the foreign policy should be to protect that security. In other words, there is a clear strategic culture in Costa Rica, and it has an obvious set of keepers.

The consensus on the nation's strategic culture is built on three traumatic events in the twentieth century. The nation's strategic culture and the axiomatic bases of its foreign policy may be understood as the gradual evolution of a collective response to these nightmares. The first was the only military rebellion against a civilian government, led by Joaquín and Federico Tinoco Granados in the years before World War I. The Tinoco brothers had grown tired of the fractious manner of the oligarchy and were particularly concerned about a group that sided with the Germans. Federico Tinoco took power in January 1917 and declared that his government would support the cause of the Allies in the war. Despite this declaration, President Woodrow Wilson decided that he would not recognize Tinoco's government and persisted in his opposition long after the war had ended. On August 11, 1919, Joaquín Tinoco, head of the army, was assassinated on the streets of San José. Federico fled the country the next day. A new "legitimate" government was elected in December and only Wilson's illness delayed US recognition of this government until August 1920.

One of the elements in the confusion over how to deal with Federico Tinoco was that Emiliano Chamorro, from Nicaragua, with his close connections to the US State Department, gave safe haven to opponents of the government and allowed them to mount expeditions into Costa Rica. The weakness produced by this internecine conflict left its mark on the Costa Rican elite, especially in how such unresolved disputes left the country vulnerable to attack from Nicaragua.[20]

The second episode is also the result of an armed insurrection: a revolution from the right, led by a group of reformers who feared that the government was shifting to the left and would undermine the nation's democratic way of life and expose it to intervention from the United States. It was led by a coffee grower, José Figueres Ferrer, who was one of the founders of the Partido Liberación Nacional.[21] Figueres's ascension was notable for establishing new precedents, such as abolishing the army.

It is important to underline the irony of making a revolution to prevent radical change and the absolutely clear sense of agency that "Don Pepe" (Figueres) had.[22] Although the phrase had not been coined at that time, he wanted to use Costa Rica's soft power. Figueres saw that in the struggle against antidemocracy, whether it was the Soviet Union and the Communist Party on the left or autocratic dictators on the right, a close alliance with the United States was indispensable. He worked constantly to build ties to leaders in the United States who understood the nationalist reformist urge in Latin America. He was a critical figure in organizing the Caribbean Legion, which had opposed dictatorships in the region, and he got his friends in the United States to support their work.[23]

The third and final episode that contributed to the strategic culture of Costa Rica is the experience of the civil conflicts in Guatemala, Nicaragua, El Salvador, and Honduras during the 1970s and 1980s and the militarization of the region, which began to spill over into Costa Rican territory. This led the government of Costa Rica to seek help to resolve the conflicts, reduce US intervention, and reduce the power of the military. Going it alone would not work. It was clear to those who governed Costa Rica that its sense of separation from the rest of Central America would continue to erode and that the distinctiveness of Costa Rica mattered less than the threat of revolution or subversion in the region to the United States during Ronald Reagan's presidency. The challenge was to find a way to resolve the civil conflicts in the region without provoking further militarization of the conflicts by US intervention. The response was collective action. In building collective action, we have the first concrete, successful manifestation of collective agency in the region. It proved to be an integral part of the transition to the post–Cold War world.

Mexico and Colombia, the geographical bookends to the isthmus, were as anxious about the combustible situation in Central America as were the Costa Ricans. With support from Brazil, which acted as an observer, and the encouragement of the social democratic governments in Spain, Germany, and France, the government of Mexico convened a meeting in January 1983 on the Contadora Island with participation by Colombia, Panama, and Venezuela. The first step was to send an observer mission to the border between Costa Rica and Nicaragua. The next was to convene a summit meeting of government leaders in Cancún, Mexico, in July. By this point, the nations in South America, no longer ruled by the military except in Chile, saw the virtue of this approach and formed the Lima Group, with Peru, Argentina, Brazil, and Uruguay, to offer support to the Central Americans seeking peaceful solutions to their civil conflicts.[24] This was unprecedented community agency.

The United States was caught in a bind. At first, the Reagan administration was irritated, but it could not publicly reject peace or the possibility of ending the conflicts. The first response to Contadora from Washington was to demand a higher level of verification in the peace process and appoint the Kissinger Commission to report on the situation. Although the sense that time was against them had driven the Central Americans and their allies in the region to work together, now time was on their side. As the civil conflicts in Nicaragua, El Salvador, and Guatemala dragged on with no side able to defeat the other, the Reagan administration, as it entered its second term in office, began to appreciate the shift in its favor in the bipolar struggle with the Soviet Union, which brought democracy support back into prominence along with public declarations of support for human and civil rights. The political opposition in Congress also came together, making executive, unilateral action more difficult. This made the hardline militarization wing of the administration step back as the government looked to shore up its relations with European allies, burnish its reputation as the defender of moral values against the evil empire, and restore the tattered relations with nations in the hemisphere.[25]

Time also had changed the political and strategic landscape in Latin America. The Cold War security framework actually reduced the scope of foreign policy autonomy in most of the countries. In South America, the military dictatorships, with their focus on the national security state, could defend their legitimacy only by declaring their allegiance to the United States and to the struggle against communism. If there were differences between them and the United States, as there were in the case of Argentina during the administration of Jimmy Carter (1976–1980), it drove the military to domestic policies of extreme nationalism to retain their legitimacy at home. The Argentine generals even attempted to get even with the United States during the Carter administration and restore their autonomy by cozying up to Cuba and the Soviet Union. In their desperation to restore their legitimacy, the Argentine military invaded the Malvinas (Falkland) Islands, insisting after the fact that they were led to believe that the United States would support them and that they were convinced they would be beneficiaries of the worldwide anticolonialism sentiment. They were tragically wrong on both counts.[26]

After Argentina's disastrous war with Great Britain over the Falklands/Malvinas in 1982, the military retreated from power and conducted elections, which were won by Raúl Alfonsín, a powerful advocate of human rights and democracy as universal core values, who had a wide following throughout Europe and the Non-Aligned Movement and reached out to the US government in his first trip abroad after the election. As Alfonsín took office in Argentina, the Brazilians were going through their own transition to democracy along with Uruguay. That left the military dictatorship in Chile alone in the region, and it quickly took on the status of pariah, the status Argentina had suffered after the invasion of the Malvinas/Falklands.[27]

As the evidence mounted that the Soviet Union would back away from confrontation with the United States, and that there was little or no threat to US security to be expected from Latin America, the Reagan administration turned its back on Pinochet and even went so far as to finance the political campaign against him that led to the plebiscite won by the forces of democracy in 1988. The US ambassador to Chile, Harry Barnes, made it clear to Pinochet that there would be active opposition to him in Washington if he were to decide to contest the results of the popular vote. The policy shift was marked with great emphasis in a formal "Statement on Support for Democracy in Chile" that was issued in December 17, 1987. This statement was drafted originally in November by the Chile Desk Officer of the State Department and approved all the way up the line to Secretary George Schultz. By way of emphasis, Assistant Secretary Elliott Abrams, who had been a powerful advocate of the anticommunist hard line in the Reagan administration, provided Schultz with a memo justifying the statement to accompany it when he transmitted the draft to the president for his approval.[28] That approval, when it came a short time later, was explicitly included in the press release accompanying the statement. As if to show Pinochet that this was not a trivial or ceremonial statement, the State Department transferred $1.2 million that had already been granted to the Centro de Asesoría y Promoción Electoral in Costa Rica to the Crusade for Civic Participation in Santiago. The money was crucial in the campaign leading up to the plebiscite, especially in adding more than a million registered voters to the rolls.[29] The US House of Representatives followed the State Department action with a resolution supporting the statement. How different the political debate over democracy in Chile was from the debate twenty years earlier over teaching the Guatemalan police how to torture their fellow citizens.

In Chile and elsewhere in the region, the transition to democracy placed the new civilian democratic governments in something of a quandary. By virtue of their declaration of support for human and civil rights, they were siding with their more than slightly tarnished model, the United States. At the same time, they tried to use their soft power to extend their autonomy from the United States. In a sense, they were identifying with the United States as it assumed the role of victor in the Cold War, a victory trumpeted as having been won as much through soft power and the virtues of its economic system as through its superior military might. The United States insisted that it was not a victory achieved through military conquest, although the Reagan administration had increased military spending so much that it virtually bankrupted the Soviet Union as it tried to keep up, and came close to bringing the US economy to its knees, but the embrace of the United States became uncomfortable in Latin America in short order.

In Central America, the drive to take agency in the peace process was spurred by the leadership of the new president of Costa Rica, Óscar Arias, who brought both the UN and the OAS into the discussion, so that the Soviet Union and Cuba would have their interests represented. In the 1970s, he worked for Figueres, who returned to the presidency of Costa Rica in 1972. Arias was elected president for the term 1986–1990. He took the peace plan presented by the Contadora group and altered it so that it better suited the interests of several actors in the region's civil wars and called together the presidents of the four countries and began what came to be called the Esquipulas Process.

At this stage, even the reactionary, oligarchical regimes in Central America began to come to terms with the inevitability of the peace process and that the process would involve major roles for external actors in addition to the United States, such as the UN, the OAS, and the growing international civil society led by major human rights organizations. Although these conservatives always had operated with one eye on the United States, they came to understand in the 1980s that the unilateral interventionism exercised by the Reagan administration would destroy them as well in its obsession with militarizing the effort to eliminate those the US government considered communist subversives. This led the rulers of Guatemala, El Salvador, Honduras, and Nicaragua to accept the peace process, even if grudgingly, and the role of outside actors. The final element in the shift in US policy was the growing power of the congressional opposition to the Reagan administration. Within this new framework, the United States retained its voice, but its capacity for action was seriously constrained. By bringing all the actors to the table, the peace process opened the possibility of achieving major reforms in the region without armed conflict. For Costa Rica, a nation without an army, the militarization of conflict in the region had been a threat to its existence. For his efforts, Arias was awarded the Nobel Peace Prize in 1987.[30]

The Esquipulas Process was a remarkable success. The structure of the negotiations and the results—the peace processes in El Salvador, Guatemala, and Nicaragua—may be considered a major part of the transition from the Cold War, which actually came to an end during the peace talks. The end of the Cold War removed the rigid, zero-sum framework of the national security state and created a more fluid security environment in the region in which the nations of Latin America could begin to seek their own agency and attempt to reformulate their relationship with the United States, which remained the most influential outside actor in the hemisphere but no longer pretended to exercise the type of hegemony that had been part of inter-American relations for a century. As the Cold War wound down, the United States began to experience difficulty in defining its security interests in the region. Marginalizing the United States in the Esquipulas Process complicated the challenges confronting the Central American countries, and at the same time opened new space for their autonomous action. In the years following Esquipulas, the more effective the peace process, the more active the resulting governments would be. Aside from Costa Rica, the most active in world affairs after the Cold War have been El Salvador, Nicaragua, and Panama. Guatemala and Honduras have retreated to their older pattern of inward-looking oligarchical governments with little space for political contestation and very high levels of internal violence.

During the Cold War, the nations of Latin America tried a variety of policies or mechanisms to free themselves from the straitjacket of the bipolar geopolitical struggle in which they had little room for autonomous maneuver. The linkage between aggressive interventionism by the United States and restrictions on individual freedom imposed by military dictatorships provoked widespread anger and anti-Americanism throughout the region. Especially among progressive groups, the United States lost its allure as a democracy with progressive values, and among groups on the right, it lost its cachet as a modernizing economy capable of increasing the wealth and well-being of their population. Those concerned with economic development and social equity also grew impatient with the United States, especially during the Reagan administration, with its insistence on market solutions to all problems and its dominance over the so-called Bretton Woods institutions, which the Latin Americans once thought would be allies in their efforts to grow and shuck off their economic dependence. Anti-Americanism expanded across the region and across the political spectrum.[31]

Historical memory had a great deal to do with the spread of anti-Americanism and with its persistence to this day. Who in Nicaragua does not remember that the United States put Somoza in power and sustained him and his family for two generations? Who throughout the Caribbean does not remember that the United States took over the Dominican Republic for twenty years and then left behind Rafael Trujillo? The coup in Guatemala engineered by the CIA in 1954 is still fresh in memory. There are those in Chile and Brazil who will not forgive the United States for provoking and supporting the military coups that ended democracy in their countries. Many throughout Latin America remember that the United States contributed to the rise of Fulgencio Batista in Cuba and the frustration of the reforms promised by the constitution of 1940 and that it took an armed revolt by Cubans to be rid of him.

The Cuban revolution continues to be the symbol of everyone's desire to blunt the hegemony of the United States. Their revolution represents the most successful example of Latin American rejection of US hegemony and the exercise of agency in world politics.[32] For that reason, nearly every country in the region has offered some gesture in support of the Castro regime and expressed its opposition to the US policy of embargo, known in Cuba and throughout Latin America as the Blockade. Most notably, the majority of the countries in Latin America have voted against the United States and for Cuba in the United Nations. Until the end of the Cold War, Mexico made support for Cuba against the United States one of the elements of its policy of nonintervention. During the brief return to power by Juan Perón in Argentina (1973–1974), his minister of economics, José Ber Gelbard, attempted to extend the life of import substitution industrialization by exporting cars to Cuba in exchange for sugar. The Argentine military tried to do business with Castro when Carter turned nasty. Raúl Alfonsín, the paladin of human rights, stopped off in Havana on the return leg of his first trip to Europe in 1983, where he had been lionized by all the social democrats on the continent. When asked why he had picked Havana to stop, he made it clear that it was important to bring Cuba back into the hemispheric community and demonstrate to the United States that fellowship with Cuba could not be prevented by unilateral policy in Washington.[33]

The problem with these efforts to express independence from the United States through defiance of its policy toward Cuba was that to the extent that foreign policy was determined by opposition to the United States or by focus on the need to express defiance of the United States, that focus distorted efforts to achieve autonomy and reduced its agency outside the hemisphere. Cuba could win agency in the world community through its defiance of the United States. Supporting Cuba, without taking a similar posture in support of the Soviet Union in the Cold War, did not automatically create more autonomy for the rest of Latin America unless they could create some alternate form of identity for the region as a whole. They were not able to do that for more than twenty years after the end of the Cold War. Without that regional identity, defiance of the United States as a goal of foreign policy had the perverse result of tying the nations of the region closer to the United States and reinforcing the control the hegemonic power exercised over those nations that consider themselves weaker. This became clear in the new century and led to efforts to create a regional organization that would be free of US control.

The drive in Central America for collective protective action against US unilateralism run amok should be taken as an early sign of the transition to a world after the Cold War. So, too, may we understand the impact of the transition to democracy in the region. As country after country made its way back to some form of democratic governance and tried to put behind it forever the experience of the national security state or the violent civil conflicts that were associated with the Cold War, they began to see themselves increasingly as part of the new world order. A crucial role in the transition to democracy and in reaching an understanding of the world that might follow the Cold War was played by a generation of students of foreign affairs who in the 1970s began to study international relations and, more specifically the United States, as a means of coming to terms with the strategic environment of the Cold War. They felt the corrosive effect the US obsession with security was having on well-being in the region. Through their studies, they sought to find more space in world politics for the nations of Latin America than allowed by the straitjacket the United States tried to impose on their countries.

As the Cold War came to an end, many of the nations in Latin America suffered another economic blow in a series of sovereign debt failures. It was the final blow to the ISI model and rendered most of the economies vulnerable to outside influence. The international agencies with power to aid stricken economies—the US Treasury, the International Monetary Fund, and the World Bank—pushed the debtors to adopt severe austerity programs that would make it virtually impossible for them to continue developmentalist programs. In most cases, the Latin Americans avoided the most severe austerity programs, but they all were forced to adopt some measure of neoliberal policies that made it difficult for them to realize their hopes for development. In response, several countries mounted fierce campaigns against the programs the international agencies tried to shove down their throats. The results of their bargaining were partially successful. Their efforts to defend themselves represent new levels of agency in the sense that the governments recognized their capacity for autonomous action in the multilateral world of finance and economics.[34]

Those interested in international relations came together under the leadership of Luciano Tomassini, a Chilean political scientist who had worked at the Inter-American Development Bank in Washington and at the Institute for Latin American Integration in Buenos Aires before returning to Santiago, where he worked at ECLA/CEPAL until his death in 2010. Using the FLACSO model of an epistemological community, Tomassini called on colleagues throughout the region to join the Latin American Network for International Relations (RIAL) and managed to raise the funds, especially from the Ford Foundation, to begin annual meetings in 1977. These meetings took place until 1992, at which time academic institutions in many of the countries took up the challenge of studying the global community and how their nations might fit into it.[35]

RIAL was a strong combination of progressive fraternity, a lobby for academic freedom, and a laboratory for the study of international affairs. It was a true epistemological community. Future foreign ministers and cabinet members such as Celso Lafer (Brazil), Rodrigo Pardo (Colombia), Dante Caputo (Argentina), Rosario Green (Mexico), and José Miguel Insulza, Luis Maira, Heraldo Muñoz, Juan Gabriel Valdés, and Carlos Ominami (Chile) came together to discuss how their nations could use international relations to speed the transition to democracy and how, once returned to democratic governance, they could create constructive roles within the international community. RIAL was an intellectual testing ground for the expression of agency in Latin American foreign policy.[36]

One of the early participants in RIAL, Luis Maira, spent his years in exile in Mexico, where he helped create the first academic center in Latin America outside Cuba for the study of the United States.[37] Together with Carlos Rico, a Mexican political scientist, and Roberto Bouzas, an Argentine economist, they founded the Centro de Investigación y Docencia Económicas (CIDE) in Mexico City. For ten years they published the

Cuadernos Semestrales de Los Estados Unidos, from 1977 to 1988, which were rigorous studies of US public opinion, the Congress, and the political currents in the United States that might help explain the twists and turns of US foreign policy.[38] The group at CIDE also organized seminars with scholars from the rest of Latin America as well as from the United States, and published one of the first studies drawing attention to the dangers of militarizing the conflicts in Central America.[39]

The political commitment of the academics who participated in RIAL is an important facet of the transition to democracy in Latin America and of the transition to the post–Cold War world. Many of those who met in the 1980s to discuss how Latin America might escape the suffocating dominance of the United States and its own military dictatorships not only pushed the framework of the formal study of international relations by adding a Latin American perspective to a field of study generally dominated by positivist scholars in the United States and Europe, they also put themselves on the line by entering government and putting their policy proposals into effect, or at least attempting to push them through the complex decisionmaking processes of democratic governance. The way members of RIAL participated in the policy process radically changed the culture of how academic debate could permeate the policy process in Latin America. Although the Chilean case is the most obvious and most significant, there are other examples in the hemisphere, such as Argentina, Brazil, and Mexico, in which public debate among academics and intellectuals became part of the decisionmaking process and policy planning. In many countries, with the transition to democracy, the diplomatic training experience came to include rigorous academic study for the first time.

As the Berlin Wall was torn down and the Cold War came to an end, the nations of Latin America and the United States were faced with challenges that were mirror images of one another. In Latin America, the challenge was how to achieve agency in a post–Cold War world in a manner that would not simply be an expression of hostility to the United States or in which foreign policy would be a symbolic rejection of the United States, but rather part of a policy that would seek to maximize the nation's interest and objectives. On the other hand, for the United States, the challenge would be how to establish a relationship with nations that with the exception of Cuba, were governed now by civilian, democratic governments, selected in regular free and fair elections, in a way that would be respectful of their new roles as agents in the global community. In the absence of any threat to its interests from outside the hemisphere, would it be possible for the United States to create relations with the nations of the region that were not based on the assumption of US hegemony? Given historical memory in Latin America, would it be possible to establish collegial relations of confidence with the United States while their nations sought to establish roles for themselves in a globalizing world? This dual dilemma is the subject of the final chapters. For the Latin Americans, the Cold War could not end soon enough.

Notes

1. The speech and its background can be found in Martin Gilbert, *Churchill: A Life* (New York: Holt, 1992).
2. Elting E. Morison, *Turmoil and Tradition* (Boston: Houghton Mifflin, 1960); Robert H. Ferrell, *Peace in Their Time* (New Haven, CT: Yale University Press, 1952); Daniela Spenser, "Forjando una nación posrevolucionaria," in Jorge Schiavon, D. Spenser, and M. Vazques Olivera, eds., *En busca de una nación soberana* (Mexico: CIDE, 2006). For the most part, the Communist Party operated without repression in most of the countries of the region throughout the 1920s and 1930s. Communists had little impact on the political process in Latin America, except in forming part of the Popular Front in Chile and splitting the socialists in Argentina into two different factions. On the other hand, where there was organization of the working class, they played an important role in the labor movements. Once the United States entered the war in Europe, communists were considered allies, although conservatives still considered them nasty people and the US government sent agents into the field to monitor their activities.
3. This point is made in Lars Schoultz, *Human Rights and United States Policy toward Latin America* (Princeton, NJ: Princeton University Press, 1981) and *National Security and United States Policy toward Latin America* (Princeton, NJ: Princeton University Press, 1987).
4. German Gúzman, Orlando Fals Borda, and Eduardo Umaña Luna, *La violencia en Colombia*, 2 vols. (Bogotá: Ed Tercer Mundo, 1962). The rate of killing in the countryside subsided for about two decades and then soared again as drug traffickers and then paramilitary bands combined with the guerrillas to kill over 300,000 people and displace more than 5 million from 1980 to 2010.
5. Piero Gleijeses, *Shattered Hope: The Guatemalan Revolution and the United States, 1944–1954* (Princeton, NJ: Princeton University Press, 1991); Stephen Schlesinger and Stephen Kinzer, *Bitter Fruit* (New York: Doubleday, 1982). The process by which first Arévalo and then Árbenz fell from grace in Washington is debated at length in the National Security Council reports beginning with NSC144 (March 4, 1953) through NSC 5902/1 (February 16, 1959), which are available through the collection of the George Washington University National Security Archives website.
6. Accepting marginal refugees was a policy Trujillo followed again after the Evian conference in 1939, when the Dominican Republic accepted several boatloads of Jewish émigrés, at the urging of President Franklin D. Roosevelt; Allen Wells, *Tropical Zion* (Durham, NC: Duke University Press, 2009).
7. Martha F. Riche, "The American Institute for Free Labor Development," *Monthly Labor Review* 88.9 (September 1975). The AIFLD soon came under the influence of the CIA and lost its credibility in Latin America. See Hobart A. Spalding Jr., *Organized Labor in Latin America* (New York: Harper, 1979). For a more general treatment of the period, see David Rock, ed., *Latin America in the 1940s* (Berkeley: University of California Press, 1994).

8. Joseph S. Tulchin, "The United States and Latin America in the 1960s," *Journal of Inter-American Studies* 30.1 (1988): 1–36.

9. Guillermo O'Donnell, "Reflections on the Patterns of Change in the Bureaucratic-Authoritarian State," *Latin American Research Review* 12.1 (1978): 3–38.

10. In Spanish, *las cosas tienen que estar atadas y bien atadas.*

11. Earlier in the century, Brazil had tried several times, without success, to seize control over the international price of coffee.

12. Juan Pablo Pérez Alfonso, *Petróleo: Jugo de la tierra* (Caracas: Editorial Arte, 1961). Pérez Alfonso was profoundly conflicted about the proper use of oil in Venezuela's development. He expressed concern for the country's dependence on one product and once referred to oil as "the devil's excrement."

13. Richard L. Clinton, "The Modernizing Military: The Case of Peru," *Inter-American Economic Affairs* 24.4 (1971); David Scott Palmer, *Peru: The Authoritarian Tradition* (New York: Praeger, 1980); Alfred C. Stepan, *The State and Society: Peru in Comparative Perspective* (Princeton, NJ: Princeton University Press, 1978); Cynthia McClintock, *Self-Management and Political Participation in Peru, 1969–1975: The Corporatist Illusion* (London: Sage, 1977); Luigi Einaudi, "Revolution from Within? Military Rule in Peru since 1968," *Studies in Comparative International Development* 8.1 (1973); Jorge Rodriguez Beruff, *Los militares y el poder* (Lima: Mosca Azul, 1983).

14. Golbery do Couto e Silva, *Planejamento estratégico* (Rio de Janeiro: Biblioteca de Exercito, Rio, 1955) and *Geopolitico do Brasil* (Rio de Janeiro: Jose Olympio, 1967); Alfred Stepan, *The Military in Politics: Changing Patterns in Brazil* (Princeton, NJ: Princeton University Press, 1971).

15. This debate and others are found in Kirsten Weld, *Paper Cadavers: The Archives of Dictatorship in Guatemala* (Durham, NC: Duke University Press, 2014), p. 110.

16. The values perspective never is absent. Sometimes it is more salient than at others. For a comparison of the Carter and Reagan human rights policies, see Vanessa Walker, "Ambivalent Allies: Advocates, Diplomats, and the Struggle for an 'American' Human Rights Policy," Ph.D. dissertation, University of Wisconsin, 2011; and, "At the End of Influence: The Letelier Assassination, Human Rights and Rethinking Intervention in US-Latin American Relations," *Journal of Contemporary History*, 46:1 (2011).

17. These episodes are recounted in Cynthia J. Arnson and Tamara Taraciuk, eds., *Argentina-United States Bilateral Relations*, Woodrow Wilson Center Reports on the Americas no. 8 (Washington, DC: Woodrow Wilson Center, 2003); Heraldo Muñoz, *The Dictator's Shadow: Life Under Augusto Pinochet* (New York: Basic Books, 2008).

18. Arnson and Taraciuk, *Argentina–United States Bilateral Relations*, chapter 4 recounts the activities of Tex Harris during the dictatorship. Another discussion of the US-Argentine relationship is Ariel C. Armony, Hector Schamis, and Giselle Cohen, *Repensando la Argentina: Antes de diciembre de 2001 y más allá de mayo de 2003*, Woodrow Wilson Center Report on the Americas no. 7 (Washington, DC: Woodrow Wilson Center, 2003).

19. On the shifting use of human rights policy, I refer to Vanessa Walker, "A Tale of Two Policies: Carter, Reagan, and Human Rights in the Western Hemisphere," unpublished manuscript in possession of the author; Andrew J. Kirkendall, "Liberal Democrats, Latin America, and the Cold War Consensus from Eisenhower to Nixon," unpublished manuscript in possession of the author.

20. Joseph S. Tulchin, *The Aftermath of War* (New York: New York University Press, 1971), pp. 66–70. More detail is in Dana G. Munro, *Intervention and Dollar Diplomacy in the Caribbean, 1900–1921* (Princeton, NJ: Princeton University Press, 1964).

21. Kyle Longley, *The Sparrow and the Hawk: Costa Rica and the United States during the Rise of José Figueres* (Tuscaloosa: University of Alabama Press, 1997).

22. In this case, I can add some personal reflections to the narrative because I worked for Figueres as his teaching assistant when he was a visiting professor at Harvard University in 1963.

23. After 1959, the litmus test of acceptable progressive positions for those in the United States was how the regime in the hemisphere viewed the Castro regime in Cuba, and Figueres always was a staunch anticommunist.

24. Jack Child, *The Central American Peace Process, 1983–1991* (Boulder, CO: Lynne Rienner, 1992); Cristina Eguizabal, ed., *America Latina y la crisis centro-americana: En busca de una solución regional* (Buenos Aires: GEL, 1989); Francisco Rojas Aravena and Luis Guillermo Solís, *¿Súbditos o Aliados?* (San José, Costa Rica: FLACSO, 1998); Jeffery Paige, *Coffee and Power: Revolution and the Rise of Democracy in Central America* (Cambridge, MA: Harvard University Press, 1997); James Mahoney, *The Legacies of Liberalism: Path Dependence and Political Regimes in Central America* (Baltimore: Johns Hopkins University Press, 2001); Charles D. Brockett, *Political Movements and Violence in Central America* (New York: Cambridge University Press, 2005).

25. Thomas Carothers, *In the Name of Democracy* (Berkeley: University of California Press, 1991). The shift by the Reagan administration was by no means complete. At this time, Oliver North in the National Security Council was organizing the funding of the armed opposition to the elected government in Nicaragua, the so-called contras, despite specific prohibition of such funding by the Congress, through the sale of arms to Iran, the proceeds from which were funneled to the contras.

26. Joseph S. Tulchin, "The Malvinas War of 1982," *Latin American Research Review*, 22.3 (1987): 123–41.

27. Carlos Escudé, *La Argentina ¿Paria internacional?* (Buenos Aires: Editorial Belgrano, 1984).

28. All of these documents, including the notations that indicate who was involved, can be found on the State Department's Virtual Reading Room, available at https://foia.state.gov/Search/Search.aspx.

29. Both Carothers, *In the Name of Democracy*, p. 157, and Paul Sigmund, *The United States and Democracy in Chile* (New York: Twentieth Century Fund, 1993), p. 168 indicate their recognition of the significance of this episode. Genaro Arriagada, who played an important role in the campaign, thinks this episode was crucial to their success. Arriagada, interview with the author, September 24, 1994.

30. Arias returned to the presidency in 2006–2010 and attempted to exercise leadership for Costa Rica in Central America, but with less success. One of his young aides during his first presidency was Luis Guillermo Solís, who, after a career in politics including several appointments as Costa Rican representation to regional organizations, was elected president in April 2014.

31. Hal Brands, *Latin America's Cold War* (Cambridge, MA: Harvard University Press, 2010).

32. The literature on the Cuban experience is vast. See Jorge I. Domínguez, *To Make a World Safe for Revolution: Cuba's Foreign Policy* (Cambridge, MA: Harvard University Press, 1987) and *Cuba: Order and Revolution* (Cambridge, Harvard University Press, 2009).

33. When asked why he had insisted on visiting Castro and by doing so to legitimating the least democratic regime in the hemisphere, Alfonsín made two points. The first was that he had told the State Department that he was making the stop, so it was not an anti-US gesture; second, it was important to strengthen the bonds among Latin American nations, irrespective of their political nature. When pressed, he confessed

that the arrogance of the United States in imposing its embargo on Cuba irritated him and that it would buttress his government's autonomy by showing his independence of the United States. Alfonsín, interview with the author, October 17, 1992.

34. These episodes are treated by Mark E. Williams, *Understanding US–Latin American Relations* (New York: Routledge, 2012), chapters 8 and 9; Vinod K. Aggarwal, "International Debt Threat: Bargaining among Creditors and Debtors in the 1980s," *Policy Papers in International Affairs* 29 (1987).

35. RIAL was given new life in 2014, with Latin American funding, under the leadership of Ricardo Lagos, former president of Chile, and Luis Maira, who had been active in RIAL in its earlier incarnation.

36. The annual volumes produced by RIAL are a record of how the expanding group of IR specialists in the region viewed the world. These volumes also are a record of their unfailing optimism about the transition to democracy in the region and their faith in the growth of Latin American agency. I was privileged to participate in many of these meetings in the 1980s and early 1990s.

37. This does not include the Center for the Study of the United States, which was part of the Cuban Foreign Ministry.

38. Rico went on to become a diplomat and was instrumental in formulating Mexican policy toward the United States in the years after NAFTA that contributed to the growing partnership between the nations. *Cuadernos Semestrales* was published from 1977 to 1988. CIDE was created in 1974. In 2014, Maira joined with Carlos Heredia to refound the center within CIDE. Maira now is director of RIAL in its new existence as the Council on International Relations of Latin America and the Caribbean.

39. Luis Maira et al., *Centroamérica, crisis y política internacional* (Mexico: Siglo XXI, 1982).

6

Post–Cold War Optimism

In the euphoria following the dramatic razing of the Berlin Wall in November 1989, President George H. W. Bush triumphantly declared the end of the Cold War and summoned the beginning of a "new world order." It was a catchy phrase, one that seemed to match the momentous quality of the events that had preceded the celebration in Berlin. While no one was quite sure what Bush meant, it was plain that he intended to convey optimism, a sense that an era of instability and threat had been left behind, and that all the nations of the world could look forward to a period of peace and goodwill. As if to add emphasis to the president's rhetorical flourish or to give it academic heft, the deputy director of the State Department's policy planning staff and a former analyst of international affairs at the Rand Corporation, Francis Fukuyama, explained that the end of the Cold War was the "end of history."[1] Following Georg Hegel, he saw in the collapse of the Soviet Union the sudden end of a terrible dialectical struggle over how the world was to be organized and the triumph of one of the contending parties.[2] With that triumph, total and unconditional, the United States and the way of life it represented—democratic, liberal capitalism—had swept all before it, and all the nations and peoples of the world would reap its benefits.

Although it simplifies things somewhat, we can think of the economic dimension of Fukuyama's "end of history" in the phrase "Washington Consensus," first coined about the same time by John Williamson, a senior fellow at the Institute for International Economics in Washington.[3] Although his optimism was more tempered than Fukuyama's, Williamson was attempting to capture the notion that there was increasingly widespread agreement, not just in Washington but all around the world, that a basic set of market responsibilities had come to be considered orthodoxy in places, such as Latin America and the developing world more widely, where for decades they had been hotly contested. He was referring, on one hand, to a set of national behaviors normally considered typical of conservative governments in the most developed countries, such as balanced budgets and financial policies that sought to curb inflation, keep exchange rates and prices free of government control, and public sector debt within certain limits. On the other hand, he was referring to the fact that these behaviors long had been the core of recommendations by the multilateral financial institutions, the so-called Bretton Woods institutions, particularly the International Monetary Fund (IMF), and the World Bank, based in Washington, DC, which had been created by the Allies after their triumph in World War II.[4]

Williamson was encouraged by the fact that many of the countries in Latin America had shifted to economic policies that made them more transparent and more competitive in the international market, a market that was itself swept up in the larger trend of globalization.[5] The linkages between rapid changes in communication technology, for example, and financial transfers of all kinds simultaneously made it easier for Latin American countries to participate in the international economy, although increasing participation exerted pressure to conform to dominant rules in that economy. The widespread sense that going along with the general consensus on opening economies would bring more benefits than costs made most governments in the region willing to follow the lead of the more developed countries, although there was a constant murmur of dissent that such policies were nothing more than intervention without armed forces and that the neoliberal attacks on the state would expose the most vulnerable elements of their populations while weakening the nations' autonomy.

Prodded and pushed by the international banks and the demands of the US Treasury, many of the governments in Latin America had widespread debt crises and grudgingly set out on economic reforms of profound significance, turning away from import substitution models of development that had dominated policymaking virtually since the Great Depression and had been an article of faith since the 1950s. Most of the countries felt that these "reforms" were imposed on them and had left them with less autonomy to formulate policies they believed would accelerate their development. It was no accident that a series of studies by the World Bank in the 1990s called into question populist social spending and inflation as tools to fight poverty and as ways to insulate developing nations from the vicissitudes of the international market. The most significant finding was that inflationary policies hurt the poor most of all.[6] The Washington Consensus seemed global in its reach and unassailable in its permanence. As Henry Kissinger told the Trilateral Commission in 1992, the changes were unprecedented in their speed and their global spread.[7] Several leaders in Latin America shared in this optimism. Óscar Arias, former president of Costa Rica and a recipient of the Nobel Peace Prize, echoed Bush's expectations of a new world order.[8]

While Fukuyama and Williamson expressed confidence that their views were widely held and they were describing the way things actually were, the end of the Cold War together with the onset of globalization set off an intense debate on the nature of this new world order and how it was to be governed. The decade after 1989 was an especially fecund period of debate over the nature of the international system. The triumphalism in the United States and Western Europe was taken by the most conservative realists as evidence that the world was unipolar and that the United States was the dominant power. The implication for the realists was that the United States could and should work its will because it was more powerful than any other country.[9] The justification for this power lay in part in the values that had driven the United States in its battle with the Soviet Union. These values were trumpeted by a group called neoconservatives, who considered themselves neo-Wilsonians in the sense of mission they made an important part of the US role as the world's dominant power.[10] They, like Wilson and Theodore Roosevelt a century before them, were willing to bring civilization, American style, to the less developed nations of the world. Among academic students of international affairs, John Mearsheimer provided a comprehensive theoretical argument for how the United States should use its power in the emerging global community.[11]

The opposition to the traditional realists came from those who saw in the new world order changes the realists failed to appreciate. To begin, they saw a large and increasing set of actors in all regions of the world who were not ready or willing to accept US hegemony. They saw an increasingly strong web of international institutions that were providing rules and guidelines for the globalized world to which the United States was a willing party and in which nations around the world were placing their confidence and support. In addition to these multilateral institutions, such as the United Nations and the World Trade Organization, both of which had enforcement mechanisms over which the United States did not exercise control, there were a number of observers who pointed to the extraordinary emergence of an international civil society of nonstate actors who were playing an increasingly important role in setting the rules for the international community. These nonstate actors were complementing the multilateral institutions in building a growing array of interlocking networks and groups that hammered out consensual rules and regulations, including the increasing reliance on the institutions and modalities of international law. These institutionalists, or neorealists as some of them preferred to be labeled, included Joseph Nye and Robert Keohane, who pointed to the use of soft power or values in building the new international system. Also aligned with the group that urged modification of the traditional realist approach were those who focused on the gradual creation of multilateral groups of states and nonstate actors who form "regimes" based on shared interests or values, including such disparate issues as trade and women's rights.[12] These regimes or sets of multilevel games came to be called "relational structures," which play a role in international affairs that the traditional realists refuse to take seriously. In addition there was a small minority of analysts who thought that the new international institutions should set the rules of the game, and these were considered representatives of the liberal school, formerly known as idealists.[13]

Two other significant currents of thought and academic analysis in Latin America critical of the realist approach are the neo-Marxists, who focus on class and seek alternatives to liberal capitalism, and the students of international political economy, who see the systemic economic structures and social inequalities of developing countries as important elements in their insertion into the new world order that belie the seeming (ir)rationality of their choices.[14] The academic debate in the United States gave little attention to Latin America and Latin Americans who studied international affairs. The latter, individually and as a group, gained their voice within the region and beyond it after the terrorist attacks of September 11, 2001.

Although the document was not immediately made public as the publications by Fukuyama and Williamson had been, the US military took a moment to take stock of what the new world order meant for the use and projection of US military power—the hard power of which realists spoke. The fruit of their reflection was a document published in 1996 by the Joint Chiefs of Staff, *Joint Vision 2010*. In that document, which had a general tone of confidence if not self-satisfaction, military leaders considered it reasonable and appropriate that the United States aim for "full-spectrum dominance" in all theaters of engagement and in all aspects of potential conflict. This was not the ravings of a mad person in a bunker. This was the considered result of a discussion across all of the major forces of the nation's military, with outside consultants and friendly academics involved in the discussions. The process began at the end of the administration of George H. W. Bush and was completed after several years of hard work in the first presidency of Bill Clinton. Reading the document twenty years later gives the reader pause. What were they thinking? Yet, when we put *Joint Vision 2010* in the context of the end of history and the Washington

Consensus, it seems all of a piece—except for the fact that no one outside the United States (certainly no one in Latin America) would have agreed with the Joint Chiefs and the fact that President Bush's initial celebration of a new world order specifically included the conviction that the international community would be ruled by collective institutions, through collegial dealings with colleagues in agreement with one another. That is not the implication of the statement written by the Joint Chiefs.[15]

Events have made a mockery of Bush's new world order. Fukuyama's end of history has been converted into a subject of ridicule in the debate that continues today over the nature of the international community. The Washington Consensus has become a term of opprobrium for a neoliberal model and an avatar for economic neo-imperialism. The opinion of the Joint Chiefs of Staff in *Joint Vision 2010* may be considered hubris brought back to Earth by events following 9/11. The peace, goodwill, and sense of an inertial, almost inevitable drive toward a world community prospering in an open international economy that had been implicit in the president's remarks are hard to find or even imagine twenty-five years later. Everywhere you turn, there is conflict, disaster, terrorism, and the threat of worse, not to mention persistent poverty, rising inequality in the developed and developing world, and massive population dislocations not equaled since World War II.

Even if history did not end in the immediate aftermath of the Cold War and if the structure and order of the international community are still far from a settled matter, the sense of vast change continues to be pervasive. There is widespread conviction that there would be no return to the bipolar struggle for hegemony between rival empires, although there are some who see in the rise of China and the resurgence of Russia hints of a return to great power conflict. In Latin America this major tectonic shift was especially powerful because it came along with the transition to democracy in many countries. The sense of permanent change was helped by the fact that many of the countries, after recovering from the debt crisis of the 1980s, stabilized their economies and began to enjoy significant profits from the increasing prices of their primary product exports.

The transition to democracy meant that the people of Latin America were free to choose their own path in the world— they had bestowed legitimacy on the process by which they would choose that path. There was much talk of a renewal of the social compact between state and people in which both recognized they were accountable to one another. The transition to democracy fulfilled the need for accountability and legitimacy that had been the necessary condition for the founding fathers in the United States. True, the quality of the new democracies disappointed many, and there were references to the need for second- and then third-generation reforms to complement the transitions; but in international affairs, no one in

Latin America questioned that a new era had begun and no one wanted to go back to the old order of authoritarian and military rule or to the hegemonic straitjacket of control by the United States. In formulating policies guiding their insertion into the new world order, the newly democratic nations of Latin America were keenly aware of the debate over the structure of the global community and wanted to be part of it. They were also sensitive to the academic debates over the global community. For the most part, Latin American leaders wanted to be realistic in their understanding of the world and be seen as sensible and realist. At the same time, their memory of unequal market exchange, IMF censure, and US hegemonic pressure made them eager to form part of various new regimes, and made them willing to be protagonists in the multilateral agencies that seemed to be so important.

After the Cold War, the nations of Latin America reached for agency in the international system with both hands. At first, US leaders saw no reason to expect that such agency would be in conflict with their own interests, given that they also saw no reason their historical hegemony in the hemisphere could possibly create tensions in inter-American relations. They expected Latin America to ride the wave of globalization with them. Even if they paid very little attention to Latin America in their discussions of the new world order, officials in the Bush and Clinton administrations were certain that economic activities would be central to their new international relationship, north or south. When the terrorist attacks in 2001 changed US strategic priorities, US hegemony in the hemisphere created bitter tensions with more than a few nations in Latin America, and the United States began to see that Latin American agency was not an unmixed blessing.

The vast military and economic power accumulated by the United States since World War II and nearly fifty years of experience in throwing around the nation's geopolitical weight served to make the United States more disposed to strut on the stage of international relations, as the Joint Chiefs of Staff demonstrated in their published planning documents. There was still the idealistic strain in US policy—a desire to do the right thing, and the missionary zeal to do humanitarian deeds in the name of democracy that was made more powerful by the sense of having "won" the Cold War. There never was the sense that the United States should solve the world's problems by itself or through the use of its own military power. The problems that soon surfaced—Yugoslavia, the former Soviet Union, Rwanda, Kuwait, Somalia, South Africa, the Middle East, and Haiti—cried out for external mediation of some sort, either because of the human misery they produced or because they threatened to spill over their borders. Yet there was no consensus, either in the United States or in Latin America, as to how the international community should go into action.

In the same manner, there was a new agenda of global issues, such as the environment, drug trafficking, migration, and pandemics that could be managed only with multilateral instruments and that called for new modes of cooperation. The agenda was long and complex; despite the sense that something had to be done in a collective manner, there was very little agreement as to how it should be addressed. The United States considered that it had earned the right to lead the international community, while giving little idea of how it was to exercise that leadership. This made many in Latin America wary of following the United States and, over time, more and more people came to see that their new urge for agency and their desire for autonomy might prove to be incompatible with US hegemony.[16]

What emerged from early discussions in the Bush administration was a package, the Enterprise for the Americas Initiative (EAI), designed to deal with the major preoccupations of the nations in the region—debt, trade, and economic well-being. Aimed at Mexico, which had surprised the Bush administration by proposing a major new trade initiative that ended up as the North American Free Trade Agreement (NAFTA) and included Canada, it included the rest of the hemisphere. There soon was talk of a Free Trade of the Americas Agreement. It was consistent with the administration's policy in the Uruguay Round of the General Agreement on Tariffs and Trade (GATT) negotiations and with the commitment of the Latin American nations to the multilateral trade reform central to those discussions. Finally, by insisting on partnership and hemispheric togetherness, the EAI was designed to still the deep-seated anxieties of Latin Americans about the residual urges of US hegemony. Despite early enthusiasm, within a few years, the EAI would join the Alliance for Progress in the junk heap of history.

There were signs of trouble from the outset. The 1980s had been a lost decade for most of Latin America. The region had gone backward in economic terms, pinned down by the heavy burden of the enormous unpaid international debt that had brought the flow of private capital to a standstill and dragged most of the hemisphere into a recession that was undermining the new and fragile democracies. In the face of severe recession, civilian governments were unable to raise the revenue to satisfy the legitimate needs of their population, and the restructuring programs imposed on them by the international banks were sapping the strength of the state precisely at a time when a strong state was needed to consolidate the new democracies and respond to legitimate social needs. Many in the region did not share the Washington Consensus or Bush's optimistic view of the world.[17]

Bush was not attracted to a program of official aid, which the leaders of the Andean nations had proposed in their preliminary meeting with him in Cartagena in February 1990. Historically, with the exception of the Alliance for Progress, the United States had responded to Latin American requests for economic help by urging them to open their markets and allow US capital to solve their problems, a modern form of dollar diplomacy. "Trade not aid" was the response of US officials after World War II to Latin American colleagues who asked for a hemispheric equivalent of the Marshall Plan. What is remarkable, in hindsight, is the degree of optimism that market opening would cure all economic and political ills in the region. Roger B. Porter, one of Bush's advisers, emphasized that the policy was about markets, eliminating barriers to trade and entrepreneurship, and reducing statism. "The challenge to Latin governments under the Bush initiative," Porter said in the fall of 1990, "is to remove obstacles to efficiently functioning markets, and to create a climate for entrepreneurship." States should not be involved in production, but should "implement regulations which safeguard foreign investments and facilitate the entry and exit of capital."[18]

In retrospect, it is remarkable that such a fuss was made over a policy initiative that quickly sputtered out and accomplished so little. All doubts and qualms were swept aside by the extreme confidence that suffused US policy planning in the aftermath of what leaders saw as the nation's triumph in the Cold War and its unquestioned supremacy in the global order. It is important to remember as well that for a decade before the Berlin Wall came down, the United States had been the subject of study after study certifying the nation's decline relative to the emerging economic community in Europe and Japan. Even the most optimistic of the studies was convinced that the days of US dominance of the international economy were over and that the best that might be anticipated in the years ahead would be some sort of tripolar world in which economic influence might be divided evenly among the United States, Europe, and Asia.[19] The end of the Cold War seemed to nullify all the talk of US decline, and the EAI was designed to buttress the US position in the hemisphere. Unfortunately, like the good neighbor policy in the 1930s and the Alliance for Progress in the 1960s, announcing a major policy shift was not enough to put it into action.[20]

Trade, at least, seems to have been an idea whose time had come. The trade "pillar" as it was called in the EAI, rested on a complex set of broad, general commitments to freer trade, known as framework agreements, which were signed with every nation in the hemisphere except Cuba, Surinam, and Haiti, and a bold commitment to create a free trade area "from Alaska to Tierra del Fuego." Curiously, almost without being asked, Latin American nations began to lower their tariff barriers and accelerate processes of trade reform begun before June 1990. There was a belief or a hope that the new world order would benefit them if they were able to adjust to its new guidelines. As the representative of the Brazilian government, Sergio Amaral, stated at hearings conducted by the US International Trade Commission in January 1992, "A sea change has taken place in Brazil's trade policies, which had an immediate impact on U.S.-Brazil trade relations."[21] Amaral complained that the United States was lagging behind Brazil and other Latin American nations in the liberalization of its trade policies. He joined the Argentine representative in Geneva, Ambassador Archibaldo Lanús, to urge the United States to take a more aggressive stance in collaboration with the nations of the hemisphere in confronting the protectionist tendencies of some European nations within the GATT. The Latin Americans were concerned they might find themselves in the near future exposed in a world market in which only the primary product exporters eliminated trade barriers while the developed countries, their logical markets, had left their trade walls as high as they had been.[22]

After the initial rush to join the new trend in the 1990s, enthusiasm in Latin America for freer trade and negotiated labor and environmental rules waxed and waned with the prices of commodity exports. As long as export windfalls were high, Latin American governments were sympathetic to international rules of trade and exchange. When the price of commodities fell, so did their enthusiasm.[23] Considering the deep-seated belief among Latin Americans in the inequity of the international markets, the staying power of free trade, and open markets more generally is a remarkable feature of the post–Cold War hemisphere even though the grand scheme of a free trade area of the Americas came to nothing.[24]

The NAFTA talks dragged both the environment and labor standards into public debate for the first time, with widely varying postures among the members of the hemispheric community. At the beginning of the post–Cold War period, the same euphoric consensus that all issues would be solved in multilateral harmony extended to consideration of protecting the environment. There was even a world summit on the environment in Brazil, where protection of the Amazon rain forest had become an international cause célèbre, especially in Europe and the United States.[25] The Brazilians were at odds with the United States on two grounds. First, the nationalist argument was that after all, it was Brazil's rainforest and the developed countries should mind their own business. The second was an argument that characterized the newest bloc on the block, the BRICS—Brazil, Russia, India, China, and South Africa—which were considered and considered themselves to be the next group of developed countries. They argued that they should not be made to follow new rules on the environment put forward by the most developed countries because they had the right to go through a period of economic growth similar to the one the developed countries had in the nineteenth and early twentieth centuries when they made heavy use of fossil fuels in their industries. This was a perverse form of structuralism combined with modernization in which the developing countries asserted the right to go through the same development stages as others had.[26] The Latin Americans were concerned that the United States might use the environment as a weapon in their trade negotiations.[27]

The environment was a blunt weapon in trade negotiations and soon lost its effect. By the end of the decade, the issue had become a question of how to deal with climate change and how to create standards to limit or reduce carbon emissions. Sustainable development, which had been a question for developing countries in the 1990s, evolved into two separate issues: one for developed countries that considered the carrying capacity of the planet, the other for the least developed countries that considered sustainability as a means of limiting poverty. This dispute slowed to a crawl all efforts to create international standards or rules for limiting the emissions of fossil fuels that are blamed for the warming trend that many consider the most serious threat to the global community. After 9/11, when the conservative wing of the Republican Party portrayed the question of the human role in climate change (which drove the campaign for environmental protection policy) as a liberal plot, environmental protection efforts shifted to international agencies. In those forums, the scientific consensus as to the human impact on climate change was given a full hearing, but the major differences among developing countries as to what to do about it made collective action very difficult. Leadership in environmental protection passed to the Europeans.[28]

In and of itself, the EAI accomplished virtually nothing and was oversold in Latin America.[29] The success of the export models built into the Washington Consensus proved to be cyclical. After a decade of slow growth, the export boom in the first decade of the new century, driven by China's extraordinary growth and voracious appetite for commodities, brought dramatic windfall profits to several countries in Latin America and renewed their interest in open markets. The core of the model—opening the economy to trade and investment—proved to be uneven in its benefits and brought unanticipated policy consequences that reduced policy flexibility of Latin American governments and undercut sustainability.[30] On the other hand, the indirect gains of EAI were not trivial. At the very least, in a worst-case scenario, the possibility of a free trade area in the hemisphere protected the Latin American nations against a resurgence of US protectionism, although nontariff barriers have become so complex and the asymmetry between the US economy and Latin American economies is so vast that true free trade is an unattainable ideal. In addition, there was a palpable increase in investor confidence in Latin America, as shown by the impressive demand for securities on a growing number of exchanges in the region along with significant inflow of private capital, although the inflows proved transient and did not have the predicted impact on development, except in the few countries most hospitable to such investments.[31]

More significant, and totally unintended by the Bush administration, the EAI provided a powerful stimulus to intraregional integration efforts, pushing them further toward realization than at any previous time. Projects such as Mercosur (Mercado Común del Sur) and the Andean Pact were strengthened, at least in the short run, and proved to be a powerful support for the self-esteem of the peoples of the hemisphere. Ironically, by pushing the Latin American nations to restructure their economies, leading them to expect great things from the EAI, and then frustrating them by bureaucratic inadequacy and partisan wrangling, the United States ended up strengthening Latin American regionalism and the determination to achieve something on their own in international affairs. Some Latin Americans considered the EAI a success by linking democracy and economic integration to legitimate the necessary, inevitable, and politically difficult policies designed to make the nations of the region "global traders."[32]   In this view, the EAI played a strategic role in preparing Latin America for greater agency in a globalizing international trade community. Intraregional trade has remained a priority even as the opposition to the Washington Consensus has become more powerful. By the end of the decade, there was a widespread consensus in Latin America that such regimes among subsets of nations were in their long-term interest.

Historically, the United States had preferred to deal with Latin American nations one-on-one and went to great lengths to discourage joint or multilateral efforts. However, in the immediate aftermath of the Cold War, the United States believed that it needed Latin America to join in the settlement of hemispheric disputes, just as it needed European and other allies to deal effectively with crises in Yugoslavia, the Congo, Cambodia, Iraq, or elsewhere, whether it was through the United Nations or other forms of collective effort. In the Western Hemisphere, the Bush and Clinton administrations wanted partners and allies to deal with crises in Haiti and Peru. Both leaders realized that they would need allies to deal effectively with drug trafficking, terrorism, immigration, and threats to the environment. That need for allies—for partners, as George H. W. Bush put it—struck many in the hemisphere as opening the way to changes in US policy that were not entirely anticipated and that ran counter to the US historic desire for a free hand in hemispheric action.

The Clinton administration built on Bush's initiatives and incorporated summitry into US foreign policy in the hemisphere. The first Summit of the Americas was held in Miami in December 1994. It is important to emphasize that the idea of the summit was encouraged in Latin America and that Latin Americans played an important role is setting the agenda, including their insistence on discussing free trade in the hemisphere. While there were dissenters, summit meetings struck most leaders as an excellent way to exercise their agency.

Aside from trade negotiations, the first collaborative efforts by nations in Latin America to increase their leverage in the international system went into making the existing hemispheric architecture more useful to them. The most significant of the Latin American collaborative efforts was to reform the OAS. Taking advantage of a willing secretary general, João Baena Soares, a Brazilian career diplomat, a group of relatively young ambassadors from Argentina, Chile, Brazil, and Mexico combined their efforts to move the OAS away from its historical position as an organization incapable of decisive action except under US leadership. It was bad enough that the OAS served as a puppet for the United States—most egregiously in 1954 in dealing with Guatemala—but the organization did not seem capable of effectively dealing with any of the issues of priority to the Latin American members.

Led by Heraldo Muñoz, the Chilean ambassador, the OAS declared that democracy was the mode of government favored by members of the OAS and that members would act to protect democracy in any member state. The first step was a public declaration by the assembled members in Santiago, Chile, of a "Commitment to Democracy," which was later converted into an official Resolution 1080 (1991). While the commitment by the members was not specific or concrete, it obviously was a great benefit to the government of Chile and any other government in the region, which was forced to look over its collective shoulder at the armed forces in its country as a potential threat or limit to their capacity to govern.[33]

At the organizational level, the Mexicans, with able support from the Argentine and Brazilian ambassadors, took the lead in creating a set of commissions, in which majority rule (not unanimity) was the mode of discussion and which would have powers to act on issues of concern to the members. The Mexicans were concerned primarily with creating a framework in which unilateral "certification" by the US Congress of countries according to their efforts to stem the flow of drugs into the United States would be delegitimated. Action by the OAS, through the new Inter-American Drug Abuse Control Commission (CICAD), was considered by members of the Congress as a viable alternative to their own work, and they agreed to end the annual ritual vote, so noxious to the Mexicans, on the condition that the OAS take on the issue.[34] The commission proved extremely useful as a forum for exploring ways to deal with drug abuse that included discussion of the role that demand played in the illegal traffic and how multilateral collaboration might prove more effective than the unilateral "war on drugs" approach favored by the United States.

The Latin Americans also were interested in creating a forum for discussing the traffic in small arms and light weapons, which had a marked destabilizing effect in a number of countries and took on increasing importance as the peace processes in Central America advanced. These conversations led in 1997 to the Inter-American Convention Against the Illicit Manufacturing of and Trafficking in Firearms, Ammunition, Explosive and Other Related Materials and then, in 1999, to the Convention on Transparency in Conventional Weapons Acquisitions. The latter expressed the link between the arms control agenda and the new concept in Latin America—that of cooperative security. The question of arms trafficking was dealt with within CICAD, which could link arms control with the struggle to contain drug traffic. Dealing bilaterally with the United States was fruitless because the influence of the domestic gun lobby made conversations with US officials too delicate. The new commission, by contrast, was ideal for making public the views of the receiving nations in the hemisphere and exploring collective action that might win some collaboration from the United States. In time, the United States became adept at using the new structure and after the terrorist attacks of 9/11, created a commission, the Inter-American Commission Against Terrorism, in which the Latin Americans proved willing collaborators.[35]

The third reform, linked to the organizational changes, was an attempt to have the OAS play a constructive role in settling historical territorial disputes, many of them left over from the postindependence era, that had burst through the veneer of tranquility in the region at the end of the Cold War. Rather than focus on how to take advantage of the new world order and exercise their agency as democratic states in a global community that seemed to share their values, nations all around the hemisphere quarreled with their neighbors over contested territory and threatened armed conflict. Within two years of the end of the Cold War, virtually every country in South America and Central America was involved in a territory dispute with its neighbors. In some cases, there were episodes of violence and the loss of life at the border.[36]

To make the OAS relevant to dealing with these conflicts, the ambassadors from Argentina, first Juan Pablo Lohlé and then Hernán Patiño Mayer, pushed the OAS into discussions of regional security. The Security Commission held meetings over a three-year period for diplomats, members of the legislatures, journalists, academics, and military officers from countries whose borders were in dispute. These meetings produced concrete results in resolving the final points of contention along the mountain border between Argentina and Chile, in creating a Special Commission to discuss the riverine boundary between Argentina and Uruguay, and in mediating among the nations in Central America to demine the Gulf of Fonseca that touched the borders of El Salvador, Honduras, and Nicaragua.[37]

The OAS was not successful in stopping the conflict between Peru and Ecuador over portions of their border on the Amazon side of the Andes. After some fruitless diplomacy, the OAS called on the group of four "friends" that had negotiated the original Rio Protocol in January 1942 to intercede. The friends—Argentina, Brazil, Chile, and the United States— with OAS backing managed to get a cease-fire and push the combatants into a slow process that culminated in a statement that established a binding procedure to resolve all differences between the two countries.[38] The final resolution was a significant step in establishing civilian control over the military in South America, and the slow speed of the peace process was due largely to the role of the military in the domestic politics of both countries. In the case of the internecine conflicts in Central America, the OAS could not generate enough confidence to settle the disputes and had to work closely with the UN, in the case of Nicaragua because of the involvement of Cuba, and with nonstate actors in Guatemala and El Salvador.[39] In all of these cases, the OAS was undermined by the unilateralism of the United States during the Reagan administration.

The transformation of the OAS should be seen as a side effect of the euphoria following the end of the Cold War. Multilateralism and instruments to strengthen democratic governance were given priority in hemispheric affair. During the Bush administration, the tone of optimism came from the top. It was conveyed and executed in an extraordinarily effective manner by Luigi Einaudi, the US ambassador to the OAS.[40] The reforms of the OAS would have been unthinkable without Einaudi's collaboration. For a few years, the OAS became an effective element in hemispheric governance and looked as if it would become the chosen instrument of Latin American agency in collective action.[41] After 9/11, the United States lost interest, the budget was gutted, and the new regionalism initiatives from Latin America served to erode the influence of the OAS.

During the Clinton administration, there was considerable effort expended north and south to create the infrastructure of community through summits—ceremonial meetings of heads of state of all the states in the hemisphere (excluding Cuba). So welcome was the first of these summits that they were imitated at the ministerial level, beginning with a defense ministerial in Williamsburg, Virginia, in July 1995. The principal virtue of the ministerial summits was that nations could discuss their shared interests and seek to resolve the significant differences among them. From the Latin American perspective, the defense ministerials were particularly effective in buttressing the new democracies in their efforts to bring their militaries under civilian control, and they made it possible for nations with border problems to meet privately without embarrassing their governments. Civilian control of the military was a touchy subject at the first ministerial. By the eleventh meeting, in Peru in 2014, it was common to include in the final document the statement that democracy was essential for the defense of the nations in the hemisphere.[42]

The progress in using ministerials to bring the military under civilian control and enhance transparency as a basic instrument of confidence building was important. At the first meeting, Canada led an entire session on the virtues of accountability to the voting public through the use of periodic, comprehensive reports on the activities and finances of the defense ministry, known as White Books. Argentine president Carlos Menem urged his minister, Oscar Camilión, to get Argentina named the host for the second ministerial. But Argentina had no White Book. So Camilión had to promise that Argentina would institute the practice of the White Book before the next meeting. To accomplish this task, the government not only had to make pubic its military activities, mission, and budget, it had to get the legislature to staff defense committees in the two chambers so that someone could read a budget. The first Argentine White Book was presented at the Bariloche ministerial in 1996.[43] The first ministerials had moments of difficulty created by the presence of several ministers who represented authoritarian governments and did their best to water down resolutions declaring that democratic values were central to the security mission of all the countries in the hemisphere.[44]

The Bill Clinton administration was more open to debate on policy questions than its predecessor (or its successor, for that matter) and the formulation of policy toward Latin America had the virtue of being about as transparent as such a process can be, and more transparent than any since. Clinton's advisers pushed him to focus his energy on pivotal states, mainly Brazil and Mexico, with Chile as the model country, and use crosscutting (intermestic) issues such as population, migration, the environment, human rights, ethnic conflict, and international finance to bring the nations of Latin America together.[45] These were issues that Clinton found interesting, and he was sympathetic to the idea of using them as a framework within which to encourage cooperation with the nations in the hemisphere. Clinton had a voracious appetite for information and thrived on sessions with Anthony Lake, his National Security Advisor, and Arturo Valenzuela, the Latin Americanist on the National Security Council, both academics, to discuss what most presidents had considered issues too complex for their consideration. Despite these signs that partnerships with Latin American countries were possible, for the most part, Clinton's attention was drawn to crises in other parts of the world, and the push for Latin American partnerships lost force.[46]

The principal centripetal force holding the Latin American nations together and maintaining their optimism at the hemispheric level in the decade after the Cold War was the transition to democracy in many of the countries. In each case, the military had become international pariahs, so in the aftermath of the Cold War, elected civilian leaders considered themselves legitimated by the international system as well as their own citizens. They moved with purpose to establish their international identity. The paradigmatic case was Chile. Not only was the civilian government a coalition with extensive international linkages, it brought into government an extraordinary cohort of foreign policy experts, many of whom had spent the dictatorship in exile studying international relations and other subjects at universities in the United States and Europe. Even before they took power, they were thinking about Chile's insertion into the global community and how that insertion was part and parcel of the transition to democracy.[47] No fewer than a dozen of the senior officers in the foreign ministry, the defense ministry, and in other government offices were academically trained experts in international relations, and all of them had participated in RIAL. A few of the cohort, most notably Augusto Varas, remained in academia, and their presence ensured that the government would be receptive to debate and dialogue with the media and the academy. In a region where foreign policy rarely had been characterized by the permeability of the bureaucracy, at one swift transition, the Chilean government became a model for the region. Confidence building in the hemisphere after the Cold War included increasing the communication between the media and the policy apparatus within countries and between countries. As the founding fathers had insisted in the case of the United States, this was the way to make the policy process transparent and make the policymakers accountable to their electorate.[48]

The new Chilean foreign policy apparatus moved quickly to establish democratic Chile's new role in world affairs on three fronts. The first was to establish the country's position in all relevant multilateral organizations—Muñoz went to the OAS, Juan Somavía went to the UN, Juan Gabriel Valdés (the son of the president of the senate and a Ph.D. from Princeton) went to Spain, Carlos Portales, (who studied at Stanford) was Director General de Política Exterior, and Alberto van Klaveren, another Princeton Ph.D. was an adviser to Portales and later head of Policy Planning and Undersecretary (Sub Ministro).

At the same time, the new ambassador to the United States, Patricio Silva, made it clear that Chile wanted to begin negotiations on a trade treaty. The Concertación government's economics minister, Alejandro Foxley, knew that was the place to establish Chile's leverage in the international system, the second front for the government. By the end of the Patricio Aylwin government, Chile had managed to divide its international trade into three equal geographic parts among the Western Hemisphere, Europe, and Asia—the only country in the hemisphere to do so. It was in one sense an anachronistic concession to dependency theorists by seeking to eliminate any possible weakness in the country's trade due to a dependence on a market or markets in one region. Anachronistic or not, it was a remarkable achievement and had the added benefit of inserting Chile into the Asian market just as China was emerging as a major player in the world economy.[49]

The third front of Chile's advance into world affairs was to focus on the country's soft power, a concept that the cohort of US-trained experts found particularly useful. Chile would tout its democratic credentials as the key to its new influence and agency in world affairs. It would be the representative of democracy and human rights throughout the world, joining as many organizations as it could. It would also follow the basic rules of the economic game, even though its social democratic supporters were less than enthusiastic about the Washington Consensus. The declaration of support for democracy by the OAS as the result of the meeting in Santiago in 1991 was the biggest achievement of the country's soft power. A few years later, Muñoz, who had been shifted to Chile's embassy in Brasília, worked with his Brazilian colleague Celso Lafer in drafting the final declaration of agreement at Doha in 2001.[50] The idea was to seek a role that would enhance the country's international reputation. Chilean views were offered and respected in a wide variety of global forums.

In Argentina, where Carlos Menem was elected to succeed Raúl Alfonsín in 1989, the primary initial goal was to reverse the historic policy of friction with the United States and make it clear that Argentina would follow the US lead in forming the new global community. Argentina was one of the few countries to send support to the United States in its effort to repel Iraq from Kuwait in 1991. It was Menem's sense that the declaration of alliance with the United States would bring immediate benefits, both political and economic. He first was rewarded with a state visit to Washington.[51] Two years later, his reward was to name Argentina a "non-NATO ally."[52]

When Argentina's ambassador in Washington, Guido di Tella, was about to return to Buenos Aires in 1991 to become foreign minister, he told the press that he wanted the two countries to be so close that it would be like "carnal relations."[53] After some time as minister, he amended his goal to making Argentina a "reliable partner."[54] To that end, he assigned one of his senior political officers to follow the US Congress and to bring Argentina's interests to the attention of US lawmakers.[55] With the goal of making Argentina appear a reliable global citizen, he established a joint commission with his counterpart in Santiago to resolve the final border disputes between the two countries dating from the end of the nineteenth century, when a treaty to determine that border had left some ambiguities with regard to the Andean watershed. He ended Argentina's semi-secret missile program and instructed his representatives in Brasília and in Montevideo to relieve tensions with the other members of Mercosur. In that manner, he expected to make Argentina relevant in the world community. He also began conversations with the British government with the hope that these would lead to formal negotiations over the Falkland Islands (Malvinas). Argentine relations with the United States had never been better than they were during the Clinton administration.[56]

In the case of Mexico, the transition was focused on domestic affairs and on NAFTA. It was the period in which the Institutional Revolutionary Party was relaxing its hold on power and may be seen as the analog to the transitions in Argentina, Brazil, and Chile from military to civilian regimes. To become a reliable partner in North America, Mexico worked to clean up its semi-authoritarian political system and create the economic institutions, such as an independent central bank, finally accomplished in 1993, that would facilitate the privatization of the economy and open the country to the opportunities offered in NAFTA. The lobbying effort by the Mexican government in support of NAFTA was unprecedented by a Latin American government. It was conducted in concert with the embassy's efforts to remove the embarrassment of the drug certification and shift discussions of how to deal with illegal drug trafficking to the multilateral forum of the OAS. To that end, Mexico played a key role in the reform of the OAS. In addition, for the first time, the Mexican government worked the US Congress to gain support for immigration reform.[57]

Brazil suffered significant political and economic instability in the first years after the end of the Cold War. But when Fernando Henrique Cardoso took office in January 1995, he asserted Brazilian agency in world affairs with a flair and impact not equaled since the Baron of Rio Branco a century earlier. Cardoso was convinced that Brazil should be a world power. To that end, in his opinion, the country had to do three things: reduce inequality (Brazil was at the time the most unequal country in the world according to World Bank data), end energy dependence, and accept its geopolitical destiny.[58] To accomplish the first, he brought Paulo Renato de Souza back from Washington, where he was operations manager at the

Inter-American Development Bank, to coordinate and expand the country's antipoverty programs. The result was the Bolsa Escola, which combined several existing state and municipal programs into a federal conditional cash transfer program that focused on keeping children in school through family subsidies. The program was so successful—Brazil's poverty was reduced by 28 percent during Cardoso's presidency and the country's Gini coefficient fell by nearly twenty points—that it was continued and expanded by Cardoso's successor, Luiz Inácio Lula da Silva, as the Bolsa Família.[59]

To begin the second task, Cardoso opened the country's national petroleum company, Petrobras, to foreign investment. Again, success was fast and astounding. Relying mainly on joint ventures, Petrobras made Brazil virtually self-sufficient in energy within a decade.[60] Cardoso also privatized a number of other state-owned companies that had become a drag on the country's development. Most notable among these was the telephone company and the giant mining company Vale do Rio Doce. In the second Cardoso government, the economy took off and with it the country's global presence.

To accomplish the third goal, he put Ronaldo Sardenberg in charge of a new Strategic Affairs Secretariat and began an ambitious program (SIVAM) to cover the entire Amazon Basin with radar using US capital to jump-start the effort. At the same time, Sardenberg began a program of studies of hemispheric and global issues that turned his agency in Brasília into a formidable think tank.[61] Cardoso established linkages between the government and the country's scholars and brought the permeability of his government to outside discussion to a level never before seen in Brazil. The country was on its way, led by a series of ambitious and effective foreign ministers. Cardoso made it clear that his goal was a permanent seat on the Security Council of the United Nations and he would assume such responsibilities in world affairs as might be necessary to justify the recognition by the world's powers of Brazil's new role in world affairs. With this, he began a debate within Brazil that continues to this day over how to exercise its new agency.[62]

With the end of the Cold War, the nations in Latin America realized they had space in the international system within which to operate and that the zero-sum power game imposed on them by the United States could no longer be sustained. In public pronouncements, US leaders made it clear they did not wish to perpetuate a relationship in which the United States asserted dominance in an open manner, as it had for the better part of a century. They called out for partnership, for collaboration with the nations of the hemisphere, although somehow they still expected the rest of the hemisphere to bow to their will in matters of regional security or at least follow them willingly. This was not what most Latin Americans had in mind as they explored the possibilities inherent in their new freedom of action in world affairs. After Menem left office in 1999, no one in Latin America wanted relations with the United States so close as to be "carnal."

The reform of the OAS offered some flexibility for the Latin Americans in dealing with controversial policy questions. The summits were useful because they could discuss issues of significance to them, which was hard to do in the OAS and almost impossible in bilateral exchanges with the United States. Clinton and his successors, George W. Bush and Barack Obama, loved face-to-face dialogue and valued direct contact with colleagues in the hemisphere, however brief. The more they met, however ceremonial the gatherings, the more reason they found to come together. Within the context of hemispheric meetings, such as those held by the OAS or the summits, it was no longer impossible to express hostility to the United States.[63]

There was a growing sense that some new regional or subregional forums were necessary to explore ways multinational collaboration might be fruitful. In this context, however, historical differences, such as those that had led to war between Peru and Ecuador or continued to disturb relations between Colombia and Venezuela, made regional cooperation very complicated. Even Mercosur, the longest-lived and most institutionalized of the subregional organizations, had its ups and downs and appeared to have hit a limit to its effectiveness, especially when one of the two larger members, Argentina or Brazil, was experiencing economic difficulties.

At the end of the last decade of the twentieth century, there were two issues on which there was widespread agreement in Latin America in opposition to US policy: the exclusion of Cuba from the hemispheric community and the US militarization of the fight to contain traffic in illegal drugs. There seemed to be no way to bring those disagreements to the fore and no mechanism, bilateral or multilateral, to resolve the differences. The frustration in dealing with these issues during the Bush and Clinton administrations partly explains why the regionalism in Latin America would look for new ways to deal with problems that would not be inhibited by the United States and why the resistance to US hegemony continued to grow over time.

The new commissions in the OAS allowed for open discussion of policy options, although there were very few concessions on the part of the United States. In the case of drug trafficking, the differences between north and south were as wide as an abyss. In the south, the producing countries could not understand why the United States did so little to reduce demand for the drugs that caused so much trouble. If there were no demand, there would be no production except for the traditional production of coca leaf, which was consumed by the indigenous peoples in the Andean region of South America. While officials in the US government did not deny that demand was a problem, they were convinced that if production were stamped out, there would be no drug problem, and so they continued with the war on drugs, which had been declared originally during the Richard Nixon administration. Without moving an inch to compromise its position, the United States pushed the Latin Americans into a zero-sum power struggle that was characteristic of the Cold War: you either help us stamp out drugs or you are enabling the traffickers. That had been the thinking (or lack of thinking) behind the certification program by Congress. Once that had ended, it was up to the OAS to maintain the theater of discussing how to end the illegal traffic in drugs without being able to discuss how to reduce demand in the country that consumed more than 75 percent of the drugs exported from Latin America. It did not help that throughout the decade, the larger countries in South America (Argentina, Brazil, and Chile) insisted that drug trafficking was not their problem and wanted no part of the debate over the solution. That changed in the new century as all of them became transit countries with significant domestic drug problems of their own.

In the first years after the Cold War, the vast majority of drugs moved from Latin America to the United States passed up the Andes, through Colombia, and then through the Caribbean over water. In some cases, drug cartels outgunned the police on the smaller islands in the Caribbean. The US Coast Guard offered to help, but the problem was national sovereignty and territorial waters. To counter the reluctance of microstates to allow the United States to take over their police function, the English-speaking countries joined forces to create a Regional Security Service (RSS) and then asked the United States to supplement their ordnance and strategic capacity. During the Clinton administration, a compromise was struck on the national sovereignty issue, and it provided that if a member of the local police were to ride on the bridge of a US Coast Guard vessel, then that vessel could enter the nation's territorial waters in pursuit of drug traffickers. This Ship-Rider Agreement was signed between the United States and more than a dozen countries in the Caribbean; by 1995, the flow of illegal drugs through the Caribbean had been virtually stopped. Moreover, as a by-product of the new cooperation among the microstates, there began a movement to bring the penal codes of the member countries into alignment, so that the RSS and the US Coast Guard could become an effective regional law enforcement collaborative.[64]

In the effort to patrol the Caribbean more effectively, the drug traffic issue overlapped with the other issue on which Latin America was unable to find an acceptable language of conversation with the United States: the readmission of Cuba into the hemispheric family. Through its insistence on ostracizing Cuba, the United States had managed to convert Cuba into a hemispheric symbol of resistance to US hegemony. Thanks to the power of the Cuban American lobby, it had become impossible to discuss the issue in the United States without stirring rapid opposition within both political parties. As far as the United States was concerned, the Cold War with Cuba had not ended.[65] This was a source of great irritation to an increasing number of countries.

As the Coast Guard increased its efforts to deal with drug trafficking in the Caribbean, the absence of channels of communication with the Cuban navy created dangerous encounters on the high seas between naval forces of the two countries. With no formal diplomatic mechanisms through which to avoid such danger, the Coast Guard turned to unofficial channels to create modes of communication that would benefit both countries by avoiding conflicts. The Drug Enforcement Administration used private contractors to establish clear communications with the Cubans to avoid the movement of drugs through Cuban territory and air space. By the middle of the Clinton administration, these unofficial links were coordinated by a special office in the Defense Department, which made sure the State Department was not in the loop. This was a case in which bureaucratic fragmentation actually facilitated hemispheric cooperation.[66] Despite these ties and Cuba's impeccable behavior, the United States refused to recognize that Cuba belonged in the hemisphere. As if in response, Latin Americans increased their efforts to create forms of solidarity with Cuba and to find mechanisms, regional or subregional, through which Cuba could be reintegrated into the hemispheric community.

At the end of the twentieth century, the question for Latin Americans was what form(s) should their agency take? The asymmetry of power between the United States and the nations of the region was not going to disappear soon. This was particularly obvious in trade negotiations, and the response of many nations in South America was to decline the US invitation to participate in free trade negotiations. However, opposing the United States, which was now possible without retribution or some form of coercion, was not by itself a fruitful form of agency. With the exception of Cuba, opposition did not make it easier to achieve national policy objectives. How to create a hemispheric community after hegemony was not going to be easy. On the part of the Latin American nations, it would require a clear understanding of national objectives and a realistic appraisal of the means to achieve those objectives. For the first time in their history, foreign policy—how to be in the world—was a part of the competition for power in democratic states. It made a difference to the voting public how their leaders would direct their actions in world politics. This was a first.

The terrorist attacks in 2001 and the mad rush of the George W. Bush administration to militarize unilateralism threw the hemispheric community into disorder in ways that were reminiscent of the Cold War. The war on terror destroyed the euphoria the end of the Cold War had generated. It also made the end of US hegemony more problematic. That meant that as the experience of agency in the world community became more familiar, it appeared inevitable that opposition to US hegemony would become adversarial.

Notes

1. The phrase first appears in his essay, Francis Fukuyama, "The End of History?" *National Interest* 16 (1989): 3–18, and was published as a book, *The End of History and the Last Man* (New York: Free Press, 1992).

2. Fukuyama saw this as vindication for the victory of the Allies over the Axis in World War II, the outcome of which had been frustrated by the Soviet Union, which created the conditions for the Cold War.

3. John Williamson, "What Washington Means by Policy Reform," in John Williamson, ed., *Latin American Adjustment: How Much Has Happened?* (Washington, DC: Institute for International Economics, 1990).

4. The triumphalism of the Allies at Bretton Woods is described in Ed Conway, *The Summit Bretton Woods, 1944: J. M. Keynes and the Reshaping of the Global Economy* (New York: Pegasus Books, 2015).

5. For an introduction to the discussion of globalization, see Thomas L. Friedman, *The Lexus and the Olive Tree* (New York: Farrar, Straus and Giroux, 1999) and *The World Is Flat* (New York: Farrar, Straus and Giroux, 2005).

6. This went counter to thinking prominent until then among authoritarian and populist regimes that state spending bolstered the support for the government and could be used to help social groups that supported the state, thereby justifying budget deficits, public debt, and inflation. See Samuel J. Morley, ed., *Poverty and Income Distribution in Latin America* (Washington, DC: World Bank, 1997); Rudiger Dornbusch and Sebastian Edwards, eds., *Macroeconomía del populismo en la América Latina* (Mexico: Fondo de Cultura Económica, 1992).

7. Henry Kissinger, "Unsolved Problems," in *Lisbon, 1992: The Annual Meeting of the Trilateral Commission* (Paris: Trilateral Commission, 1992).

8. Óscar Arias, "The Quest for a New World Leadership," Woodrow Wilson Center, Latin American Program Working Paper no. 199 (Washington, DC: Wilson Center, 1992).

9. A powerful voice for the unipolar concept was Charles Krautheimer, a syndicated columnist for the *Washington Post*, whose views can be seen in his *Democratic Realism: An American Foreign Policy for a Unipolar World* (Washington, DC: American Enterprise Institute, 2004).

10. Perhaps the most significant neoconservative voice was William Kristol, the founder and editor of *The Weekly Standard*.

11. John Mearsheimer, "The False Promise of International Institutions," *International Security* 19.3 (1994/1995); "A Realist's Reply," *International Security* 20.1 (1995); and "Realists and Idealists," *Security Studies* 20.3 (2011). An offshoot of the realist approach is rational choice theory, which adapts the methodology of microeco-

nomics to political action by insisting that all political action is the result of a careful calculation of costs and benefits in the action or policy. Although rational choice is powerful in a number of US university political science departments—mainly because of its use of mathematical methods, which are considered neutral and correct—in the positivist sense, it has made few contributions to the IR debate in the United States and has had little impact in Europe or Latin America. In fact, in Latin America, rational choice is considered a modernized version of modernization theory, designed to relegate developing nations to positions of weakness and inferiority.

12. As a sample, see John Ikenberry, *New Thinking in International Relations* (Boulder, CO: Westview Press, 1997); John Ikenberry, Anne-Marie Slaughter, Thomas J. Knok, and Tony Smith, *The Crisis of American Foreign Policy: Wilsonianism in the Twenty-First Century* (Princeton, NJ: Princeton University Press, 2008). Slaughter is best known for her work on the growing strength of international law, "International Law and International Relations Theory: A Dual Agenda," *American Journal of International Law* 87.205 (1993) and "The Real New World Order," *Foreign Affairs* 183 (1997): 183–97. A realist critique of Slaughter is Eric Posner, *The Perils of Global Legalism* (Chicago: University of Chicago Press, 2009). On regimes and their complexity, see Vinod Aggarwal, *Debt Games* (New York: Cambridge University Press, 1996), which adapts game theory (and its rational choice assumptions) to multilayered interactions among states and nonstate actors that create rules with power to influence state and nonstate behavior.

13. See, for example, Daniel H. Nicholls, "Relational Structures: Counterhegemony and Material Power: A Network Approach to Hierarchy and US Power Projection in the Americas," Ph.D. dissertation, University of London, 2015. On how information is learned and shared in these regimes, see Laura Gomez-Mera, "The Impact of International Agreements against Human Trafficking: Evidence from Latin America," paper presented at the Annual Meeting of the Latin American Studies Association, San Francisco, May 23–26, 2012, and "The Diffusion of Global Prohibition Norms: Sex, Labor, and Organ Trafficking," paper presented to the Annual Meeting of the International Studies Association, San Francisco, 2013.

14. See, for example, Benjamin J. Cohen, *Building Bridges: The Construction of International Political Economy* (Princeton, NJ: Princeton University Press, 2008) and *International Political Economy: An Intellectual History* (Princeton, NJ: Princeton University Press, 2008). Cohen includes Keohane and Nye, among others, as important contributors to the growth of international political economy (IPE). He has had a major influence on several Latin American students of international affairs. For a recent Latin American discussion of IPE, see Juan Pablo Luna, "Representación política en América Latina: Hacia una nueva agenda de investigación," *Política y gobierno* 14.2 (2007).

15. See http://www.dtc.mil/jv2010/jv2010.pdf. Five years later, still before 9/11, the Joint Chiefs produced *Joint Vision 2020*, which was less extravagant. After Iraq and Afghanistan, President Obama issued his own version of the government's strategic plan, which recognized limits to the projection of US power.

16. The invasion of Panama in 1989 to oust the military strongman Manuel Antonio Noriega, even though the OAS had been used as a fig leaf, had made others nervous that the United States would use its power in an unilateral manner without paying adequate attention to Latin American interests. Bush hoped his economic effort, the Enterprise for the Americas Initiative, would calm those fears and create a wellspring of goodwill toward the United States, while supporting the US efforts toward worldwide free trade.

17. The Washington Consensus stirred opposition from the very beginning. Many on the left would not grant to advocates of orthodox market forces the notion that these were

the only answers, and they insisted that the new democracies could reform their economies without strict adherence to market orthodoxies. See, for example, Luiz Carlos Bresser Pereira, José María Maravall, and Adam Przeworski, *Economic Reforms in New Democracies: A Social-Democratic Approach* (Cambridge: Cambridge University Press, 1993).

18. Roger B. Porter, "The Enterprise for the Americas Initiative: A New Approach to Economic Growth," *Journal of Interamerican Studies* 32.4 (Winter 1990): 2. In testimony before the International Trade Commission two years later, Deputy Assistant Secretary for Inter-American Affairs David R. Malpass insisted that the EAI would be a cure-all for Latin America.

19. The classic statement of what has come to be called "imperial overreach" is Paul Kennedy, *The Rise and Fall of the Great Powers* (New York: Random House, 1987). Other examples of similar arguments are David P. Calleo, *Beyond American Hegemony* (New York: Basic Books, 1987); Josef Joffe, *The Limited Partnership* (Cambridge, MA: Ballinger, 1987) (Joffe changed his mind more than twenty-five years later and published a book in which he argued that the United States had not declined); Joel Krieger, *Reagan, Thatcher and the Politics of Decline* (New York: Oxford University Press, 1987). For a very different opinion, see Henry R. Nau, *The Myth of America's Decline* (New York: Oxford University Press, 1990); Lester Thurow, *Head to Head: The Coming Economic Battle among Japan, Europe, and America* (New York: William Morrow, 1992).

20. Bureaucratic confusion doomed the EAI. See Don Abelson, "Energy Policy in the Western Hemisphere," Latin American Program, Woodrow Wilson Center, Working Paper no. 195 (1991); Sydney Weintraub, "The New US Economic Initiative toward Latin America," *Journal of Interamerican Studies* 33.1 (Spring 1991): 1–18. The lack of staff was a constant preoccupation of the USTR, for example, see the interview with Carla Hills in the *New York Times*, May 2, 1992, ii, 2. At the end of 1992, it was still USTR policy to do one treaty at a time and consider Mexico not finished until Congress had ratified the treaty. Ernest R. May had underscored the difficulty involved in shifts in what he called "axiomatic" or underlying policies.

21. See *New York Times*, May 2, 1992, A35.

22. Archibaldo Lanús, "Una perspectiva desde Genebra," Relaciones Argentina-EEUU, presentation to FLACSO seminar, Buenos Aires, March 6, 1992.

23. There have been winners and losers in NAFTA. On balance, the Mexican middle class has grown enormously in the years since the treaty was put into effect, and trade between the two countries has increased more than five times.

24. The Washington Consensus always stirred opposition. See, for example, Bresser Pereira, Maravall, and Przeworski, *Economic Reforms in New Democracies*; Efraín Gonzales de Olarte, *El Neoliberalismo a la Peruana* (Lima: Instituto de Estudios Peruanos, 1998); Efraín Gonzales de Olarte, ed., *Nuevos rumbos para el desarrollo del Perú y América Latina* (Lima: IEP, 1991).

25. The United Nations Conference on the Environment and Development, June 3–14, 1992. For a review of the impact of the conference on environmental impact, see Luis E. Sanchez and Peter Croal, "Environmental Impact Assessment, from Rio-92 to Rio+20 and Beyond," *Ambiente y sociedade* 15.3 (December 2012).

26. Rubens Ricupero, *Trans Atlantic Futures* (Washington, DC: n.p., 1992). Ambassador Ricupero warned that it would be a major bone of contention in any negotiations for a free trade agreement.

27. Indeed, there was evidence that environmental groups were prepared to do just that. Again, however, it is important to point out that these groups had already raised the specter of unfair disparities in environmental regulations in that they were discriminating against Latin Americans by inserting these concerns into the debate over NAFTA and EAI.

28. The environment continues to be an argument between realists and their opponents. The former point to the foot-dragging by the most powerful nations, while the institutionalists point out that leaders such as Barack Obama in the United States are capable of negotiating significant agreements with China, considered to be the strategic opponent of the United States.

29. Peter Hakim, "The Enterprise for the Americas Initiative," *Washington Quarterly* 15.2 (Spring 1992). Also see his "The Enterprise for the Americas Initiative, What Washington Wants," *Brookings Review* (Fall 1992).

30. Working Group on Development and the Environment in the Americas, *Foreign Investment and Sustainable Development: Lessons from the Americas* (Boston: GDAE, 2009). On the shortcomings of globalization, see Joseph E. Stiglitz, *Globalization and its Discontents* (New York: Norton, 2002); and Joseph S. Tulchin and Gary Bland, eds., *Getting Globalization Right* (Boulder, CO: Lynne Rienner, 2005).

31. GDAE, *Foreign Investment and Sustainable Development*.

32. Felix Peña, *Competitividad, democracia e integración en las Américas* (Rio de Janeiro: Getulio Vargas, 1992).

33. The declaration was followed by the Inter-American Democratic Charter (2001) and then, in the new regional organization CELAC (from which the United States was excluded), the Democratic Declaration (2013). See Heraldo Muñoz, "The OAS and Democratic Governance," *Journal of Democracy* 4.3 (1993).

34. This deal was facilitated by the cooperation of the newly appointed drug czar, General Barry McCaffrey, who had served as the chief of Southern Command and worked closely with his Latin American colleagues, who sensitized him to the outrage provoked by the certification process. McCaffrey, in collaboration with the Woodrow Wilson Center, facilitated access to Senator Charles Grassley, who was cochair of the International Narcotics Caucus and worked out the details directly with the OAS ambassadors. The hero of this effort was Arturo Sarukhán, who in the beginning was the "Drugs and Thugs" officer in the Mexican embassy. Sarukhán returned to Mexico to be a special consultant to Minister Rosario Green, then became the first Mexican representative to the MEM meetings of the CICAD-OAS. Congress ended its certification program once and for all when Sarukhán was chief of staff for Policy Planning under Minister Jorge Castañeda. By that time, Senators Chris Dodd and Tom Daschle were the key supporters of the move.

35. For studies of this period of growing influence of the OAS, see Andrew Cooper and Thomas Legler, *Intervention without Intervening?* (New York: Palgrave Macmillan, 2006); Viron P. Vaky, and Heraldo Muñoz, *The Future of the Organization of American States* (New York: Twentieth Century Fund, 1993); Monica Herz, *The Organization of American States* (New York: Routledge, 2011).

36. David Mares, *Violent Peace: Militarized Interstate Bargaining in Latin America* (New York: Columbia University Press, 2001).

37. Francisco Rojas Aravena, ed., *Cooperación y seguridad internacional en las Américas* (Caracas: Nueva Sociedad, 1999) summarizes the collaborative work of the OAS, FLACSO, and the Wilson Center. Documents recording the results of OAS commission meetings were published by the OAS and are available online. Including academics in the policy process was an important expansion of the penetrability and accountability of the new democracies in the region. The concept of cooperative security was useful at the time, but it did not stick. A decade later, when regionalism became important, there was little talk of cooperative security. The Defense Council of UNASUR was charged with defining regional security and chose not to do so.

38. The original conflict, 1942, is chronicled in Bryce Wood, *The United States and Latin American Wars, 1932–1943* (New York: Columbia University Press, 1966);

the solution to the conflict in the 1990s is in Gabriel Marcella and Richard Downes, eds., *Security Cooperation in the Western Hemisphere: Resolving the Ecuador-Peru Conflict* (Miami: University of Miami Press, 1999); Hal Klepak, *Confidence Building Sidestepped: The Peru-Ecuador Conflict of 1995* (Ottawa: FOCAL/York University Press, 1998).

39. Cynthia Arnson, ed., *Comparative Peace Processes in Latin America* (Washington, DC: Wilson Center Press, 1999).

40. Einaudi became such an effective spokesman for the expanded OAS that at the end of his diplomatic career, after he had retired from the US Foreign Service, he was elected assistant secretary general of the OAS in 2000, and then became acting secretary general from 2004 to 2005, when Secretary General Miguel Ángel Rodríguez of Costa Rica resigned suddenly. He was succeeded in May 2005 by José Miguel Insulza of Chile. Leadership and timing counts in hemispheric affairs.

41. The roles played by Muñoz and Einaudi are clear examples of how leadership influences the policy process.

42. For a sympathetic evaluation of the summits, see Javier Corrales and Richard E. Feinberg, "Regimes of Cooperation in the Western Hemisphere: Power, Interests, and Intellectual Traditions," *International Studies Quarterly*, 43.1 (1999): 1–36. The ministerials are described on the OAS website. Corrales and Feinberg see the ministerials as part of a periodic surge of "hemispherism," which they understand as part of regime creation. They take the optimistic position that each surge constitutes "many steps forward followed by some steps backward" (p. 3).

43. Slowly, all of the major countries in the hemisphere have come to produce White Books. Not surprisingly, in countries such as Chile and Brazil, where the military had arrogated to itself control over defense and where the military had in the past determined when it should take over the government, there was significant resistance among the armed forces to this move toward transparency and accountability.

44. It is worth noting that the agenda of the conference was set by assistant secretary of Defense Joseph S. Nye, Jr. and that preparations for the conference included several seminars with the academic Latin Americanists in the Washington area, conducted by Nye. The permeability of the US government to open debate on policy was greater in the Clinton administration than it was under his successor, George W. Bush, and the difference had an impact on the policy process.

45. Robert Chase, Emily Hill, and Paul Kennedy, eds., *Pivotal States* (New York: Norton, 1999).

46. Lake and Valenzuela held regular sessions in the White House with a broad spectrum of the Washington think tank corps. This made the Clinton administration more respectable in the eyes of many in Latin America and served as a model for increasing the permeability of the policy process in Latin America. Lake is currently executive director of UNICEF; Valenzuela, after a period as assistant secretary for Latin America in the Obama administration, returned to his post as professor at Georgetown University.

47. Augusto Varas, ed., *Hacia el Siglo XXI: La proyección estratégica de Chile* (Santiago: FLACSO, 1989).

48. Francisco Rojas Aravena, ed., *Cooperación y seguridad internacional en las Americas* (Caracas: Nueva Sociedad, 1999); Joseph S. Tulchin and Francisco Rojas Aravena, eds., with Ralph Espach, *Strategic Balance and Confidence Building Measures in the Americas* (Stanford, CA: Stanford University Press, 1998); Rut Diamint, ed., *Control civil y fuerzas armadas en las nuevas democracias latinoamericanas* (Buenos Aires: University Torcuato di Tella, 1999) and *Sin gloria* (Buenos Aires: EUDEBA, 2015).

49. Ironically, twenty years later, when the price of copper collapsed, as did the

prices of other commodities, Chile was found to be too dependent on the export of one commodity and on one market for that commodity, China.

50. *New York Times*, November 11, 2001. The front page of the *Times* carried a photo of Muñoz and Lafer at the final session of the conference.

51. At that visit, the president of IBM-Argentina, Ricardo Martorana, gave a speech to the US Chamber of Commerce in which he praised Menem's leadership and promised that the new pro-US policy would restore Argentine greatness. This was a sign that not all had changed in Argentina's view of the world.

52. Author's interview with Foreign Minister Domingo Cavallo, September 22, 1991.

53. In Spanish, *relaciones carnales*. Later, Di Tella repented of his attempt at humor and settled for "close relations."

54. Author's interview with Guido Di Tella, April 23, 1995.

55. In this, the Argentines were following the Mexican lead in the NAFTA talks in lobbying US lawmakers to achieve national objectives.

56. The official history of this period has been prepared by Andrés Cisneros and Carlos Escudé and is available online at http://www.ministerioderelaciones exteriores.gov.ar.

57. At this time, Mexico had the good fortune to incorporate into the decisionmaking circles of the ministry an extraordinary cohort led by Sarukhán, Andrés Rozental, and Carlos Rico, who worked closely with leaders with academic sympathies such as Rosario Green, Olga Pellicer, and later Jorge Castañeda.

58. On Brazil's strategic interests before and after Cardoso became president, see Ricardo Sennes, *As mudanças da política externa brasileira nos anos 80* (Porto Alegre: UFRG, 2003); Ricardo Sennes, ed., *Brasil e a política internacional* (São Paulo: IDESP, 1999).

59. The Bolsa programs have been studied intensively by the World Bank and the UNDP and generally given very good grades. Scholarly studies have been more cautious, finding fault in the program's efficiency. For a broad overview, see Sônia M. Draibe, "Social Policy Reform," in Mauricio Font and Anthony Peter Spanakos, eds., *Reforming Brazil* (Lanham, MD: Lexington Books, 2004).

60. A series of factors, domestic and international, have caused the energy program to stumble in the second decade of the new century.

61. Led by Luis Bitencourt and Thomaz Guedes da Costa, both with doctoral degrees from US institutions.

62. Cardoso continued his reflections on globalization and Brazil's role in world affairs in *Charting a New Course: The Politics of Globalization and Social Transformation* (New York: Rowman and Littlefield, 2001).

63. The only exception to this is the 2005 Mar Del Plata meeting, in which Argentine president Néstor Kirchner made the situation so unpleasant for George W. Bush that the latter turned to his advisers and asked, "What am I doing here?"

64. Stopping the flow of drugs through the Caribbean only drove it onto land. From 1995 to 2013, 95 percent of the drugs coming out of Latin America into the United States came through Mexico. Beginning with the Calderón administration in Mexico in 2008, Mexico and the United States began a military campaign to stanch the flow of drugs. By 2012–2013, nearly 25 percent of the flow had returned to the Caribbean. See the report by David Lewis, in *Manchester Trade*, May 24, 2014, http://www.ManchesterTrade.com.

65. Joseph S. Tulchin and Rafael Hernández, eds., *Cuba and the United States: Will the Cold War in the Caribbean End?* (Boulder, CO: Lynne Rienner, 1991); Joseph S. Tulchin, Andrés Serbin, and Rafael Hernández, eds., *Cuba and the Caribbean*

(Wilmington, DE: SR Books, 1997). At one of the seminars at the Wilson Center in 1991, a middle-level manager in USIS told the visiting Cubans that they did not understand that it was the Cuban American lobby, not the State Department, that determined US policy toward Cuba.

66. The Defense Department took the same position on Cuba as it did on homosexuals in the military: "Don't ask, don't tell."

7

The End of Hegemony
and the Evolution of Agency

Although the end of the Cold War presented Latin American countries with opportunities to play new roles in the world with greater autonomy, most appeared at first to have little sense of how they should use the space opening for them. Few in the region offered suggestions as to what sort of community they wished to form in the hemisphere, and fewer still tried to participate in the broader conversation as to what sort of international community they should work to form, although this would change in the new century. In contrast to this official diffidence, in several countries, notably Argentina, Brazil, Chile, Colombia, and Mexico, there was a dramatic increase in the academic consideration of these issues and public discussion of them. Around the hemisphere, courses in international relations (IR) were added to university curriculums, multiple graduate programs in IR were introduced, and there was a profusion of journals, academic and semi-popular, on the subject. Mass- circulation newspapers in Argentina, Brazil, Chile, Colombia, and Mexico added correspondents with true expertise in foreign affairs. IR had become a hot topic for discussion and a matter for public policy.[1] This expansion of the public discussion and the increasing academic sophistication is crucial in the evolution of Latin American agency. First, it makes the discussion more reasonable and brings a wider range of theoretical approaches and policy options into the arena. Second, it makes the policy process more permeable, which increases its transparency and credibility. Third, it puts the nation's exploration of national interests into a global framework, which enhances the possibilities for agency. In all of the major countries, Argentina, Brazil, Chile, Colombia, and Mexico, credible academics with international scholarly reputations played important roles in policymaking and participated in the increasingly rich public debate on international affairs.

For the better part of a decade after the Cold War, the primary external issue with which most of the countries dealt was the thorny problem of solving border conflicts with their immediate neighbors, some of which dated from the colonial period. These conflicts were inextricably bound up with internal questions of the role of the armed forces and historical legacies of military rule and authoritarianism that had fixed national identities with heavy overlays of nationalism focused in belligerent fashion on one or more of their neighbors. As a consequence, for many of the countries, peace and security meant first freeing themselves from internal threats of military dominance and settling scores with their neighbors. That is why in the first decade after the Cold War most of the attention to questions of autonomy and agency dealt mainly with confidence building between neighbors and attempts to strengthen the institutions of internal civilian governance so that it might be possible to debate or discuss a foreign policy that was not frozen into historically fixed metaphors of aggressive nationalism. Agency in the global system was something of a novelty, even a luxury, when people were still shooting at one another along virtually every border. In the Andes between Chile and Argentina, they did so frequently, until Argentine president Carlos Menem decided serious countries with pretensions to international agency should not do such things. The borders between Colombia and Ecuador and between Venezuela and Colombia were the sites for frequent armed incursions and battles. The most serious was the war between Peru and Ecuador, which required a community effort to resolve. In none of these episodes was the hegemonic power, the United States, more than a cooperative member of the community in the search for peace. Absent any reasonable fear of external intervention or subversion, the United States did not attempt to impose its will on the contestants.

In the new century, the nations of Latin America wrestled with three interlocking issues. The first, and most difficult in the countries that had only recently navigated the transition from authoritarian to democratic regimes, was how to stabilize the institutional matrix within which an autonomous foreign policy might be formed. That meant, most of all, the consolidation of civilian control over the armed forces and establishing public forums for policy discussion and debate. Accountability and impunity were still relatively new topics. The second issue was to determine what the nature of autonomous foreign policy might be. Did freedom from US hegemony necessarily mean opposition to the United States, or was partnership possible despite the legacy of history and the obvious asymmetry of power between them? Finally, how should they exercise their agency in the international community?[2] How much responsibility were they willing to assume by sitting at the table at which the rules of the international community were formulated?

This last item has been the subject of intense debate throughout the region for two decades. The fact of the matter is that in global terms, US hegemony had served as a cost-free entrée to global affairs for many of the nations of Latin America. If any of them participated in solving conflicts or in wars, as Brazil did in World War II and Argentina did in the Gulf War, it was at the behest of and under the leadership of the United States. Autonomous of US cover, each global player assumes some responsibility for its own actions. Those that do not are known as free riders, a criticism commonly leveled against Latin America. The question posed in capitals around the hemisphere in the new century is what is the cost of joining the rulemakers of the international community?

Linking all of these questions was the drive to put together regional and subregional groups, either to satisfy the sense that larger markets were more efficient than small ones, as ECLA/CEPAL had been suggesting for decades, or through some iteration of the Bolivarian notion that the nations had common histories and common values that would bind them together. By the second decade of the twenty-first century, regionalism would become the dominant theme in collective efforts to form a Latin American identity and community that somehow would be free of US hegemony.[3] Despite significant effort, ideological differences among the nations were a powerful inhibiting force making the formation of communities more difficult. These differences continue to this day.

Brazil's bold move to demand recognition as a great power, including a permanent seat on the UN Security Council, did not appeal to any other countries in the region. Most considered it a leap too far. On the other hand, none wanted to make their way by hitching their wagon to the leadership of the United States, as Menem had tried in the 1990s. Menem's successor, Fernando de la Rúa, thought respectful friendship between Argentina and the United States was close enough. Anyway, within months of de la Rúa's inauguration, Argentina virtually imploded and by 2001 suffered the worst economic crisis it had experienced in more than a century. Argentina would not be a player in the international community to be reckoned with for some time.

The only significant initiative to forge community in the region came from Venezuela, where Hugo Chávez took office in 1999, declaring his determination to achieve "socialism for the twenty-first century." Invoking the Bolivarian dream, he also offered to lead a new regional organization, the Bolivarian Alliance for the Peoples of Our America (Alianza Bolivariana para los Pueblos de Nuestra América, ALBA), that would oppose the United States and the imperialism it represented. With the windfall profits from a rapid increase in the price of oil, Chávez reached out to countries with the promise of cheap oil and his project of a more just and autonomous Latin America. The center of his alliance was Cuba, where he had become an acolyte of Fidel and Raúl Castro. He won more support as the years unfolded as newly elected progressive governments joined the alliance, first Daniel Ortega in Nicaragua (2006), and the region's first indigenous president, Evo Morales in Bolivia (2006), then Rafael Correa in Ecuador (2007), and for a brief time, Manuel Zelaya in Honduras (2008). Chávez tried to pull Mercosur into his orbit, but Brazilian president Luiz Inácio Lula da Silva resisted his blandishments. This was an ideological movement that set itself against the imperialism and neoliberalism of the United States.

So long as the international price of oil stayed above US$90/barrel, the break-even point for the government, Chávez had billions to play with. In 2014 the price of oil collapsed, and his successor, Nicolás Maduro, discovered that the international pretensions of ALBA and Petrocaribe, the institutional mechanism for selling oil to friendly nations at special rates, were impossible to sustain. Outside the hemisphere, Chávez only seemed to be interested in tweaking Uncle Sam's nose. He invited the Russian navy to conduct maneuvers within Venezuela's territorial waters in the Caribbean; he visited Iran and invited the Iranian head of state to Venezuela; he signed enormous joint venture deals with the Chinese, none of which came to anything for nearly a decade. Nothing in his foreign policy nor in what he claimed for ALBA could be taken as the framework of an international community except an ideology he called socialism for the twenty-first century and anti-Americanism. Amid all of these gestures, Venezuela maintained its oil exports to the United States and its subsidized oil shipments to the Commonwealth of Massachusetts.

In Mexico, the Party of National Action (PAN), with Vicente Fox as its candidate, came to power in 2000 as the first opposition party to govern Mexico in more than seventy-five years. Fox's platform called for deepening the friendship with the United States, increasing bilateral efforts to control the drug trafficking violence along the border, strengthening the institutions that guaranteed political democracy and market efficiency, and putting Mexico into the world community. Given the inhibited nationalism that had marked Mexico's foreign policy under the Institutional Revolutionary Party (PRI), this last goal was remarkable. Under the PRI, the Mexican armed forces had no specific mission to enhance the nation's sovereignty and no blue-water navy. It kept to itself in international affairs and kept a low international profile. In his bold new foreign policy, Fox was influenced by two intellectuals, Jorge Castañeda Gutman and Adolfo Aguilar Zínser, who believed that the time had come for Mexico to take its place in the world. Castañeda was named foreign minister and Aguilar Zínser became national security adviser.[4] As in Argentina, Brazil, Chile, and Colombia, the transition to democracy and the opening of the policy process to debate and scrutiny was an indispensable prelude to Fox's determination to mark Mexico's agency.

Fox and US president George W. Bush made a photogenic pair in their cowboy boots and hats when they met on the Bush ranch in Texas after both of them were newly installed. Fox took away from the meeting the sense that the new US government would be attentive to issues the Mexicans found sensitive, such as immigration and the massive amounts of small arms sold in the United States and shipped to Mexico to be used by the drug cartels, which now controlled the shipment of more than 80 percent of the drugs that entered the United States from Latin America. To bring Fox closer, Bush invited him for a state visit in September 2001.

Castañeda thought the time was ripe for a major overhaul of the hemispheric community as well as Mexico's role in it, and he prepared a powerful speech for Fox to deliver in Washington. The speech called for terminating the Inter-American Defense Treaty (known as TIAR in its Spanish initials) that had been an instrument of US domination for half a century. Fox suggested replacing it with an agreement that would recognize the autonomy of the nations in the hemisphere and alter the focus of the TIAR from a concern with external threat to a consideration of threats internal to the community, such as international crime. The speech was delivered in Washington on September 9, 2001, and was well received. But timing is crucial. Two days later, terrorists took down the World Trade Center Twin Towers in New York and plowed an aircraft into the Pentagon. It was no time for revising security treaties that considered external threats. There was an external threat to the hemisphere and it had attacked the United States. In powerful contrast to the Mexican posture, Celso Lafer, Brazilian foreign minister, instructed the Brazilian representative to the regular meeting of the OAS General Assembly then in Lima to invoke the TIAR as the hemispheric response to an external attack. Lafer followed this with a major addess in Washington on September 21, 2001.[5]

Castañeda never recovered from this unfortunate sequence of events. Fox was left embarrassed and lost confidence in his foreign policy advisers. Castañeda turned his attention to Latin America and accomplished a number of significant goals in putting Mexico back into the Latin American community. Aguilar Zínser was sent to the United Nations, where he held Mexico's position with conviction when the Bush envoys tried to bully him and the other Latin American representatives into following the US lead in attacking Iraq.[6] Fox succeeded in giving Mexican foreign policy a new framework and set the country on the path to taking an important role in the hemispheric and the global communities while maintaining a special relationship with the United States in which Mexico was treated as a partner. It was during the Fox administration that the Ministry of Foreign Affairs (SRE) began a mammoth publication project that put a huge chunk of the ministry's archive online. This came along with a significant increase in public funding of international studies at the graduate level in universities throughout the country, that resulted in a dramatic increase in the public discussion of foreign affairs and a rich effusion of publications dealing with Mexico's foreign affairs and foreign policy.[7]

In Chile, the foreign ministry fully intended that its soft power would be of even greater value outside the hemisphere than within it and was somewhat surprised that there were obstacles in its path. The major problem was the strategic culture that focused obsessively on protecting the territorial conquests of the War of the Pacific. The Chilean armed forces controlled a portion of the nation's copper profits as a royalty (regalía) and used it to maintain the most sophisticated military equipment in South America. All of the threat scenarios followed in the study centers of the several forces considered invasions from Peru and Bolivia as the nation's primary threat. The senior officers would not consider responsibilities outside the hemisphere, such as UN peacekeeping, because they said they could not divert assets from protecting the national territory. It took more than a decade for the Concertación to change the thinking of the senior officers to allow for an international role that would better suit the new image of the country.[8]

Another obstacle for Chile in leveraging its soft power was the set of compromises the Concertación had forged with the military regime when it took power in 1990, compromises the leadership considered essential for the stability of the new civilian government. All of the compromises amounted to an avoidance of a public reckoning of the abuses of the military regime. Principal among these was to leave the former dictator General Augusto Pinochet free to sit as a lifetime senator and influence his military colleagues on active duty. That compromise came back to haunt the government of Eduardo Frei Ruiz-Tagle in 1998, when a Spanish judge issued a warrant through Interpol for Pinochet's arrest for crimes against humanity while he was in London for medical care. In responding to this challenge, Frei and his successor Ricardo Lagos had to think through the domestic cost of Chile's role in the evolving international community.

Although he was not happy about it and certainly did not do it deliberately or with pleasure, Pinochet became a symbol of the slow, halting progress in the reconstruction of an international community in the aftermath of the Cold War, in which peoples and their governments were in agreement as to what constitutes acceptable behavior. No state follows the code of good behavior all the time; but in the aftermath of the Cold War, there was a growing consensus that human rights should be protected, that states cannot violate the human rights of their citizens with impunity, and that systematic use of force against ethnic or political minorities is inappropriate. Moreover, there was a growing network of civil society institutions that worked assiduously for the preservation of these rights. What was not clear at the time—and not fully clarified to this day—is how the international community is to enforce this code of good behavior. The central question is impunity. How will violations of the code be challenged and punished? Who will enforce the code? At the time of the warrant for Pinochet, the international action in Kosovo, when NATO used military force to oust Serbian president Slobodan Milosevic, was taken as a model. Afterward, Kosovo did not appear to be widely applicable, because the massive military pressure exerted by the forces of NATO under the leadership of the United States depended so heavily on the institutional integrity of NATO and the geographical proximity of Kosovo to the European heartland. The genocide in Rwanda, for example, produced consternation but little action on the part of the NATO allies and no response from the nations of Latin America.[9]

Perhaps the case of East Timor might be more to the point for the slow development of international agency in Latin America. The United States and its European allies quickly arrived at the decision that the Indonesian government was behaving badly and the Indonesian armed forces, through the paramilitary groups they controlled, were part of the problem, not part of any possible solution. An election had been held with international observers in attendance in which a large majority of the citizens of East Timor had voted for independence from Indonesia. Maverick elements of the armed forces decided they would not honor the results of that election and proceeded to drive the leaders of the independence movement into hiding and use force to repress the movement. As in Kosovo, geography played an important part in what happened next. Because of where East Timor was, none of the European nations had any interest in sending troops, nor did the United States. Australia, which was close enough to be very concerned with what happened there and capable of doing something about it, was not about to send troops to the island on its own responsibility. US secretary of state Madeleine Albright declared that the "international community" should deal with the problem. US representative to the UN Richard Holbrooke, who, with National Security Adviser Anthony Lake, had done so much to deal with Kosovo, took the lead in hammering out an agreement that the Indonesian government could accept and that would provide sufficient freedom of action for the Australian troops and their allies on the ground. The United States promised to provide "logistical support" to the peacemakers. The United Nations was given the job of establishing order on the island—peacemaking and peacekeeping—and providing the East Timorese with advice and support in setting up their new democracy.[10] In this sequence, a Brazilian, Sergio Vieira de Mello, a senior offical at the UN, played an important leadership role.[11]

There are two elements in the denouement in East Timor relevant to Latin America. The first is the importance of procedural democracy and the value of international verification. There was at that time a veritable world-wide army of election observers and experts who were available on short notice to go anywhere at any time to help anyone hold a fair, clean election. These election experts work for the UN, the World Bank, the Organization of American States (OAS), and the Carter Center; they are nongovernmental organizations (NGOs), independent contractors, scholars, and concerned individuals. They form a tight network that is in constant communication. The Brazilian government agreed to send Brazilian citizens to East Timor to help in the elections and in keeping the peace afterward.

The second element is the power of international NGOs that operate in the fields of human rights and the protection of democratic rights of peoples, especially ethnic minorities, throughout the world. These organizations are the most significant new actors in the international arena in the aftermath of the Cold War, part of the new international civil society. They are frontline troops in the formation of an international community in what are known as regimes of behavior surrounding specific issues or sets of issues. Their importance brings us back to Pinochet.[12]

Pinochet's arrest in London on October 17, 1998, was the result of a combination of the two elements that were important in driving the international community to action in East Timor. First was the fact that the Chilean courts had been unable or unwilling to prosecute the general for the crimes he was alleged to have committed as the head of state in Chile. He operated in the senate with impunity and continued to exercise his influence within Chile, especially within the armed forces. He denied having committed any crimes; the armed forces denied having been involved in any crimes; the courts would not prosecute senior officers for crimes of which they were accused. Enter the international NGOs and Spanish judge Baltasar Garzón. Their strength was the growing international consensus around the questions of due process and human rights which made a fairly robust regime. The European nations had signed formal agreements in defense of both in which traditional arguments of territoriality were subordinated to the broader community. The end of the Cold War meant that any strategic arguments in defense of repression and the national interest were no longer valid. Even Margaret Thatcher's angry insistence that the British valued Pinochet because he had been Britain's ally in the Falklands/Malvinas War was of little use in refuting the demands of the international community. The impunity with which Pinochet operated in the face of the accusations was his undoing.

When Pinochet got off a plane in Chile in March 2000, after the British courts decided that he should not be extradited to Spain because of his supposed poor health, he walked without benefit of any support to his limousine. The newly installed president, Ricardo Lagos, indignantly called for judicial examination of the cases against the former dictator. Within weeks, a Chilean court came up with an ingenious way to get around the amnesty law of 1978 and prosecute members of the armed forces for violating the human rights of Chilean citizens during the dictatorship. As the judicial proceedings dragged on, the courts again excused Pinochet because of his poor health. He died in December 2006, with 300 cases pending against him. After his death, information came to light that the former dictator had squirreled away millions of dollars in international bank accounts. Many Chilean conservatives who were willing to accept his violations of human rights were outraged by this dishonesty. The unequivocal actions of the Lagos government buttressed Chile's soft power under the new international regime.

Next, Judge Garzón went after the military in Argentina, asking the Argentine government to extradite the leaders of the repression during the dictatorship. At first, the Menem government invoked the same arguments of territoriality that the Chileans had used to reject Garzón's former request. His successor, Fernando de la Rúa, determined that the Argentine courts should decide and in the short period of his government, before the collapse of 2001, he began the judicial proceedings. After his election in 2003, Néstor Kirchner pushed the judiciary to get on with their task, and they did so. The same year Garzón issued the warrant for Pinochet, Hipólito Solari Yrigoyen, an Argentine politician, published *Human Dignity*, in which he chronicled the evolution of the international norms of human rights in the previous fifty years.[13] In the decade after the Cold War, the community of nations made great progress toward rejecting impunity for crimes against humanity, and, at least on occasion, showed that it was willing to pay a price to protect human dignity anywhere and everywhere. Chile and Argentina, among others in Latin America, learned how that affects their autonomy and their agency.

Even after dealing with Pinochet, Chile's soft power continued to be hampered by its success in the nineteenth-century War of the Pacific. Peru and Bolivia, vanquished in that war, had territorial claims against Chile, despite treaties both had signed certifying their loss of territory. In the period of revived border disputes in the region, it was clear that these countries would not allow regional groups to have any power or create any viable regional architecture as long as Chile held onto that territory. Chile's position was that the treaties had settled the matter. Year after year, Peru and Bolivia brought their dissatisfaction to the OAS and the UN, just as Argentina did in its dispute with Great Britain over the Falklands/Malvinas. After years of debate, the Chilean military finally accepted the reality of renegotiating the peace treaties and the territory involved. In this shift in strategic culture, the new Chilean participation in peacekeeping and other forms of global collaboration, as well as Pinochet's trial, played important roles. Under Lagos, with Michelle Bachelet as minister of defense, the civilian government moved to consolidate its control over the armed forces. They even renegotiated the terms of the royalty on copper sales that went to the armed forces, although they could not eliminate it completely. Bachelet's transparency moves included creating the White Book of the Chilean armed forces in which the budget, including the royalty, was made part of the public record. Emboldened by this progress in civilian control, Lagos approached his Bolivian counterpart with a proposal to open discussions about the boundary and about a solution to the Bolivian claim for an outlet to the sea.[14] The Bolivians refused to talk.

Seizing the moment, the Peruvians took their claim over the maritime boundary between the two countries to the International Court of Justice. After years of stonewalling the Peruvians and the court, the Chileans finally agreed to discuss their differences, and in January 2014 the court decided the dispute and allocated about two-thirds of the area to the Peruvians.[15] The loss of disputed waters was of trivial economic consequence since most of the fisheries in the area were controlled by Chilean companies and Chilean investments in Peru more than made up for any losses in the fisheries. As the dispute was being decided in The Hague, the Chilean government reiterated its offer to the Bolivians. Instead, the Bolivians preferred to put their claim to the court in the form of a demand for the return of territory taken by Chile after the war. That dispute has not been resolved, but Chile has shown itself ready to make amends. In September 2015, the court recognized Bolivia's right to negotiations with Chile over the territory in dispute. In a step designed to link the peaceful resolution of the dispute with Peru to Chile's soft power, in November 2015 President Bachelet announced the creation of a huge maritime preserve to protect the marine life of the eastern Pacific.

In another step to establish their role in the international community, Heraldo Muñoz, then ambassador to the United Nations and following the East Timor model, took the lead to give peacekeeping a Latin American identity. Muñoz maneuvered through the Security Council, on which Chile was sitting in April 2004, a mission for the stabilization of Haiti, MINUS-TAH, which would not include the United States.[16] Muñoz began by getting the Brazilians to accept leadership of the new mission, which would give the mission legitimacy. In this way, Muñoz wanted to show the entire world that Latin America, a region of peace, could act in concert to keep the peace. MINUSTAH certainly demonstrates Latin American capacity for agency. It also suggests that Latin Americans fell into the trap of Wilsonian missionary zeal: troops may be able to stop violence, but they cannot create stable democratic government without the willing and capable cooperation of local actors. Peacekeepers cannot create democratic governance.[17] The MINUSTAH effort was a marked exception to the post–Cold War pattern of Latin American reluctance to take the lead in international community actions. It set a precedent, but has not been followed very frequently.

The terrorist attacks of September 11, 2001, put a stop to community building in the Western Hemisphere despite Brazilian efforts to rally the hemisphere behind TIAR. For the remainder of the Bush administration, the United States retreated to the unilateralism and zero-sum thinking about foreign policy that had characterized the Cold War period. There had been warning signs of trouble ahead for Latin America even before the terrorist attacks. In matters of defense and foreign policy, the new president surrounded himself with former officials in his father's government, such as Dick Cheney and Donald Rumsfeld, with grudges to settle. A number of senior advisers were notorious neoconservatives with strong Wilsonian views about the exportability of US values. Most specifically, the president nominated as assistant secretary of state for Latin America a Cuban American, Otto Reich, known for his hardline views on Cuba and Venezuela. This nomination suggests that apart from trade and the bilateral relationship with Mexico, Bush was prepared to see relations with the hemisphere through the myopic lens of the tortured relations with the Castro regime in Cuba.[18] That meant that any expressions of sympathy for Cuba would be considered subversive and hostile to the United States, precisely at a time when such expressions in Latin America were becoming more widespread and insistent.[19]

The terrorist attacks had the unhappy consequence of exacerbating the persistent asymmetry of agendas between the United States and Latin America. None of the countries in Latin America considered terrorism a threat to their national security, although the Argentines twice had been victims of such terrorist actions.[20] But most of them were willing to go along with the kind of technical cooperation the United States requested to make trade and travel between them more secure. Most striking, the government of Argentina went out of its way to cooperate. In the brief tenure of his government (January 2002–May 2003), President Eduardo Duhalde authorized the transformation of Buenos Aires from the dirtiest port in Latin America to the first smart port that would inspect all cargo headed for the United States before it left Argentine territory. That program of full cooperation was maintained by the new government of Néstor Kirchner despite the president's propensity for anti-American rhetoric.

The invasion of Iraq drove a wedge between the United States and Latin America. Chilean president Lagos was offended by the US demand to support the invasion. In the United Nations, Ambassador John Bolton demanded of Muñoz and Aguilar Zínser that Chile and Mexico vote with him in the Security Council. They refused. The damage done to US relations with Latin America by the war with Iraq and the war on terrorism went far beyond the personal and was long lasting. The principal wedge of divergence between north and south was the remilitarization of security, similar to the manner it had dominated Central America during the Cold War. This time around, it was less a matter of escalating civil conflict into civil wars with external actors than it was a matter of having the United States rely heavily, almost exclusively, on the military as a response to anything that came close to touching on security. No matter how hard the Latin American insistence that the problem was not military but one of crime or drug trafficking, the United States had no answer other than to throw more military at the problem. The bottom line was that the military had the assets and the networks. Although he no longer was president of Brazil, Cardoso gave an eloquent speech to the French national assembly expressing the general feeling in Latin America that the struggle against terrorism was not a war and was not a clash of civilizations.[21]

In Central America, the security issues confronting the subregion were mainly crime and violence, often but not always associated with international drug trafficking, and the need to organize effective preparations for the certain but unpredictable natural disasters that occur so frequently. Here, the resources belonged to the Pentagon, and they are trained to share those resources with counterpart armed forces. The problems, however, are social and civil and require building effective state responses by countries whose civilian institutions are still weak and unprofessional. The US government was sensitive to this asymmetry; but in the absence of multilateral cooperation in dealing with gangs, drug trafficking, immigration, and natural disasters, the default option left the initiative in the hands of the Pentagon. When the leadership of Southern Command was confronted with this dilemma, its response was that they had no other effective interlocutors. Without sufficient resources in some other unit of government, efforts by the Pentagon continued to have the unwanted consequence of stunting the development of civilian democratic institutional responses to crime and violence. For their part, none of the governments in Central America came up with a coherent or effective policy to deal with the asymmetry between military action and civic capacity. In Guatemala and Honduras, where the governments were still controlled by conservative elites, it was useful for domestic purposes to keep the military involved. Costa Rica, with no army, was an obvious outlier.

This heavy historical legacy and the asymmetry of power between the United States and Latin America affected bilateral military relations in several ways. First, it produced mission creep. The war on drugs was a clear example. Country after country, from Mexico to Argentina, was captured by the lure of valuable military hardware delivered through existing channels to expand the mission of their military to take on the struggle against the illegal traffic in drugs. Although few denied that the struggle required civilian institutions and laws, in the short run, no one wanted to spend the time and energy creating or strengthening those institutions. The asymmetry of civilian control over the military in the United States and the imperfect control in Latin America confuse the dialogue between US military and Latin American colleagues and between US leaders and their Latin American counterparts. Where civilian control was consolidated, military dialogue became more fluid.[22]

Faced with the challenge of the US return to unilateralism under George W. Bush, the Latin Americans became more active in defining their participation in various forms of community, networks, and regimes, with and without the United States, in specific issue areas, such as security and trade. Ironically, the Latin Americans took over the leadership of the hemispheric defense ministerials because it suited them and gave them a forum in which to discuss such issues as the Falkland Islands (Malvinas). During the Bush administration, there were defense ministerials held in Chile in 2002, Ecuador in 2004, Nicaragua in 2006, and Canada in 2008. There also was a proliferation of meetings at the bilateral and subregional level with the purpose of building confidence and consolidating civilian control over the armed forces. Potentially the most significant initiative was the effort to create a regional security framework within the Union of South American Nations (UNASUR), although very little progress has been made in the decade since it was founded.[23]

The global trade regime has become more complicated over the past twenty years, but the nations in Latin America were becoming more comfortable exercising their agency at different levels within this regime, whether it is the World Trade Organization (WTO), Mercosur, or any number of proliferating associations concerned with trade, investment, or financial dealings. In these regimes, Brazil has played a leading role and has not been afraid to use the rules to defend its national interests against the United States, China, or any other possible adversary. By using the dispute resolution mechanisms of the WTO and the Inter-American Development Bank (IDB), among other organizations, the Brazilians have shown the way for other nations in the region on how to become rulemakers incrementally on their own terms, in a relatively nonadversarial manner. There have been cases in which nations in Latin America have chafed at the confining features of rule-based communities, even without US hegemony. For example, Venezuela withdrew from the IDB's dispute resolution agreement when it did not want to accept third-party determination of the value of properties confiscated from foreign investors. Perhaps more significant, the Venezuelan government, with some echo from Argentina, Ecuador, and Bolivia, denounced the Inter-American Commission on Human Rights, but none of these states has withdrawn from the OAS.[24] Chávez, with ALBA, promised a new form of community, an anti-American community. He also promised to integrate Cuba into the hemispheric community through ALBA. But by limiting ALBA's collective agency to anti-Americanism, Chávez actually reduced the effective agency of its members within the hemisphere and the wider global community. At the hemispheric level, ALBA offered a progressive message that was attractive to a number of states in the region that had no intention of joining it.

In the midst of this leftward tilt, along came Barack Obama, the first African American president of the United States. He came into office opposing George Bush's wars and promising a collegial approach to international affairs and a less assertive approach to global leadership. Expectations around the world were so high—unrealistically high—that if you read the European or Latin American press in the months following Obama's election, it must have appeared as if the world's problems were about to be solved. In many ways, he reminded observers of the response to John F. Kennedy's election in 1960—he was charming and well spoken, his wife and children were delightful, and he had beaten a man who was as *antipático* as it was possible for a politician to be. Obama said all the right things and seemed so in tune with the interests of democratic countries in every region of the world.

Certainly, part of the euphoria around the world had to do with the deep resentment toward the previous administration, especially its bellicose rhetoric and unilateralism. Instead of the ugly American, Obama seemed like the good-looking American.

In foreign policy, things began badly for the new administration. The economic crisis that had exploded in the last year of the Bush administration was only getting worse as Obama took office, and it was spreading around the world. As if this were not distraction enough, it was made clear almost immediately that the local partners in both theaters of war, Iraq and Afghanistan, were not going to behave the way Candidate Obama had hoped they would, and President Obama, because of his campaign platform, was locked into a long, conflicted debate among his advisers as to how to conduct what soon was called "his war" in Afghanistan. In other crisis spots to which the candidate had offered a new approach, much the same thing happened. The Iranians were not interested in dialogue, the Israelis dug in their heels in opposition to a two-state settlement with Palestine, the Russians were not ready to settle all of the differences between them and the United States, and the Chinese took an increasingly belligerent posture in Asia and in multilateral institutions of all types. In the case of the Russians, Obama was able to secure a significant if modest reduction in nuclear arms in the early months of 2010.

With regard to Latin America, there was not much material to go on during the campaign. There were hints about a change in policy toward Cuba, hints about immigration reform, and a bold statement about a new approach to the problem of drugs in the United States and drug trafficking.

Beyond that, analysts only had to go on a stated preference for multilateralism and an eagerness to seek partners—the same word used by George H. W. Bush almost twenty years earlier—in the solution of common problems. But almost at the start of the new government, a crisis in Honduras put the government in a very bad place. Even in the new century Honduras was still a penetrated polity, if not quite a client state.[25] In January 2006, José Manuel Zelaya Rosales took office as president of Honduras. Although a member of the commercial and agricultural elite that had dominated the country for decades, he began almost immediately demonstrating a certain independence of action by expressing admiration for Hugo Chávez and extending popular participation in politics. By 2008, he declared his intention to join ALBA and had begun a campaign to hold a national referendum to change the constitution so that popular groups would have more power in running the country. He was opposed in this effort by the majority of the elite and their representatives in the national chamber of commerce and congress. What happened in the following year hews so closely to the pattern of penetrated politics set a century earlier by Chandler Anderson and his Nicaraguan client Emiliano Chamorro that the differences between the two episodes are more instructive. First and foremost, the US Congress played a critical role in shaping the actions on the ground and contested the government's declared policy. Second, there are more international actors in the twenty-first century than there were before, and most of them were trying to act in a manner that would reduce the hegemonic influence of the United States, but they were unwilling to operate without the collaboration of the United States. Also, in Honduras, the United States was trying to create a new policy, one in which partners were crucial to enforcing the rules of the community.

The Honduran Chamber of Commerce asked their lobbyist, Lanny Davis, to have the US government switch its support from President Zelaya to Roberto Micheletti, the head of the congress. In this episode, Davis did not head to the State Department, as Anderson had done a century earlier, even though the secretary of state was Davis's good friend Hillary R. Clinton. He headed instead to the Senate Office Building, where he had an appointment with the chief of staff of the junior senator from South Carolina, Jim DeMint. Davis's job was to convince DeMint to support the campaign sponsored by the Chamber of Commerce in Honduras to defend the congress against what they called the antidemocratic aspirations of President Zelaya. The congress of Honduras was cooperating with the Supreme Court to prevent Zelaya from calling a referendum to change the constitution. The military, at the moment, was quiet.

The argument Davis made was that the Honduran congress and Supreme Court were defending democracy against the subversion of the president. It was an important part of his argument that Zelaya seemed to be falling under the influence of Hugo Chávez, who was seen by many conservatives as a threat to hemispheric stability. Even conservatives who did not focus much of their attention on foreign affairs, of whom DeMint was one, were happy to see any friend of Chávez as an enemy of the United States and any enemy of Chávez as a friend of the United States. Davis knew that Congress was his best bet. He also represented, among others, Laurent Gbagbo, the former dictator of the Ivory Coast, whose democratic credentials were not particularly strong, so he knew his way around the offices of the most conservative, business-friendly members of Congress. DeMint proved to be a perfect target. He had blocked the appointment of Arturo Valenzuela as assistant secretary of state.[26] He considered talk of multilateralism in the hemisphere to be anti-American. And, Davis knew, he already had been approached by Otto Reich, who considered Chávez to be the most evil person in the world after the Castro brothers.

Davis got DeMint to fly to Tegucigalpa at the crucial juncture in the standoff between the congress, which had induced the armed forces to force Zelaya to flee with his wife to the Brazilian embassy, and the international community (including the United States), which refused to recognize Micheletti as chief of state. Not only did DeMint succeed in frustrating the policy of the US government, he succeeded in blocking all efforts by the international community to get rid of Micheletti or allow Zelaya to return to power. Ultimately, the strategy of Davis's clients succeeded. A few months later, in elections that had already been scheduled, a new president, Porfirio Lobo Sosa, was elected. The discussion immediately shifted to when and how to allow Honduras to reenter the international community. Brazil and Venezuela tried to keep Honduras out of the OAS, but were ultimately outvoted. Davis had done his job well.[27]

From the very beginning of this episode, OAS was involved and enjoyed the cooperation of the Obama administration. Immediately after the coup, a special assembly of the OAS was called, in keeping with the procedures specified in the Democratic Charter signed in Chile in 1991. That assembly asked the secretary general to go to Tegucigalpa and report back. He returned in a matter of days to indicate that neither side appeared willing to compromise. The OAS supported the ongoing initiative by the former president of Costa Rica, Óscar Arias, and provided him with a senior staff member, the Chilean diplomat John Biehl. Secretary General José Miguel Insulza headed a delegation of Latin American foreign ministers to Honduras in August in what proved to be a final effort to use the OAS as an instrument of regional governance. The OAS refused to accept the ambassador sent by Micheletti's provisional government, and the United States withdrew the visas held by Micheletti and others in his government. Finally, US assistant secretary of state Thomas Shannon and his deputy,

Craig Kelly, achieved an agreement under which Zelaya would be invited back, the constitutional amendments would be shelved, and the presidential elections would proceed as scheduled, without Zelaya as a candidate. Micheletti would not be allowed to continue as president. Brazil and Venezuela opposed this deal because they insisted that Zelaya should be returned to office immediately. The governments of Central America disagreed and wanted the elections to go through.

At the last minute, Micheletti and the Honduran congress backed away from the agreement. However, as the presidential elections approached, the United States announced that it would recognize the results if the observers considered the elections to be fair. That broke the consensus within the OAS to impose sanctions on Honduras and, led by the new Colombian president, Juan Manuel Santos, with the United States in agreement, the nations of South America put together enough votes in the OAS to lift the sanctions.

What is noteworthy about this episode is that the Obama administration tried to avoid behaving like a hegemonic power. The president and his advisers saw the coup as an ideal situation in which to apply the new policy of multilateralism in the hemisphere. The Central Americans didn't fully trust him. More important, the Hondurans didn't believe him. The OAS could maintain its consensus to follow the Democratic Charter, but the consensus broke down over how to enforce that charter. Nonintervention was a powerful force within the organization. Both Brazil and Venezuela wanted Zelaya returned to power, but were reluctant to allow the OAS to be the instrument of their policy and would not cooperate with the United States to accomplish their goal. Lula, Brazil's president, was in the middle of a period in which he was trying to create space for Brazil in world politics as a major player, especially with his trip to Iran. When DeMint told the crowd at the airport in Tegucigalpa that the US government did not have the will to force the *golpistas* from power, he was correct. Without a consensus, the hemispheric community was impotent. In the face of DeMint's assurance, the head of the *golpe*, Micheletti, felt he could violate any agreements the US representatives had forced him to negotiate. There is always wiggle room in a penetrated polity. The radical change in US policy toward Latin America had been frustrated.

These failures had the perverse consequence of emboldening Daniel Ortega to reduce the democratic space in Nicaragua and allowing the government of Guatemala to reduce the pressure on the military to carry out the terms of the peace accord. Neither the US government nor the OAS had the desire or the power to enforce these rules, and the United Nations, which had brokered the peace accord, was powerless without US support.[28] Only President Mauricio Funes in El Salvador was able to maintain momentum toward a reconciliation among battling political factions by calling on the international community to support his efforts to consolidate democracy in El Salvador, and that partly explains why Obama decided to stop off in San Salvador on his way back from Chile as part of his first visit to Latin America in March 2011. It was a sign of things to come when he cut short his visit because of the unfolding crisis in Libya.

While this failure of US government influence may seem surprising in the context of the long history of US relations with the countries of Central America, it is not surprising given the terms of Obama's new policy to seek collegial relations with Latin America. More surprising was the failure of new actors to play an effective role in the region. The failure of the OAS to bring about a negotiated, compromise peace; the failure of the regional effort led by Óscar Arias of Costa Rica; and the failure of Brazil to win any supporters for its position indicate that the legacy of history in Latin America is heavier than many observers believed. The legacy of US hegemony and intervention cannot be lifted by a conscious policy decision in Washington to become more collegial. It is a matter as well of patterns of behavior in which the states of the region find it difficult to agree on the rules of their community and even more difficult to agree on whether and how to enforce those rules. In the cases of weak states, it is a matter of state incapacity where an elite captures the state and prevents measures to make them accountable to their citizens or their own laws. Such governing elites continue to use foreign policy as an instrument to maintain their domestic power in Honduras and Guatemala and in other countries in the region.

The Honduras episode also appeared to undermine the progress in Central America in stitching together a fabric of regional cooperation that took as its central purpose solving regional problems in a peaceful manner without reference to outside actors. What had begun in the 1980s was considered throughout the region as a positive development that would buttress the struggle for stability and democracy in all of the countries. Had the delicate fabric of Central American regional cooperation been torn to shreds? As it turned out, the Latin Americans began to seek solutions to their problems without the United States and have come to understand that one way to exercise agency can be the effort to establish a Latin American identity. In the last chapter, we consider how this might play out. The new regionalism in Latin America is the central issue in the effort to build a hemispheric community with rules. Trade regimes and international consensus on value and rights are relatively easy to shape; they are based on shared values and interests and participation is essentially at the discretion of each participant. Enforcing rules requires a totally different level of commitment. The questions posed for consideration in the final chapter have to do with the consequences of the end of US hegemony, for both the United States and Latin America, and how the nations of Latin America expect to exercise their agency in the hemisphere and in world politics.

Does any of the Latin American nations care if they are relevant in world politics? Then China entered the hemisphere.

Notes

1. On the issue of autonomy in the period following the end of the Cold War, see Juan Gabriel Tokatlián and Leonardo Carvajal, "Autonomía y política exterior en América Latina: Un debate abierto, un futuro incierto," *Revista CIDOB d'afers internacionals* 28 (1995): 7–31; Juan Gabriel Tokatlián and Roberto Russell, "From Antagonistic Autonomy to Relational Autonomy: A Theoretical Reflection from the Southern Cone," *Latin American Politics and Society*, 45.1 (April 2003): 1–24.

2. An early example of a skeptical view of Peru's insertion into the global community is Alejandro Deustua, "La política exterior peruana," *La república*, January 26, 2001.

3. Pia Riggirozzi and Diana Tussie, eds., *The Rise of Post-Hegemonic Regionalism*, United Nations University Series on Regionalism 4 (London: Springer, 2012); Andrés Serbin, Laneydi Martínez, and Haroldo Ramanzani Júnior, eds., *El regionalismo "post-liberal" en América Latina y el Caribe: Nuevos actores, nuevos temas, nuevos desafíos* (Buenos Aires: CRIES, 2012).

4. As in the case of Chile and Brazil, international training had a major influence on both men, Castañeda at Princeton and Aguilar Zínser at Harvard. While Castañeda relied on the skilled diplomatic corps for his backup, especially Carlos Rico and Arturo Sarukhán, Aguilar Zínser brought into the presidential palace a group of university professionals in IR, led by Raúl Benítez Manaut, the likes of which had never been seen in Mexico. Clinton's use of academic professionals in the NIC was a model for Fox. His successor, Felipe Calderón, brought in Rafael Fernandez de Castro from ITAM to be his top adviser on international affairs.

5. See Celso Lafer, *Mudam-se Os Tempos Diplomacia Brasiliera, 2001–2002*. (Brasilia: FUNAG/IPRI, 2002). See also www.espaçoacademico.com.br/015 /15pra.o1.htm; www.scielo.br/scielo/php?script=scl_arttext+prd=50034.

6. Bush sent representatives to a number of capitals in Latin America to win support for the US war in Iraq, but they were uniformly unsuccessful. In one case, President Lagos of Chile threw the envoy, Otto Reich, out of his office because he found Reich's bullying unseemly. Ricardo Lagos interview with the author, March 15, 2003.

7. See for example, Guadalupe González González, "Un siglo de política exterior mexicana (1910–2010): Del nacionalismo revolucionario a la intemperie global," in Maria Amparo Casar and Guadalupe González González, eds., *Mexico 2010: El juicio del siglo* (Mexico: Editorial Taurus, 2010); Guadalupe González, "México en America Latina: Entre el Norte y el Sur," in Ricardo Lagos, ed., *America Latina: ¿Integración o fragmentación?* (Buenos Aires: Edhasa, 2008). Foreign policy got major coverage in the first published National Development Plan of the government of Enrique Peña Nieto (2014). In the same fashion as the Mexican SRE, the Argentine ministry put online more than fifteen volumes of documents and articles; see Alberto Cisneros and Carlos Escudé, eds., *Historia General de las relaciones exteriores de la Argentina, 1806–1989*, 20 vols. (Buenos Aires: Grupo Editor, 2000); http://www.argentina-rree.com/home_nueva.htm. In the same spirit, the Argentine Council on Foreign Relations (CARI) has put its publications online at http://www.cari.org.ar /recursos/libros.html. There are at least a dozen Brazilian journals dedicated to foreign affairs. All are available online.

8. On Chile's strategic culture, see Felix E. Martin, *Chilean Strategic Culture*, Findings Report 10 (Miami: Florida International University Press, 2010). This is one

of a series of reports on the strategic culture of Latin American nations available online at the FIU-ARC website.

9. It is worth noting that ten years later, during the crisis in Syria, prominent members of the governing coalition in Chile, Sergio Bitar and Jorge Heine, called for Chile to take note of the crisis and participate in some multilateral form of resolution to the conflict; *El Mercurio*, September 13, 2013. On the general problem of states that do not obey the code of conduct and what the United States would like to do about it, see Robert Litwak, *Rogue States* (Baltimore: Johns Hopkins University Press, 1996); Robert Litwak, *Regime Change: U.S. Strategies through the Prism of 9/11* (Baltimore: Johns Hopkins University Press, 2007); Robert Litwak, *Outlier States: American Strategies to Contain, Engage, or Change Regimes* (Baltimore: Johns Hopkins University Press, 2012).

10. One of the chief UN officers in the peacemaking corps was a Brazilian, Luis Bitencourt, an original member of the Brazilian Strategic Planning Center. He later joined the Wilson Center and worked on the Creating Community project.

11. See Samantha Powers, *Chasing the Flame* (New York: Penguin, 2008). On the foreign policy of the Cardoso government, see Carlos Eduardo Lins da Silva, "Politica e comercio exterior," in Bolivar Lamolinie, et al., eds., *A Era FHC* (Rio de Janeiro: Cultura Editores, 2002.)

12. For two different views on the growing power of an international community, see the essays by Jessica T. Mathews, "Power Shift," *Foreign Affairs* 76.1 (1997): 50–66, which stresses the importance of nonstate actors and international civil society; Anne-Marie Slaughter, "The Real New World Order," *Foreign Affairs* 76.5 (1997) 183–197, which stresses what she calls the disaggregated state. A more complete statement by Slaughter is her *A New World Order* (Princeton, NJ: Princeton University Press, 2004); a more complete argument in favor of nonstate actors, especially in the field of human rights, is Kathryn A. Sikkink, *The Justice Cascade: How Human Rights Prosecutions Are Changing World Politics* (New York: Norton, 2011); and Margaret Keck, *Activists Beyond Borders: Advocacy Networks in International Politics* (Ithaca, NY: Cornell University Press, 1998). Daniel C. Thomas, "Boomerangs and Superpowers: International Norms, Transnational Networks and US Foreign Policy," *Cambridge Review of International Affairs* 15.1 (2002): 25–44 offers a theoretical bridge between the two approaches. Other regimes that play important roles in the establishing of rules for the international community are the trade regime and the environmental regime. On trade, see Vinod K. Aggarwal, Ralph Espach, and Joseph S. Tulchin, eds., *The Strategic Dynamics of Latin American Trade* (Stanford, CA: Stanford University Press, 2004).

13. Hipólito Solari Yrigoyen, *La dignidad humana* (Buenos Aires: EUDEBA, 1998).

14. Sergio Bitar, *Un futuro comun Chile, Bolivia, Perú* (Santiago: Aguilar, 2011).

15. This settlement is summarized at www.GIS-info.com/Chile.

16. Muñoz secured the prior approval of the United States through conversations with Secretary of State Condoleezza Rice, who happened to have been one of his classmates in graduate school. For an overview of MINUSTAH, see Arturo C. Sotomayor, *The Myth of the Democratic Peacekeeper: Civil-Military Relations and the United Nations* (Baltimore: Johns Hopkins University Press, 2014).

17. Ten years later, as foreign minister in the second government of Bachelet, Muñoz moved to take the lead on behalf of UNASUR to facilitate negotiations in Venezuela between the government and the opposition. Again, his purpose was to give the intervention a Latin American identity. Lula was eager to have Brazil assume this leadership role in Haiti even though it caused considerable internal debate. See Carlos Eduardo Lins da Silva, "Futbol, pas e riscos para o Brasil no Haiti," *Politica External* 13.2 (2004). Sardenberg was Brazilian ambassador to the UN at the time.

18. Congress would not confirm Reich's appointment, but he remained in the White House as senior adviser to the president. It was he who in 2002 applauded the coup against Chávez in the short period before Chávez reasserted his authority in Venezuela, thereby giving credence throughout the hemisphere to the notion that the United States had engineered the coup. Paul Wolfowitz, Rumsfeld's second in command, is reported to have told Bush that Iraqis would welcome US troops in Baghdad with open arms, exactly what Allen Dulles had told Eisenhower with reference to the invasion of the Bay of Pigs.

19. For a Latin American view of the ideological composition of Bush's circle, see Jesús Velasco, *Neoconservatives in U.S. Foreign Policy under Ronald Reagan and George W. Bush* (Washington, DC: Woodrow Wilson Center Press, 2010).

20. First was the attack on the Israeli embassy in Buenos Aires, March 17, 1992, which killed 29 people and wounded 242. The second was the bombing of the Argentine Jewish Association (AMIA is its initials in Spanish), July 18, 1994, which killed 85 and wounded hundreds. Neither of these crimes has been solved. For many years rumors circulated in Argentina and in Washington that the Iranians had funded a cell of Hezbollah in Paraguay to carry out the attack, and in December 2014, a special prosecutor in the case, Alberto Nisman, indicated he was about to indict the president for making a deal with the government of Iran to close the investigation of the case. In January, Nisman was found dead in his apartment, in a case that remains unsolved.

21. Text is in *Folha de São Paulo*, October 31, 2003.

22. The complexity of the security dilemma in Latin America is summarized in Joseph S. Tulchin, Raúl Benítez Manaut, and Rut Diamint, eds., *El rompecabezas* (Buenos Aires: Prometeo, 2006). During the Bush administration, national and subregional security issues are described in the series Woodrow Wilson Center Update on the Americas, "Creating Community" (No. 1, October 2001 to No. 27, August 2007), available online.

23. Rut Diamint has been a prolific analyst of this regime; see, for example, "La Historia sin fin: El control civil de los militares en Argentina," *Nueva Sociedad* 213 (2008): 95–111; "Nouveaux profils de pouvoir militaire," in Renée Fregosi, *Armees et pouvoirs en Amerique Latine* (Paris: IHEAL, 2004); "Confianza y conflicto en América Latina," in Julio César Theiler, Claudio Maíz, and Luis Felipe Agramunt, eds., *Los desafíos de la integración en el siglo XXI* (Santa Fé: Universidad Nacional del Litoral, 2011); "Latin America and the Military Subject Reexamined," in David Mares, ed., *Debating Civil-Military Relations in Latin America* (Sussex: Academic Press, 2014); "Conducción civil de las políticas de defensa," in Marcela Donadio, ed., *La reconstrucción de la seguridad nacional: Defensa, democracia y cuestión militar en América Latina* (Buenos Aires: Prometeo, 2010); and "Security Communities, Defence Policy Integration and Peace Operations in the Southern Cone: An Argentine Perspective," *International Peacekeeping* 17.5 (2010): 662–67.

24. On trade regimes, see Vinod K. Aggarwal, "Reconciling Multiple Institutions: Bargaining, Linkages, and Nesting," in Vinod K. Aggarwal, ed., *Institutional Designs for a Complex World: Bargaining, Linkages, and Nesting* (Ithaca, NY: Cornell University Press, 1998); Laura Gomez-Mera, *Power and Regionalism in Latin America: The Politics of Mercosur* (South Bend, IN: University of Notre Dame Press, 2013). Others have discussed the "learning process" in various regimes; see Covadonga Meseguer and Abel Escriba-Folch, "Learning, Political Regimes and the Liberalization of Trade," *European Journal of Political Research*, 50 (2011): 775–810; Sean Burges, "Brazil's International Development Co-operation: Old and New Motivations," *Development Policy Review* 32.1 (2014).

25. John H. Coatsworth, *Central America and the United States: The Clients and the Colossus* (New York: Twayne, 1994). Coatsworth sees the clients with some ability

to maneuver and wring concessions, within limits, from an asymmetrical relationship. This is different from my view of the situations in penetrated polities in which contestants for power use the United States as an actor in their efforts to gain power or hold onto it. Those who win owe a certain amount of subservience to the United States, which is usually expressed in foreign affairs and less so in how they use their power in domestic affairs. My focus is on the process of contestation, how it limits the expansion of democratic governance, and how it restricts agency, even as it leaves some wiggle room to defy the United States. Coatsworth focuses on the asymmetry of power, which is never in question.

26. Valenzuela, in his hearing before the Senate Foreign Relations Committee, had indicated the administration's view that the move against Zelaya was a coup. These hearings can be reviewed at the committee's website (http://www.foreign.senate.gov/). For Valenzuela's later comments on the episode, see his speech to the OAS and his press conference, both available at http://honduras.unembassy.gov/sp (various dates in November 2009).

27. In her memoirs, Hillary Clinton, *Hard Choices* (New York: Simon and Schuster, 2014), p. 266, the former Secretary of State, claims that she opposed Zelaya's return from the very beginning and was the determining force in achieving that goal. There is no contemporary evidence to support her claim. My version follows all of the contemporary reporting in US and Latin American newspapers, which has been confirmed in personal correspondence with Valenzuela and Insulza. See also Abraham F. Lowenthal, "Obama and the Americas," *Foreign Affairs*, 89.4 (2010): 110–24. Lowenthal credits Assistant Secretary Thomas Shannon for brokering the agreement that Insulza says he negotiated. He and Lowenthal agree that neither side kept the bargain. Mark Weisbrot of the Center for Economic and Policy Research in Washington wrote a piece for *Al Jazeera* ("Hard Choices: Hillary Clinton Admits Role in Honduras Coup Aftermath," *Al Jazeera American*, September 29, 2014), in which he criticized Clinton's version of the events and blamed the United States for the coup. As Insulza pointed out, not even Zelaya accused the United States of involvement in the coup.

28. William Stanley, *Enabling Peace in Guatemala: The Story of MINUGUA* (Boulder, CO: Lynne Rienner, 2013).

8

Agency After Hegemony

It is clear in retrospect that President Barack Obama was naive or overly optimistic in his expectation that the nations of Latin America—individually or collectively—would embrace his project of a posthegemonic partnership in the pursuit of common goals. It was not a notion that won wide acceptance even in the United States. Whether out of habit or out of direct rejection of the idea that the United States would no longer assert its dominance in the hemisphere, the majority in Congress and many senior officials responsible for conducting relations with Latin America (in the Pentagon and Southern Command, the US Trade Representative, Homeland Security, and even the State Department) were not prepared to accept the proposition that the United States was not a leader in important policy questions. This remained true even though, after the frustrating experiences in Iraq and Afghanistan, most were sensitive to the limits of US power. Most decisionmakers and most scholars who informed the policy debate had taken the lesson that despite unequaled military and economic power, the use of that overwhelming power, what the military called supreme dominance, could not guarantee specific political outcomes or protect US interests. Unlike Woodrow Wilson in Mexico, Haiti, and the Dominican Republic or Calvin Coolidge in Nicaragua, Obama saw that the use of US military force in Iraq or Afghanistan did not produce the desired outcome and could not do so in Libya, Syria, Ukraine, or elsewhere. Power is not a zero-sum category.

The lesson that Obama took away from this experience—what came to be called the Obama Doctrine—was that although the president must appear to his domestic constituents to be strong in the face of threats and willing to use the nation's hard power where necessary, long-term protection of national interests required the projection of power in collaboration with partners, and in the long run, because of its core values and its economic capacity, the United States was best served in strengthening rule-based communities. The best tactical approach for this strategy indicated engagement with all, including countries with which the United States has disagreements, such as Cuba and Iran. As the president put it in his National Security Strategy published in February 2015, "The question is never whether America should lead, but how we should lead."[1] It is clear that the Obama Doctrine is optimistic in that it assumes that through engagement, the United States can alter or influence the behavior of rogue states to conform more closely to the shared rules of the community while at the same time enhancing the national interests of the community's members.

The dilemma posed by the Obama Doctrine in hemispheric affairs is that despite the diplomatic rhetoric, most US policymakers believe that the asymmetry of power in the hemisphere means that the United States is bound to lead and the nations of the hemisphere should follow with good grace.[2] Latin American policymakers, in contrast, will go to extraordinary lengths to avoid following that lead and avoid US hegemonic control, even if that appears to go against their own interests. In other words, US leaders see no cost in the history of hegemony, whereas Latin Americans feel that the United States must pay a very significant price for that hegemony, but they are not certain what that price should be. Even in those cases in which the Obama administration offers a different narrative to guide hemispheric relations, as it did in dealing with the coup in Honduras in 2009, many in the hemisphere cannot assimilate the language of change in US policy.

A second problem with Obama's search for partners in Latin America is that there is no such unitary actor as "Latin America" who might respond to US proposals in a rational manner, nor has there ever been. In questions of national interest or strategic objectives, there are many deep fissures that divide the countries in the hemisphere. Even in the days of extreme hegemonic pretension by the United States, as in the Caribbean Basin before World War I or during the Cold War, such unified responses from Latin America were few and far between and came at considerable cost to both sides. Ironically, just as Obama recognized the end of US hegemony and reached out the hand of partnership, the only thing on which a majority of Latin Americans agreed by way of response was that they would not allow the United States to use partnership as a mask for continuing its dominance in the hemisphere. Again, in the Honduran episode, several countries refused to join the United States in putting pressure on the *golpistas*, even though their stated policy objectives were the same as those of the Obama administration.

Since the end of the Cold War, Latin American leaders have been seeking forms of regionalism without the United States through which they might express their agency in collective action that would reject US hegemony while enhancing their national interests. Despite their many disagreements, they are seeking ways to express their common identity, autonomous of the United States, through regional organizations that, as Heraldo Muñoz, Chilean foreign minister in 2014, put it, stress "convergence within diversity."[3] This may be the most important reason the Obama partnership project made so little headway until the VII Summit of the Americas in April 2015 when he shook hands with Raúl Castro. In every country in the region, policy decisions as to how to respond to Obama's offer of partnership are seen through the historical prism of resentment of US hegemony. The calculation of the costs and benefits of partnership is skewed by constraints either of domestic politics or how decisionmakers thought they would be viewed in their neighborhood in terms of their defiance of US hegemony.

The militarized unilateralism of the Bush administration made it clear to Latin American leaders that they would protect their national interests best by reaching out to other nations rather than retreating into a defense crouch, as they had done in the face of the paranoid anticommunism of the Cold War. If they did not, they would be crushed by the insistence of the US government that they follow US leadership whether it was in the war on terrorism, the war on drugs, or some other issue the US government considered vital to its national interests. In the years since 9/11, there has been growing determination among Latin American leaders to join communities of actors and networks in which they can be proactive and in which they feel autonomous of the United States. These communities and networks might be composed of states or nonstate actors; they might be issue oriented or interest oriented; they might be called regimes or networks. In a few cases, such as ALBA, they might be driven by ideology. In all of the efforts to create community, there was the sense that each nation could exercise its agency in the hemispheric and global arenas, while each of them would have greater agency at the global level if they were to consolidate a hemispheric community.

A crucial buttress to this growing sense of agency has been the accountability and credibility provided by the emergence of the policy process in democratic governance. The process still varies widely from country to country, but it is dramatically more evident even in the least robust democracies of the region than it was only one generation ago. As they have become increasingly confident in the expression of their agency, leaders in Latin America have become enthusiastic supporters of transnational networks and increasingly respectful of soft power. In this, globalization and the Internet have played important roles.[4]

The explosive increases in the exchange of information and in trade, international investment, and consumption, together with macroeconomic stability, have nearly doubled the middle classes in all of the nations of Latin America. Information technology has transformed countless lives. Just a little more than one generation ago, in countries where people had to wait in a line to make a long-distance telephone call or couldn't use their phone line if it was raining, there is now cellular service that makes it possible to communicate from anywhere in the world to anywhere else in the world, (almost) whenever they wish. More people feel they are part of a great global village. The centripetal forces of globalization have encouraged optimistic assumptions about the forward progress of change throughout the world similar to the optimism in the immediate aftermath of the Cold War expressed in the discussion of the end of history and the Washington Consensus. In this case, the optimists point to countless studies from around the world that sustain their vision.

In Latin America, the double revolution—globalization and the transition to democracy—established the conditions for the policymaking process that had been lacking in so many countries and had marked a critical difference between the United States and Latin America since independence in how they understood world politics. Together, the dual revolutions had a profound impact on long-standing nationalistic policies in communications, strategic commodities, and the transfer of capital that had dominated policymaking in Latin America since import substitution industrialization in the 1930s and that had exerted pressure on leaders to look inward. Although there were exceptions, more countries in the region than ever before had stable macroeconomic conditions and predictable rates of exchange. With the Internet, democracy, and economic stability, policymaking became a matter of quotidian concern, and impunity became harder to hide. The growing interest of the Latin American public in foreign affairs is a central feature of their emerging agency in world affairs as is the epistemological community of foreign policy experts with their increasingly sophisticated theoretical framework for understanding policy.[5]

Of course, not everyone is optimistic about globalization, and not everyone thinks the forces of change mean progress. There are moments or occasions when not everyone agrees as to how the rules of the game are to be formulated or there might be multiple games being played, which makes fixing rules more difficult. Roque Sáenz Peña pointed out at the first Pan American meeting in Washington in 1889 that Argentina was not interested in joining a hemispheric customs union or creating institutions for a hemispheric community because it already was part of a global community through its trade and investment links with the United Kingdom and Europe. Until she left office in December 2015, the president of Argentina, Cristina Fernández de Kirchner, might have told her colleagues in the Organization of American States (OAS) that Argentina is not interested in closer collaboration because it already is an important part of a global trading community centered around an axis of exchange with China, which for the past decade and more has been buying enormous quantities of Argentine soybeans at historically high prices, has provided much needed liquidity in a series of currency swaps, and promises to provide the capital necessary to expand Argentine petroleum production and the national infrastructure. Kirchner also did tell her colleagues that the international financial system has to be changed so that it would be impossible for a federal judge in New York to hold the Argentine government hostage because it refuses to pay a few hedge funds that had not accepted new discounted bonds for those on which Argentina had defaulted in 2001.[6] Whereas Sáenz Peña and his colleagues felt themselves proud to be part of global progress and civilization in the nineteenth century, Kirchner and others question that the process was either as inevitable nor as geopolitically neutral as its proponents suggested.[7]

Skeptics convoked the first antiglobalization conference in 2001 and, as the World Social Forum (WSF), have held annual meetings around the world since that first conference.[8] The WSF is a mélange of civil society organizations and government representatives. They are hostile toward a capitalist system they consider imposed on people around the world by those nations, led by the United States and the so-called Bretton Woods institutions, that benefit from the asymmetry of economic power and the rules that govern the dominant system. The opposition to the existing rules of the game and the desire to create a new world order has become the central source of tension in the global community, especially following the financial implosion in the United States in 2008. As China challenged its Asian neighbors by moving to control islands in the China Sea, Russia challenged Europe and NATO by seizing Crimea and sponsoring separatists in eastern Ukraine. In Latin America, China became an important trading partner and a critical investor, thereby offering nations an option to the United States.[9] While opposition to rules of the game gave to the agency of individual nations or nonstate actors greater potential significance at a specific moment, the question of responsibility or accountability for their actions remained dangerously fuzzy.[10]

The most concrete proposal to alter the rules of the game and shift the global balance of power was the consolidation of the group of emerging powers known as the BRICS—Brazil, Russia, India, China, and South Africa. First coined by a Wall Street analyst to refer to a set of potential fields for investment, the acronym caught on at an informal meeting of foreign ministers during the UN General Assembly meeting in 2006. After some preliminary meetings to fix the protocol of such a diverse group with varying agendas that overlapped only on matters of international econom-ics and their wishes to change the dominant system, there was a summit meeting of national leaders in Yekaterinburg, Russia, in 2008. Since that time, there has been a summit meeting each year, rotating hosts from one member country to another. To begin the second cycle of meetings, the sixth summit in Fortaleza, Brazil, in 2014, issued a very ambitious Decla-ration and Action Plan in which they committed themselves to ministerial meetings every two years, called for peace in many of the world's hot spots, and declared their intention to launch a development bank. The latter potentially was the most significant because it would project the influence of the countries as a group to many others in the international community. The declaration also specified that Russia and China sympathized with the interests of India and Brazil in playing a more prominent role in the United Nations. Thus far the BRICS bank has done nothing and the organization has given few signs of life outside of the summits.[11] In 2015, China an-nounced the new financial institution, the Asian Infrastructure Investment Bank, to compete with the Bretton Woods institutions. Despite the fact that the United States opposed the new bank, many US allies were among the forty-six founding members. The bank's director says the new institution will be "lean, clean, and green." It remains to be seen how the rules are set and enforced at the new institution.[12] Several nations in Latin America were enthusiastic founding members of the new bank. The lack of capital continues to be the single most important factor in the development plans of most countries in the region.

Outside the hemisphere, the majority of the nations in the world still look to the United States for leadership, even though they might not be will-ing to follow the United States if action is contemplated. In none of the global hot spots—Crimea, Syria, South China Sea, Libya—did a Latin American nation take an active role, although in several there was some dis-cussion about the crisis and how important it would be to take an active role in its solution.[13] There are nations, such as Russia, China, Venezuela, and Iran, that declare themselves opposed to US pretensions to lead the world community and have taken concrete steps to weaken or counter that leader-ship and have made their ideological opposition to the United States quite clear. Much more frequent are proposals put forward on one issue or an-other—trade, the environment, humanitarian relief, the rule of law, protec-tion of human rights, the trade in poached ivory, and so on—which are not intended to oppose the United States but express differences of opinion and reflect very different foreign policy positions. These differences should be understood as the normal give-and-take in a fluid international community rather than adversarial attacks on the leader of the international pack.

Globalization optimists are fervent believers in an international com-munity with shared core values and rules, a community in which the

United States is still a leader but without the degree of dominance it enjoyed at the end of the Cold War. In this community most of the complaints are directed at leaders and countries considered to be in violation of the community's shared values and most of the debate is over how to enforce the rules.[14] It is a community with increasing popular participation expressed through social media as well as through more traditional modes such as street demonstrations and voting, which they saw as representing the popular demand for freedom and accountability.[15] Throughout the community, globalization brought dramatic increases in the diffusion of services, products, and ideas.[16] No one thinks the emerging global community will be easy to hold together. Not only is there continued dissent with regard to specific rules, there is profound uncertainty over how the rules are to be enforced.[17] In some cases, action is promoted primarily by nongovernmental actors, as in the campaign against human trafficking; in others, states have attempted to create a global consensus in their favor, as in the effort to stop hunting elephants for their ivory.[18] Even Obama's most avid defender of enforcing the community's rules, UN ambassador Samantha Power, recognizes that building consensus is difficult.[19] Some of the optimists, who expected the United Nations to play a major role in reducing conflict, are disappointed in its limited success in dealing with major upheaval and the displacement of people.[20]

But such disappointment is misplaced, as it seems to call for a return to the euphoria after the Cold War and George H. W. Bush's new world order. There is no doubt that the UN has played an important role in setting rules and reinforcing core values. And, where the context and domestic allies made it possible, even enforcing the rules, as in ousting the president of Guatemala, Otto Pérez Molina, for corruption in September 2015. As part of the peace process in that country, the parties asked the United Nations to monitor conditions in Guatemala. After a few years, in 2007, the International Commission Against Impunity in Guatemala (CICIG, its initials in Spanish) was created. In 2014, President Pérez Molina allowed the renewal of its mandate. Through the years, the largest portion of the CICIG financial support came from the United States. The members of CICIG acted in response to the demands of enormous public outcry and street demonstrations, virtually without precedent in Guatemala, against the corruption of the government. First, the vice president resigned and a few months later, with the support of CICIG, local courts indicted the president for his part in the corruption scandal and forced him from office.[21]

Another example of effective UN work in the creation of a normative network is the activity of the United Nations High Commission for Refugees (UNHCR) in creating rules and a framework in the treatment of refugees. It is a network that bridges hemispheric and global action by its members. The effort to coordinate hemispheric policy in dealing with refugees began with the Mexican effort to protect the rights of Mexican citizens who were undocumented residents of the United States. To strengthen their hand in negotiating with the United States, the Mexicans called a hemispheric meeting to consider "Asylum and International Protection of Refugees in Latin America." Three years later, in Cartagena, Colombia, a second meeting produced the Declaration of Cartagena, which defined refugee status and laid out a set of obligations by all members of the community to protect the rights of such people. That was followed twenty years later by the Mexican Plan of Action (2004) and a decade after that by the Brazilian Plan of Action (2014). As part of their membership in this community, each state has created its own legislation or executive rules, generally in collaboration with the local office of UNHCR. In most cases, the legislation was designed to deal with local issues, such as Peruvians and Bolivians in Chile, Guatemalans in Mexico, and Colombians in Venezuela. Even so, in a number of cases, most notably Brazil, the rules were applied to coordinate the assimilation of refugees from outside the hemisphere. Brazil participated in the international effort to deal with the huge wave of refugees fleeing conflict in the Middle East and North Africa, taking in several thousand. By 2015, Brazil's government, together with 96 civil society organizations and in cooperation with UNHCR, provides the largest refugee system in Latin America.

A few optimists are becoming disenchanted with the evolution of the international community. Although they never slipped into the antiglobalization camp of WSF,[22] they are concerned that there has been a decline in the quality of democracy and that antidemocratic regimes continue to hold sway in many of the world's critical countries. They are concerned that the rush to open markets produced dramatic increases in inequality, which blunts the democratic aspirations of popular participation. Some liberals and progressives who during the Bush administration had argued for less unilateralism by the United States and more collegial behavior were nonplussed by the Obama approach to foreign policy and urged him to be more decisive.[23] Conservatives denounced Obama as weak and accused him of undermining US dominance in world affairs.[24] It seems that working out the tactics of a posthegemonic national strategy—in the world and in the hemisphere—as the president put it, was going to be "complicated."[25]

Obama may have read the public better than his critics on the left and the right. After ten years of war in Iraq and Afghanistan, which cost trillions of dollars and thousands of lives—and demonstrated yet again that overwhelming US military power could not force the Iraqis to be democratic any more than Woodrow Wilson could shoot the Mexicans into democracy 100 years earlier—the US public was loath to become involved in another war in the Middle East or anywhere else. While there were insistent voices for more forceful action against China, against Russia, against Syria, against Iran, even against Venezuela, there was no proposal as to how US objectives would be met more successfully by such action.

The Obama Doctrine in Latin America sought to enhance cooperation through a variety of modest programs, conducted for the most part at the Cabinet or department level, which sought to enhance partnerships with key countries, such as Brazil, Chile, and Mexico. The president also offered specific responses to intermestic issues where domestic politics required some action, such as immigration, through an executive order offering a path to citizenship for millions of illegal immigrants and the relatively small aid program for Central America through which the administration sought to reduce the flow of illegal immigration from the violent countries of the northern triangle (El Salvador, Guatemala, and Honduras).[26] In all of these efforts—in drug trafficking, immigration, economic development—Obama found it difficult to rouse the active participation of "partners" in the region, and for some, he could not win the cooperation of Congress.

Obama's most dramatic move to improve community in the hemisphere was the announcement in December 2014 that the administration had concluded years of secret negotiations with the government of Cuba and would move to renew normal diplomatic relations between the countries. This move had an immediate, profound effect in Latin America and may prove to be the key to freeing the United States and Latin America from the stultifying animosity deposited over a century of US hegemonic pretension.[27] The rapprochement between Cuba and the United States and the reincorporation of Cuba into the hemispheric community is central to the ongoing debate in Latin America as to how autonomy and agency are to be expressed. With the transition to democracy and an acute appreciation of soft power, there was a growing realization that opposition to hegemonic pretension no longer is sufficient justification for foreign policy.[28] As Chile's former president Ricardo Lagos put it, the normalization of relations between Cuba and the United States will have a "transcendental" impact on Latin America and on Latin American relations with the United States.[29]

The end of hegemony has opened space for autonomous action whether in trade or in the exploitation of natural resources or in the organization of new regional organizations without the United States.[30] Latin Americans have an opportunity to formulate their own policies and gain control over their own destiny.[31] The dilemma is how to deal with the United States. Hegemonic or not, the United States is still the most powerful country in the hemisphere, and many of the Latin American countries are tied to the United States through trade, investment, immigration, or the violence of the illegal traffic in drugs. To date, regionalism without the United States, except as a means of building consensus or to strengthen existing regimes of cooperation, continues to be more a Bolivarian dream than a multilateral instrument for collective action.[32]

The most notable effort to build hemispheric architecture without the United States is CELAC, the Community of Latin American and Caribbean States (La comunidad de estados Latinoamericanos y Caribeños), which grew out of a meeting in Mexico in 2010 of the Rio Group and was formalized at a summit meeting in July 2011 in Caracas. The Rio Group itself had been one of the informal efforts of South and Central American nations to operate independently of the United States to preserve the peace in the region when they considered US militarization during the Reagan administration to be inappropriate and a threat to their national interests. In that sense, CELAC represents a continuation of earlier efforts to create a venue for Latin American collective action. Canada and the United States are excluded, as are the European territories in the Caribbean; Cuba is included. The presidents of Bolivia, Ecuador, Nicaragua, and Venezuela attempted to insert a flavor of ideology into the effort by expressing the hope that CELAC would be a weapon to end US hegemony. But that was not why Felipe Calderón, president of Mexico and the host of the original Rio Group meeting in 2010, supported the effort on the grounds that the region could not go on so divided. At the Caracas meeting in December 2011, Venezuelan president Hugo Chávez and the president of Chile, Sebastián Piñera, who represented the two opposite poles of the region's ideological spectrum, were appointed to frame the regulations for the new organization. The message of the majority members of CELAC, led by the Brazilians, was to muffle ideology. To take something of value from the OAS, which had been the only hemispheric organization until CELAC's creation, the members followed up a decade of effort to support democracy in the hemisphere by passing the Declaration for Democracy at the summit of 2013.

Here, one problem with CELAC was brought into high relief. By admitting Cuba, the members agreed to close their eyes to the nature of the regime there. There is no democracy in Cuba. The same issue came up when the opposition in Venezuela complained that the regime was systematically reducing the space in which to express their dissent. On several occasions, there were violent clashes between the opposition and the government, and it was pointed out that the latter were heavily reliant on Cuban military advisers, who had no experience with peaceful political contestation. When the violence escalated in February 2014, it was UNASUR

(Union of South American Nations) that attempted to intervene and bring the adversaries to the negotiating table, not CELAC.

As an organization that declares itself to be hemispheric and to defend democracy as the only mode of governance legitimate for its members, CELAC carries two major conundrums: it bars the United States and Canada, so it will be difficult to discuss truly regional issues, and it includes Cuba in an organization that declares democracy to be the only legitimate form of government. Despite these problems, it may well be a regional organization that provides the context in which a Latin American identity is forged. There are other cases, as in Ecuador and Bolivia, in which the space for contestation is shrinking. CELAC has not come up with a response to this dilemma.

Given the many schisms that divide the countries of Latin America, subregional groups seem to offer the greatest possibility in the short run of consensus or convergence. The most notable of these is UNASUR, which was created in 2008. There has been some effort to institutionalize UNA-SUR by creating a secretariat with an office in Quito, where the headquarters building was completed in 2014, and organizing a defense council, with an office in Buenos Aires as the Center for Strategic Defense Studies, also established in 2008. In handling the growing violence in Venezuela, UNASUR was paralyzed by the adherence of its members to the historic goal of nonintervention, which in this case came into conflict with the commitment to democratic governance. When the United States announced in February 2015 that it was imposing sanctions on several members of the Venezuelan government, UNASUR spoke out against US intervention in the domestic affairs of the nations in the region. Convergence within diversity is a laudable goal, but for the moment the only rule members of the CELAC/UNASUR communities appear willing to enforce is nonintervention by the United States in their internal affairs. In this early stage of development it is clear that fragmented vision among the members of these organizations makes it difficult to formulate collaborative strategies for integration and makes it virtually impossible to formulate common positions in the international system. Strict adherence to national autonomy and to nonintervention also sets limits to institutionalization of any of these organizations.[33]

Neither UNASUR nor CELAC seems interested in dealing with actors outside the hemisphere, such as China, which might play a role in insulating Latin American nations from US hegemony. The new Chinese-led development bank might well prove to be a factor in the evolution of regionalism in Latin America. For the moment there is no evidence that China intends to undermine the US position in the hemisphere.[34] Mercosur, which is a smaller, regional group with a narrower agenda, is engaged with the European Union in trade negotiations. At the time of this writing, the talks have stalled because the two principal members, Argentina and Brazil, cannot agree on their barriers to trade.

On balance, it seems that the creation of new regional organizations in Latin America will help all of the countries there come to terms with their agency in the international system. At the moment, new organizations like CELAC are treated with optimism, as if they might finally achieve the Bolivarian dream of Latin American unity. It is more likely that the growth in mutual confidence among the members will take time and effort. In this process, it is important to keep in mind that the nations of the region have as many issues that separate them from one another as they have elements to bring them together. Yet each new organization is a forum to work out historical differences and rivalries, and each makes it more possible to resolve the remaining territorial disputes that prevent any true integration. This is also true of the summit meetings that occur every two years. Even in the short period in which UNASUR and CELAC have existed, both have given evidence of their potential to deal with regional instability through mediation.[35] Heraldo Muñoz, now foreign minister of Chile, who, as Chile's ambassador to the OAS, played a critical role in the Declaration of Democracy in the OAS in 1991, also played a role in getting CELAC to include a democratic declaration in 2013. He has been a frequent and forceful advocate of Latin American regionalism, focusing on achieving a Latin American identity. For Muñoz, although there are problems ahead, the effort is liberating and the direction in general is positive. As he has made plain, for Chile, regionalism is part of its multilevel agency within the international community. For Chile, Latin American regionalism should enhance Latin American agency in world affairs.[36]

The president of Costa Rica, Luis Guillermo Solís, has taken almost exactly the same position, that all new regional organizations offer Latin American nations a voice and a forum in which to exercise their agency. Solís saw no conflict between CELAC and the OAS. He anticipated these groups would have a positive influence on the region and help member countries find ways to reconcile their differences. He expressed no sympathy for ALBA[37] where fiery anti-American rhetoric serves as a sort of membership badge more than anything else. The challenge that confronts the new regional organizations is to allow members to become more confident in expressing their agency to achieve their objectives and interests without feeling confined within restrictive forms of collective agency. The key to meeting this challenge is creating a sense of community. Chile and Costa Rica are two of the nations in Latin America (Uruguay and Brazil are others) that are comfortable in dealing with communities outside the hemisphere. They have learned to participate in making rules and have come to terms with the rules of the wider community. For all of these nations, regional or hemispheric organizations are useful as instruments in achieving their goals and protecting their interests.

There is increasing evidence that countries in the region are willing to create smaller communities based on affinities on political matters or convergence of interests. That was the case in the creation of the Pacific Alliance in 2011 among Chile, Peru, Colombia, and Mexico.[38] The alliance not only lowered trade barriers among the members, it quickly moved to establish common rules of dispute resolution, share logistical regulations for trade, and other elements that constitute the threads of a community fabric. The speed of progress in the relatively new alliance indicates a sharp divide among those countries disposed to cooperate with one another and that have the state capacity to organize cooperation and those countries that are wary of cooperation. It also suggests that there is a set of countries in the region that see their future in opening to the outside world and are willing to make the compromises of national sovereignty and nationalism necessary to strengthen community. Those also are the countries that see their future tied in some way with the United States.[39] The success of the Pacific Alliance made it easier for Chile, Peru, and Mexico to join the much larger Trans Pacific Partnership, which was signed October 6, 2015.

Ultimately, how each country grasps the opportunity of its agency in international affairs is a matter of its own capacity and aspirations. In South America, the key country is Brazil. It is the only country that has asserted for itself the status of global power and considers itself the hegemonic power within South America. When President Fernando Henrique Cardoso came to power in January 1995, he was convinced that Brazil should be a global rulemaker and that to fill that role, the country had to end its dependence on imported energy and technology, the ultimate strategic commodities, and reduce inequality, which deprived Brazil of the influence (soft power) necessary to sit at the table with the world's other great powers. He was determined to maintain the political stability and economic balance he considered indispensable in a global economy. To an amazing degree, he was successful. So successful that his successor, Luiz Inácio Lula da Silva, continued and extended the social programs that moved the index of social welfare, continued the fiscal policies that kept the currency stable, and kept within the rules of the game so that political stability was maintained. It was only in energy that Lula slipped. His party could not help itself from taking advantage of Petrobras as a cash cow. Cardoso opened Petrobras to foreign investment and within a few years the joint venture turned Brazil into an energy powerhouse, with vast deepwater reserves available for exploitation. After a little more than ten years of rapidly expanding production, Petrobras fell victim to a huge scandal and, in the midst of the uproar over illegal payments to political parties and leading politicians, production in Petrobras stagnated. During the presidency of his successor, Dilma Rousseff, the scandal in Petrobras threatened to undermine her ability to govern.

The Petrobras scandal exacerbated the growing malaise in the country created by the general slowdown in the economy, which was primarily a response to the decline in Chinese demand for Brazilian commodities. That malaise, which began in 2013, sent hundreds of thousands of people into the streets of the country's cities and nearly cost Dilma her bid for re-election in 2014. As the Petrobras scandal unfolded in 2015, the street demonstrations resumed, now with demands for Dilma's impeachment. The scandal makes it more difficult for Petrobras, the most indebted national oil company in the world, to attract the foreign investment it needs to exploit the massive deepwater (presalt) reserves. The decline in oil prices will make it difficult for the government to benefit from the export of oil, and the weakness of the economy together with the polarization of Brazilian politics in general will make it harder for Dilma to govern. That in turn will weaken the capacity of Brazil to project its influence overseas. Indeed so severe are Dilma's internal problems in 2015 that she gave very little attention to foreign policy in her second term.

With all of these problems, Brazil remains the most powerful country in Latin America. Lula thought his predecessor's plan to make the country a world power was an excellent idea. However, his advisers were split over how that new agency was to be exercised. One group, led by the foreign ministry, Itamaraty, thought that global influence would best be achieved by extending the country's historical influence in South America, the so-called Rio Branco model without pushing too hard to make rules at the global level except to support multilateralism and mediation to solve conflicts. Others in his group of intimates, who were old colleagues from the decades of the Cold War, refused to contemplate Brazil's activity on the global stage if it would appear as if the country were following the lead of the United States. This group was more interested in the ideology of anti-Americanism than they were in the pragmatism of Rio Brancismo. In one critical episode, Lula was convinced to join Recep Tayyip Erdoğan, now the president of Turkey, to negotiate with the government of Iran to rein in Iran's nuclear program. Lula's trip to Iran in 2010 was ill timed. It came precisely as the United States was shepherding through the UN Security Council a resolution to impose sanctions on Iran for not allowing international inspection of its nuclear program. Instead of showing him as a new world leader, the trip dashed whatever expectations Lula had of exercising greater influence at the international level.[40] The timing of his visit was especially unfortunate given that the United States, along with the major European powers, including Russia, were about to begin a round of talks that produced an agreement in 2015 to lift the sanctions on Iran in return for concessions to halt its efforts to create a nuclear capability for a decade. Brazil could have beeen a party to these negotiations had it not moved at the wrong time.

The debate over how or in what manner Brazil should exercise its influence regionally and globally has been going on for more than a decade. The failure to produce a consensus, either during Lula's two terms or in Dilma's two, has undermined Brazilian efforts to use its undeniable economic power and its blue-water navy, plus the great respect it enjoys, to increase its agency. The question for Brazilians seems to be whether the country should maintain its historic role as a dominant country in South America or whether it should aim for a role in the UN Security Council and for a wider role in world affairs, through either the BRICS or other organizations.[41] Brazil's hegemonic pretension in South America is a constant leitmotif in UNASUR and other regional organizations. Argentina, most prominently, sets itself against Brazilian pretensions and is not alone in attempting to find a "soft balance" with Brazil, and the only thing that prevents such a balance is the lack of state capacity and internal instability in Argentina and other countries.[42] Brazil's sense of its own power and how to use it reflects a heterodox combination of realist calculation of power and interest with heavy reliance on historical and cultural values.[43]

A close study of the Brazilian foreign policy process also reminds us of the emphasis Ernest May placed on the influence of strong leaders and the role of national nightmares in the decisionmaking process. From Rio Branco to Cardoso to Celso Amorim, the imprint of strong personalities is all over Brazilian policy, and all of them stress the great value of diplomacy over the use of harsher elements of hard power. Among members of the PT (Workers Party), there has been added the notion that Brazil can play a leadership role in the anti-establishment movement, a form of soft power, which appeals to countries in the BRICS group but has very little resonance in Europe or the United States. It also has resonance with the ALBA nations by demonstrating Brazil's progressive credentials, which have been crucial in keeping Venezuela in check. In the debate, there is no doubt that Brazil is a nation fully aware of its agency, consciously exercising it in forums or regimes in various geographic levels and in a multitude of issue areas, using its hard and soft power with equal confidence.[44] Brazil's military participation in MINUSTAH, a Chilean initiative, was crucial to the Latin American role in that UN peacekeeping effort. The dilemma remains—once the Petrobras scandal is overcome—how to modernize the Rio Branco model to allow Brazil to become a global rulemaker without losing its leverage as a regional power in South America.

Chile is another country in Latin America for which the new regionalism must complement (not replace or constrain) its efforts to exercise agency in the global arena. Chile continues to use its soft power to exercise its considerable international influence at the regional and global levels. After years of negotiations, it survived the decision of the International Court of Justice to settle the maritime boundary between Peru and Chile.[45] With the return of President Michelle Bachelet to power, Chile has moved to establish Chile's role as a rulemaker in the region. When the violence in Venezuela escalated early in 2014, Muñoz put together a group of UNASUR ministers to mediate the conflict. He stated that the effort was to give a Latin American identity to the intervention.[46] By implication, he pointed to the possibilities inherent in the new regionalism without the United States, although he made it clear that the identity to which he referred would not in any way be anti-American. Chile represents the moderate view of the future of Latin American regionalism. It works with CELAC and UNASUR while it continues to support the OAS. Alone among the nations of Latin America, it seeks moments when the nation's influence can be felt and where the national interests of the country can be advanced by agency on the global stage. Chile has indicated that it is prepared to pay the price for global influence and evaluates its agency within that framework.

Like Brazil, Chile follows a modified neorealist approach to the projection of its power, using advocacy of rules-based order and energetic participation in a wide variety of relational networks and multilateral institutions, a strategy that demonstrates a high level of state capacity. It maintains a blue-water navy and a well-equipped army and air force.[47] It participates in UN peacekeeping and collaborates actively in many multilateral organizations. Its principal weaknesses in the projection of its power have been energy dependence and rising inequality. In her second term, President Bachelet presented an ambitious program of economic and educational reforms designed to reduce inequality and broaden access for the working class and the rapidly expanding middle class to the benefits of the nation's economic development over the past three decades. The debates over these reforms, along with a series of financial scandals, threaten to push Chile toward the same sort of polarization and paralysis that has hobbled Brazil, which would have the effect of weakening its agency.[48] Still, the soft power that was such a valuable asset during the previous democratic governments continues to serve the country as a rulemaker at the global level. The country also uses a trade strategy that distributes risk among a wide range of markets. It is a founding member of the Pacific Alliance (with Peru, Colombia, and Mexico), and plays an active role in the larger Trans Pacific Partnership. It is a reliable partner and rulemaker in a wide variety of rules-based communities at the regional and global levels. In one of many ways Chile gains influence through a combination of soft and hard power, it is the only country in the region with a true sovereign wealth fund that has enough money to make a difference, although not enough to reduce inequality while the price of copper is soft. The creation of the fund was part of the Concertación government's efforts to bring the Chilean military under civilian control. Since the 1950s, the military had control over a special royalty earned on the export of copper, funds that required no public oversight. In the first Bachelet administration, that royalty was put under civilian control, although first claim on the funds still belongs to the armed forces. The legislation for the transfer of the royalty also created the sovereign wealth fund.[49]

The inability to resolve the dispute with Bolivia over the territory that Bolivia was forced to sacrifice at the end of the War of the Pacific remains a stain on the nation's soft power escutcheon. Peru has been satisfied. Bolivia is not. That is the pending territorial agenda in South America. By making the political sacrifice to compromise with Bolivia, the Bachelet administration appears willing to give up territory to enhance its stature in the region and the world as a country that can be relied on to adhere to its core values. When asked if Chile would accept the ruling of the International Court in the dispute with Bolivia, Muñoz responded by asking if Bolivia would accept the ruling. Chile consistently follows the rules.[50]

The Argentine case is today, as it has been repeatedly over the past century, an example of how agency can be counterproductive in the sense that foreign policy may aim at specific objectives but because it is badly calculated and executed, distorted by short-term demands of domestic politics and a powerful sense of Argentine exceptionalism, it ends by undermining the stated objectives of that policy. Cristina Fernández de Kirchner, who took power after her husband, continued what supporters describe as the Kirchner project of anti-Americanism. Néstor Kirchner allied his government with Chávez in Venezuela as part of his project. At the IV Summit of the Americas in Mar del Plata in 2005, he went out of his way to embarrass President George W. Bush, who withstood the affront with uncommon grace. Both Kirchners treated foreign policy principally as an instrument of domestic politics and used relations with neighbors, such as Uruguay, as opportunities to demonstrate to their political base how independent and decisive Argentina could be.[51]

In her second term, Cristina Kirchner trumpeted as symbolic of her resistance to imperialism a long-running dispute with bondholders who refused to accept the terms of the national debt restructuring negotiated in

2005 and 2010, following the mammoth default of 2001. These holdouts—Kirchner referred to them as vulture funds—sued the Argentine government for payment on the original bonds they held. In a long series of legal battles, the New York and later US courts found for the holdouts and insisted that Argentina must pay them if they were to continue paying the holders of the restructured bonds, pari passu.[52] In the early stages of the legal battle, Kirchner declared publicly that Argentina would never negotiate with the vultures. In the denouement of the dispute, after an appeal to the US Supreme Court was denied, the original judge in the case held that the banks servicing the payments on the restructured bonds could not use Argentine funds for the payments without violating US law. The Argentines complained that this violated their sovereignty and called for a restructuring of the international financial system so that disputes were not resolved by the US courts. To strengthen their hand in the dispute, when the Argentines signed an agreement with the government of China to build several dams in the southern region of the country, they insisted that their contractual agreement would be arbitrated under British law in London. This attempt to undercut US influence over the international rule of law in bond cases suggests how ineffectual their effort would be. In one sense, the globalized financial community is more sympathetic to the interests of debtors than it had been when Calvo warned against arbitrary use of power by the strong against the weak. The holdouts used courts—in New York, Las Vegas, and Ghana—to win their dispute and did not invoke the armed force of their government to protect their rights.[53] Dispute resolution under the current system has become complicated, but there still are mechanisms based on the marketplace to coerce sovereign states into behavior they consider counter to national interests. For this reason, the government of Venezuela under Chávez canceled its membership in the World Bank's dispute resolution program in 2004 as it was canceling contracts with some international petroleum companies. Ten years later, in an effort to get some international oil companies to help Venezuela increase production by the national oil company PDVSA, the Nicolás Maduro government agreed to rejoin that facility and committed to a contractual deal with some of the same companies under which disputes would be resolved by specified international procedures.

The Kirchner government raised an interesting, even important question about how the international financial market is dominated by a few powerful states and managed to their advantage through the application of the rule of law in one or another of the major financial centers (New York or London). This was one of the considerations in the creation of the financial instruments proposed by the BRICS. In a touch of exquisite irony, the Argentine embassy in Washington joined with Professor Joseph Stiglitz, one of the heroes of the WSF, and New York University to sponsor an essay contest seeking reforms of the international financial system. More significant was the diplomatic victory scored by Argentina at the October 2015 meeting of the World Bank/IMF in having introduced into the final resolution a recommendation that sovereign bond contracts include a clause that barred the isolated action of holdouts to refinancing of defaulted bonds.[54] Notwithstanding this effort, Argentine influence in world affairs has suffered a dramatic decline as a result of the government's approach to exercising agency. Similarly, Argentina has set itself against Brazilian aspirations for a permanent seat on the UN Security Council, which has not helped regional consolidation in Mercosur or in the defense council of UNASUR, and its behavior toward Uruguay in the dispute over paper mills constructed with Finnish capital in the River Plate has made nervous those countries that favor peaceful resolution of disputes. Within a single generation since the return to democracy in 1984, Argentina has managed to dissipate the influence and goodwill it enjoyed in the 1980s as well as the close ties with the United States forged in the 1990s. The willfulness in these disputes undermines the effort of the Argentine government to win international support in its efforts to recover the Malvinas Islands, still under anachronistic British control as the Falklands.

To their credit, the Kirchners used the extraordinary boom in commodity prices to invest heavily in social programs. Their focus was on poverty alleviation and subsidies to buttress the middle class. Their success was remarkable. The poverty rate declined by 25 percent from 2003 to 2010 and housing mortgages increased nearly 100 percent. To take advantage of the increasing price of oil, the national petroleum company, YPF, then controlled by the Spanish giant Repsol, was producing a surplus that could be exported and further increase the government's revenues to maintain a balanced budget and stable exchange rate. Hard currency reserves soared. The good times ended when the financial crisis exploded in the United States and economic growth in China slowed. Commodity prices flattened, and the price of oil collapsed in 2014–2015 so that the government's coffers no longer overflowed. To continue the largesse of their social programs, the government turned to policies of price fixing, especially for public services and energy, and printing money. That led Repsol to stop investing, and production stagnated. The government responded by renationalizing YPF. Within five years, Argentina flipped from an energy export surplus worth about US$10 billion/year in 2007 to an energy import bill of nearly US$15 billion in 2013. The central bank's reserves fell to stomach-wrenching levels, inflation accelerated, and because of the dispute with the holdouts, Argentina and YPF were forced to borrow money at rates nearly double those of the current international market. Argentina's capacity to influence international affairs was low and sinking.

The Argentines have shown considerable sensitivity to international norms when it suits them, again driven by the short-term needs of domestic politics. Kirchner was highly intolerant of the media opposition to her regime, although she has made a great deal of her human rights record and insisted on prosecuting the military for crimes against humanity. The Spanish judge, Baltasar Garzón, who had placed Pinochet under house arrest in London and pushed the Chilean government to begin judicial proceedings against the former dictator, had prosecuted an Argentine naval officer for crimes against humanity while he was still protected in Argentina by an amnesty law the Kirchner government later overturned. Garzón subsequently was disbarred for excessive zeal in attempting to prosecute Spaniards who had served dictator Francisco Franco for their crimes against humanity. As if to return the favor Garzón did for Argentina by prosecuting the navy captain, an Argentine judge issued arrest orders for twenty former Spanish officials, invoking the principle of universal jurisdiction for human rights violations.

The opposition to Kirchner, as well as opposition within Peronism, foiled her attempt to amend the constitution to allow her a third term in office and her influence over the movement declined rapidly, along with the impact of her foreign policy on domestic politics. Given its failure to support Brazil or Chile in their aspirations on the global stage or its lack of reliability in dealing with other members of UNASUR, Argentina's influence within the region also has declined sharply. So long as foreign policy remains the servant of short-term domestic political objectives, that low level of influence is not likely to change. The new president, Mauricio Macri, elected in November 2015, has promised to settle with the holdouts and return Argentina to its former position in the international community.

No country in Latin America has done more since the end of the Cold War to increase its agency in world affairs than Mexico. After the inhibited, inward-looking foreign policy of the PRI during its seventy-five years of semi-authoritarian rule and after the frustration of Fox/Castañeda's effort to reform the hemispheric security architecture, Fox and his successors, Felipe Calderón and Enrique Peña Nieto, took a more cautious or modest approach. But at no time was there a retreat from the conviction that the country has a role to play in world affairs. The country's leaders founded their global agency on a strong relationship with the United States and a successful management of its partnership in North America. The road to a deeper relationship of mutual trust with the United States was a long one and not easy to navigate.[55] First, there was the task of eliminating the certification of its effort in the war on drugs, which culminated in success in 2001. Then there was the successful effort to change the attitude of the United States toward control over illegal immigration by demonstrating Mexico's commitment to discharging its national responsibilities in a dedicated and serious manner. Foreign policy and Mexico's role in the world became a subject of study in the Mexican academy and a subject of debate in the press and other media.[56] Once it became clear that Mexico could and should play a role in world affairs, serious discussion of strategic issues began to put the country into a broader context. For example, there was debate as to whether Mexico should have a blue-water navy, especially once it had joined the Pacific Alliance with Chile, Peru, and Colombia. The United States was supportive of this change in strategic doctrine because it considered Mexican naval power useful in combating drug trafficking and illegal movement of persons and monitoring the Pacific in general.

In dealing with the flow of drugs from Mexico into the United States, Calderón made the fateful decision in 2008 to call out the armed forces rather than putting his efforts and resources into improving the police and the judicial system. After some time, that effort did reduce the violence and the flow of drugs. Given that the consumption of drugs in the United States has not changed significantly, the Mexican effort has diverted a significant portion of the traffic back into the Caribbean, where it had been in the early 1990s. As the campaign against the drug cartels began to take effect, the cartels moved into Central America, provoking dramatic increases in migration into Mexico and through Mexico into the United States. With their commitment to agency, the Calderón and Peña Nieto governments have strengthened their ties to the smaller nations of Central America and have worked together with the United States to deal with both problems. The flow of migration reached crisis proportions in 2014, when nearly 50,000 children, mainly from Honduras and Guatemala, were herded through Mexico and into the United States, confronting the Obama administration with an acute domestic problem.[57] To a degree never before achieved, the problem was dealt with through collaboration between the Mexican and US governments, while most of the Central American governments remain in a state of denial.[58] Together with the United States, Mexico is attempting to deal with the lack of state capacity in the Central American countries. Mexico pledged to be a responsible regional actor as part of its strategic plan to become a more significant actor on the global level. For the moment, the most effective cooperation between the two governments to limit migration is payment by the United States to Mexico so that Mexico can keep Central American migrants from crossing Mexican territory into the United States, certainly no solution to the problem.

In debating its new agency on the global stage, the Mexican government and Mexican analysts have been mindful of the same issues that are of concern to the foreign policy communities in South America: energy, strategic commodities, information, the quality of democratic governance, the rule of law, and the elements of soft power. In dealing with energy and information technology, Mexico is hampered by the crony capitalism created during the long years of control by the PRI. Pemex, the national oil company, had become bloated by patronage and used too long as a cash cow for the state. President Peña Neto pushed through radical reforms of Pemex—along with equally ambitious programs for education reform—that would allow foreign capital back into the energy sector for the first time since the expropriation of foreign-owned companies in 1938 in an effort to increase production. The first auction of exploration lots in the Caribbean Basin in 2015 were a disappointment, but the process of opening had begun, and the second round, six months later, was very successful. In communication and information technology, the process is slowed by the monopolist's struggle to keep competition to a minimum. In dealing with poverty and inequality, the Mexican state has created a set of programs that manages to provide social services and subsidies for the most needy. Although the situation is far from perfect, so long as economic growth continues, even at moderate rates, the state is able to maintain programs that alleviate poverty and slowly reduce inequality.

The most serious issue that affects Mexico's exercise of international agency is democratic governance—the level of crime and impunity associated with the illegal traffic of drugs and corruption. Over the past two decades, tens of thousands of Mexicans have been killed as a result of organized crime. In cooperation with the United States, the Peña Neto government unfurled a major program of police reform and created a new corps of federal police in an effort to return the military to their barracks. Though the number of deaths has declined over the past few years, there continue to be episodes of horrific violence with disturbing evidence that the local and federal police are involved in the crimes, either by committing acts of violence against citizens or by accepting bribes to look away while gangs conduct their violent business.

The perception of impunity and the failure of the rule of law, especially with reference to the forces of law and order, is profoundly disturbing to the Mexican public. The impact was greatest in the aftermath of two episodes that threatened the nation's social stability. The first was the disappearance on September 26, 2014, of forty-three students at a teachers college in Ayotzinapa, in the state of Guerrero, who had gone to the neighboring town of Iguala to steal some buses parked there for transportation to a demonstration. The federal government announced that the students had been kidnapped by a drug gang with the active participation of the local police and that an investigation was being started to find the students and determine what exactly transpired. Months later, the official report stated that the students had been killed and their bodies incinerated in a local dump and that those responsible were being prosecuted. Just before the first anniversary of the grizzly event, a panel of experts created by the OAS Inter-American Commission for Human Rights at the request of some parents of the students called into question the government's investigation. While the resolution of the students' kidnapping was still unfolding, the head of the Sinoloa drug cartel, Joaquin "El Chapo" Guzmán escaped from the high-security prison in which he had been incarcerated. The sense of insecurity in Mexico and the surrounding aura of corruption and impunity will be a brake on Mexico's ambitions to become a major player in global affairs.[59]

Two other countries in South America, Colombia and Peru, appear eager to play bigger roles in hemispheric and world affairs, but each is held back by historical and seemingly intractable problems. Colombia, which has outstanding natural resources and an excellent system of rules and regulations for dealing with the international market and is fairly stable politically, cannot exercise agency in international affairs in a serious manner until it settles the fifty-year-old struggle with guerrilla groups that occupy about one quarter of the national territory and, in concert with international drug cartels, manage a billion-dollar business in crime and corruption. The peace talks in Havana have the backing of the United States and many friendly states in the region and are moving toward a resolution, expected early in 2016. Once that peace agreement is achieved, the state must demonstrate its capacity to deal with the residue of bands of armed criminals who roam virtually unopposed throughout the southern rural part of the country. And, as part of the healing process, Colombia must find a way to assimilate and settle more than five million people who have been displaced by the violence over the past decades. The mere act of establishing peace with the guerrillas will give the Colombian government enormous prestige in the international community. How they use that new space remains to be seen.

The Peruvian case is less clear. After years of instability and dealing with a violent insurgency, the Shining Path, the country has settled into a mode of semi-stability and considerable prosperity, thanks to the boom in the price of the country's mineral exports. Driven mainly by the construction boom in China, Peru's exports, principally iron and copper, increased sixfold in the decade from 2002 to 2012, to nearly $46 billion. Even as the price for its metals has softened, the exports continue to bring in considerable revenue, although not nearly as much as before the slowdown in China, beginning in 2013. The problem in Peru is incompetence and a maddening inability to organize the population in anything so structured as political parties. The congress is a mess and the president for the past three terms, each elected in peaceful orderly elections, has been unable to provide any leadership, although all of them have been friendly to foreign investors and to market opening. Without political parties or any coherent organizations in civil society and without leadership, the country seems to drift along. So long as it drifts, it is difficult to establish a coherent foreign policy. And, the question remains how long a country can drift before trouble sets in.

The problem in Central America is that all but Costa Rica and Nicaragua continue to behave as penetrated polities to some degree, as they have since the early years of the twentieth century. Panama has a chance to play a major role with the newly expanded canal, but it can't seem to get its politics cleaned up or deal in a constructive manner with its rural population of mestizos and Afro-Panamanians who need to be assimilated into the national society. Guatemala and Honduras are still locked into the traditional pattern of internal factional struggles within an elite that controls the economy, the state, and the armed forces. Under these conditions, foreign policy remains a moot point. Both have lost control over portions of their territory to Mexican drug cartels. On the bright side, there are new elements in the elites that appear to be more sensitive to affairs outside their country and may give a more cosmopolitan aspect to dominance, which would lead to a greater sense of participation in world affairs. The strong links between these social movements and the international civil society are behind the successful effort to have CICIG help the Guatemalan judiciary gird its loins to oust President Otto Pérez Molina in September 2015 because of the widespread corruption in his government.

El Salvador looked for a while as if it might move in this direction because former members of the left-wing guerrilla movement were elected to public office, but its capacity to control its own territory has been compromised by the cancer of organized crime, especially gangs in the cities. Panama has begun to assume a more autonomous foreign policy and expand political contestation a little, prodded by the dramatic international attention brought by the massive expansion of the canal, expected to be ready in 2016. Nicaragua has signed an agreement with a Chinese investor to build a canal, but that appears to be many years off.

A path forward has been created since the end of the Cold War, what some call a new stage of Central American development: the diaspora and remittances from the emigrants together with the changing pattern of trade and investment in the region.[60] The increasing importance of the international community increases the opportunity for agency by opening these societies to outside influence. Even in Guatemala and Honduras—along with Paraguay the most retrograde states in the hemisphere—nonstate actors and community-wide codes of behavior are important, though their application is uneven. These players bring to the action transnational networks and norms, which are felt with particular strength at the subregional level.

Costa Rica and Uruguay represent an interesting new category of very small states, one in Central America and one in South America, which are enjoying significant influence in the international community as a consequence of their stability, their public advocacy of core values such as human rights and democracy, and their deliberate exercise of agency based on this influence and advocacy. Both countries explicitly reject military solutions to dispute resolution. Costa Rica has no military; Uruguay's is too small to be considered a measure of the country's hard power; both are social democracies and play by the rules of the international market to attract foreign investment; and both were strong allies of the United States during the Cold War.[61] Uruguay was the only nation in the hemisphere to come to the rescue of the Obama administration by taking prisoners from the Guantánamo prison. The president of Costa Rica, Luis Guillermo Solís, has indicated his support for CELAC, although San José continues as the seat of the Inter-American Court of Human Rights. Uruguay also supports CELAC, but its former foreign minister, Luis Almagro Lemes, was elected in 2015 to succeed the Chilean José Miguel Insulza as secretary general of the OAS. Almagro has insisted that the OAS and CELAC complement one another and has vowed to strengthen the hemispheric institutions. These two, along with Chile, with their firm stand on the defense of core values, will prove to be key players in bridging the gap between the OAS, with its ties to the United States, and the newer regional organizations.

The nations of Latin America are coping in a wide variety of ways with their new sense of agency and the impact it has on their relationship with the United States. Whether the United States can let go of its century-long hegemony remains to be seen; under any circumstances the autonomy and agency of the countries in the region have reached historic levels and cannot go back to an earlier level. It is clear that all the countries, large and small, understand they have roles to play in the world community. At the regional level, there is a sense that all can be rulemakers and that their nascent regional organizations can help maintain regional peace and stability, even as there remain great differences among them. It is also clear that anti-Americanism is losing its force as a foreign policy, although the historical legacy of US intervention and US exceptionalism weigh heavily on the decisionmaking in many Latin American countries and continue to inhibit their exercise of agency outside the hemisphere.[62] So long as hemispheric organizations concentrate on bridging differences, they will be useful in creating a sense of identity and community and less useful in establishing rules of conduct.

That the new organizations in the region have no clear mandate for setting rules also inhibits the exercise of Latin American agency outside the hemisphere, where rulemaking carries with it consequences and costs. The Latin Americans for the most part, though they protested vigorously against US hegemony, have been free riders in the global community for many years. Especially now that the process of public policy is so important, as is public discussion and debate, they must ask if they are willing to pay the price of active participation in the global community and how such participation enhances the well-being of their people. These are questions that were scarcely raised at the time of independence, two centuries ago. They are questions most Latin Americans didn't dare to ask when under the thrall of US hegemony. Now they are growing accustomed to asking them and are learning to live with the consequences of the answers.

There are grounds for guarded optimism. There is no doubt that the revolutionary effects of globalization have brought the nations and the peoples of Latin America into closer and more regular proximity to world affairs than ever before. The world market for commodities, especially China's remarkable growth and demand for goods, brought enormous revenues to many countries in the region in the first decade of this century. Today, with commodity prices flat or soft, the development model for commodity exporters is again undergoing intense debate, within a more democratic framework than at any other time in history. The Latin American countries understand that they should benefit from such windfalls; yet only Chile has been able to establish a true sovereign wealth fund. Colombia and Mexico have made efforts to create compensatory savings institutions to husband their resources or use the money to pay for social welfare programs. Venezuela and Argentina have used the money primarily to buy domestic political support for the sitting government; with the decline in oil and soy prices, there is very little left in their reserve funds.

The rapid expansion of the middle class in many Latin American countries hasn't just produced an explosive growth in consumption. It also has led to a historic increase in the domestic demand for capital, in the form of individual debt and mortgages and in the form of loans to start or expand small and medium-sized businesses. Information technology has made innovation easier, and the demand for investment capital has increased to unprecedented levels precisely at the time when breathtaking amounts of private capital are available at the touch of a few computer buttons. Capital will go where it anticipates profit and where it feels relatively safe. Again, with Venezuela and Argentina as the major exceptions, most of the countries have maintained macroeconomic stability with low inflation, which makes it easier for them to participate in the world economy. With Chile in the lead, many of the countries in South America have made progress in the rule of law and in making more transparent the regulatory framework that makes domestic and foreign investment legally viable. Most of the countries today are in a good position to formulate and maintain policies that spur growth and enhance the quality of life of their people. Capital and communication technology, two of the three strategic commodities that drove US policy in the hemisphere up to World War II, are now easily accessible to any country. The third of the magical triumvirate, energy, is also more abundant in the region than it has been at any time in the past, although domestic nationalist restrictions on foreign capital have hurt production in several countries. Most of the countries in South America have the resources to be energy independent.

New technologies have made it economically feasible to exploit certain oil and gas deposits that were considered unviable just ten years ago. By the end of the current decade, it is anticipated that the United States will become one of the world's major energy exporters and OPEC will lose its geopolitical clout.[63] That means that countries with large unexploited energy deposits, such as Bolivia or Argentina, will have greatly increased economic potential, if they can bring their resources to the international market. It also means that countries with proven reserves, such as Venezuela, Colombia, and Argentina, or those such as Brazil, Peru, and Mexico with hints of such reserves, must decide how they wish to pay for the enormous investments that will be required to find and exploit those reserves. To put it differently, how will energy independence affect their agency? At the moment, three of South America's largest potential energy producers have shot themselves in the foot by making bad political decisions. Argentina and Venezuela have virtually shut themselves out of the international capital market. In Brazil, Petrobras has been rendered temporarily inoperable by a massive corruption scandal. Until the scandal is resolved, Petrobras cannot tap the international markets for the capital it needs to exploit fully its massive pre-salt deposits of petroleum. Mexico, which only in 2014 created the legal framework for foreign capital to return to the petroleum industry for the first time since the Cárdenas expropriation in 1938, may be able to increase its production by the end of the decade, but not before. Ecuador has guaranteed its production and market in petroleum with a huge contract signed in 2013 with the Chinese state petroleum company, exchanging its energy independence for the financial resources necessary to keep its populist government in power. In other words, energy independence is a matter of political will in most of the countries in the region

The new player in the development game is China. Since its extraordinary expansion at the end of the twentieth century and continuing into the first decade of the twenty-first century, China's demand for raw materials literally transformed the economies of several countries. The purchase of Argentine soybeans paid for the populist programs of Néstor and Cristina Kirchner. The sales of copper provided a strong foundation for Chile's growth, including the social programs of the progressive Concertación governments. The purchase of Brazilian commodities made Lula's work much easier and provided the capital to keep the national development bank going. Venezuela and Ecuador mortgaged their petroleum to China in return for capital to keep their governments afloat. Chinese banks, Chinese construction companies, and Chinese state companies of all sorts are key players in the economic development of virtually every country in the Western Hemisphere. The role that China will play is not fully scripted. Even at this early stage, however, it is clear that the Chinese are a new player in the game. To this date, their participation is not political or geopolitical, but that may change.[64] The Chinese investment bank has declared that it will be both clean, that is, free of corruption, and green, that is, sensitive to environmental concerns.[65] In this way, the Chinese signaled that they will follow the rules of the larger international community. In organizing the large Trans Pacific Partnership, the United States indicated that it would try to make sure that they would continue to be rulemakers in the world trade community and have every intention to block China's moves to take over that role.

Bolivia has the same potential with its massive lithium deposits, said to be the largest in the world. At the moment, the government of Bolivia has decided it does not wish to exploit the lithium or significantly increase the production of its huge reserves of natural gas. While the government of Evo Morales has succeeded in renegotiating existing contracts with foreign energy companies to significantly increase the royalty payments to the state, it does not feel confident—it has become captive of the ALBA rhetoric of victimhood—that it can retain control over the massive investment by foreign capital required to exploit the lithium in the high desert to the west of the Andes. The geological fact that the lithium lies in Chilean and Argentine territory as well as Bolivian soil may account for some of Morales's caution. An optimist would see the lithium as an opportunity of historical proportions for regional cooperation among the three countries. In the same spirit, the resolution of Bolivia's claim to an outlet to the sea might well be a game changer for the region. Would a bargain that entailed an outlet to the sea for Bolivia and energy security for Chile along with a dynamic partnership between Bolivia and Chile to exploit the lithium deposits be appealing?

Globalization and the recent boom in commodity prices have made it plain that the nations in Latin America are in a position today to control their own development destiny for the first time in their history. In doing so, their new experience in agency will be of enormous benefit. None of the countries in the region remains in thrall with the international division of labor or with import substitution industrialization, and none is a victim of dependency on a manipulated international market. There is a broad consensus that the state is a legitimate actor in the market, that the state can make decisions to increase production, that the state can act to protect the most vulnerable elements of the nation's population without resorting to inflationary or populist policies that weaken the economy. That is not likely to change any time soon. While accumulating experience in a variety of trade regimes and in subregional or regional market groups, the nation-state has at its disposal an arsenal of policy instruments more varied and potent than at any time in history. Their membership in international regimes today gives them opportunities to discuss the rules that govern exchange. Calvo would be proud. Can governments be made accountable? Will they become responsive to the needs and will of their people?

In December 2014, President Obama announced that the United States and Cuba would move to restore normal diplomatic relations. Doing so will not be easy. The Republican phalanx of Cuban Americans who have kept US policy frozen since the Reagan administration, despite the end of the Cold War, now sit in critical positions in the US Congress. The embargo is the result of legislation and can only be lifted by an act of Congress. The executive can move toward normal relations, but until or unless the embargo is lifted, it will only be half a job. One thing the executive could do to please the Cubans was to remove Cuba from the list of states aiding terrorism. That was not difficult as the most involved units of the US government have considered Cuba free of such taint for twenty years. In making his announcement, Obama made it clear that in the calculation behind the policy he weighed two factors heavily: the need to improve US influence or interests in Latin America and recognition that the embargo failed to achieve its stated objectives. He declared that it was wrong to allow a minority of a small minority to distort the rational calculation of US interests. To follow up on the decision, officials of the two governments met to ease friction between them, and the two presidents met at the VII Summit of the Americas in Panama in April 2015, the first such meeting in over half a century, to discuss their reconciliation. The second obstacle to easy relations between the countries is the fact that Cuba is not a democracy. It is not a market economy for that matter, but that does not appear to be a deal breaker. The lack of political freedom and of respect for human rights will be hard to ignore and it will be hard for the Cuban governing elite to meet their critics halfway on this matter. The Cubans insist that progress cannot be made until the embargo is lifted and that requires action by Congress, which is unlikely. The United States has made it clear that the alliance in Congress necessary to remove the embargo requires some concessions by the Cubans on the political issues between them. And, in commercial or economic matters, the United States has indicated that it is willing to remove restrictions within the powers of the executive if the Cubans make it possible for US businesses to operate in Cuba. That creates a dilemma for the Cubans as they appear ambivalent on how to balance their control over the economy against gains offered to them by opening to foreign capital. Change in Cuba will not be easy.

On the long road to normal relations, the nations of Latin America will have to decide how their defense of democracy should be balanced against their support for Cuba in its defiance of US hegemony. For the past half a century, Latin Americans have looked to Cuba, even if only with furtive glances, as an example of agency in world affairs. Today, they are virtually unanimous in supporting the readmission of Cuba into the regional community. They have been unanimous in supporting annual Cuban resolutions in the UN to end the noxious embargo imposed by the United States. The policy of the United States in banning Cuba from the OAS is a major factor in the decline of that institution's influence and in the creation of ALBA and CELAC. The new secretary general of the OAS, Luis Almagro, has indicated he will move to bring Cuba back into the organization. Although it may seem somewhat miraculous at this stage, with Fidel Castro ill and in retirement and his brother Raúl aging fast along with the remnants of the revolutionary generation, and with the economy suffering significant deficiencies, Cuba continues to represent successful agency in a changing world. Cuba solved its energy deficiency by making itself indispensable to the leadership of Venezuela. It won Brazilian gratitude and support by providing thousands of doctors at a time when the lack of primary health care was one of the principal sources of disaffection with the Rousseff government. In return, Brazilian capital with support from the national development bank has built a new deepwater port in Mariel that may prove to be a major factor in the region's economy. Quietly and without any tension with other nations, Cuba sent hundreds of health workers to western Africa to help in the response to the terrifying Ebola pandemic in 2014–2015. Boldly, it invited the United States to attend a meeting in Cuba of ALBA nations to coordinate a regional strategy on the prevention and control of Ebola. The Cuban government has offered to coordinate a hemispheric program to train health professionals to implement an Ebola prevention and control plan. Its efforts won the praise of the *New York Times* editorial board and the public support of the US Centers for Disease Control and Prevention, as well as Secretary of State Kerry.[66]

Perhaps the key initiative by Cuba to enhance its status within the hemispheric community has been its role in promoting peace talks between the government of Colombia and the guerrilla group FARC. Those talks, which have continued for more than two years and, at the end of 2015, look as if they will be consummated successfully within a matter of months, have drawn unofficial representatives from the United States, Chile, and other friends of the peace process. That collective action will have a major positive impact on the growing community in Latin America, and that the United States has played an important role may improve its ties to the hemispheric regional organizations.

It is not easy to build international community. Interests, culture, and history divide the nations from one another. It is not just the Western Hemisphere that finds it difficult to organize in a collegial manner for the benefit of the community. Take one issue or problem: immigration. It tears at the fabric of society in the United States. There is no consensus on how to deal with the accumulated migration into the United States that has left a population of undocumented residents estimated at 11 million people. Haitian migration into the Dominican Republic has precipitated a crisis in which the government of the Dominican Republic threatens to expel all undocumented migrants. Such action would create a humanitarian crisis of unprecedented proportions. Now look at the surge in migration into Europe. For decades, there has been a constant flow of illegal immigrants into southern Europe from North Africa. Today, the situation is radically different. Hundreds of thousands of people are moving from the Middle East and the Caucasus into Europe, pouring across borders into Hungary and France, and throwing themselves onto freight trains passing through the tunnel to England. More than ten thousand biked across Russia into Norway. It is estimated that millions of people are displaced by the conflicts from Afghanistan to Syria and/or have been driven out of nations in Africa. The Europeans appear no better at dealing with the issue than do the leaders of the United States. Several groups have proposed walls like the one that the United States started to build on the border between Mexico and Texas. Efforts to resettle illegal immigrants have bogged down. It isn't just a European problem. What about the millions of displaced people in South Asia?

There are conflicts in many places in the world. Insurgent groups, terrorist groups, and other organized armed groups are in conflict with governments from Syria to Thailand. There is armed violence in several African countries. How can the international community deal with this conflict? The vision of a rules-based community enforcing the peace that President Obama has tried to share with other leaders seems just that—a vision. There do not seem to be enough nations willing to become part of the solution. In a recent public address, General Martin E. Dempsey, chairman of the Joint Chiefs of Staff, called on the member states of the United Nations to increase their participation in peacekeeping. There is not sufficient concern for the violent upheavals and multiple wars around the world.[67] Indeed!

There are many ways to be in the world. In the United States, the political dysfunction that characterizes the relations between Congress and the executive have led to a series of measures that restrict US influence, what Moisés Naím called *auto goles* (self goals).[68] Congress refused to fund the Export-Import Bank, it refused to fund the reforms of the IMF, it refused to increase the capital of the Inter-American Development Bank, and it has made it difficult to participate in any free trade negotiations, although the Obama administration did succeed in negotiating the Trans Pacific Partnership, the largest trade agreement in history and one that will improve environmental controls, enhance intellectual property rights, and set standards for the protection of labor.[69] These actions contributed to the formation by China of the new Asian Infrastructure and Investment Bank, which the United States has refused to join. You cannot participate in making the rules of the community if you don't join. Obama understands that as the most powerful country in the world and the country in which more innovation occurs than in any other and the country in which more intellectual property is created in a year than in the rest of the world combined, the United States is in a position to benefit more from a rules-based community than anyone else and that it is in a position to lead any community of which it is a member. But, he also understands that by joining a community, the other members can be rulemakers and that there is a cost to sharing the benefits of the community.

In Latin America, Cuba has more experience in exercising agency in the global community than does any other nation in the region, but that may change in the next few years.[70] Now that the foreign policy process has become so important and so prominent in most of the countries in Latin America (with Cuba as a marked exception), we can expect that where the process is transparent and the flow of information is not obstructed, the foreign ministries will begin to formulate—and make public—what they think about global crises, such as the violence in the Middle East, the structure of the international financial system, the neutrality of the Internet, and how to handle international pandemics. They also will become more confident in dealing with troublesome issues within the hemisphere, such as political violence in Venezuela, international drug trafficking, and criminal violence.

For the moment, with the exception of Chile and Brazil, the nations of Latin America appear uncertain about their role outside the hemisphere. Here, the optimists are correct: it is impossible to stop globalization and it is increasingly difficult to deny to the people of the region their aspirations for a better life and more freedom, even in those countries in which leaders hope to perpetuate themselves in power and limit political contestation and the expansion of democratic space. In dealing with these fundamental issues, the new regional organizations do not yet appear to offer solutions, and no one appears to be in a position to resolve the historical differences that divide the countries or eliminate the differences among them. There is more diversity than convergence.

As cautious optimists, we may expect this to change as regional organizations provide forums for open discussions of common problems. As cautious optimists, we see the growing evidence that globalization, especially in the massive increase in the flow of information and money, has made it possible for all the nations in the hemisphere to participate in a wide variety of regimes and networks and in a reciprocal fashion, to make all governments and civil society permeable to the influence of the outside actors, state and nonstate. All nations are in the world. The nations of Latin America are in the world to a degree and in more ways than ever before so that the shape and rules of the international community are more important to them than ever before. Globalization opens to all an expanding panoply of opportunities for agency. As US hegemony declines and as Cuba loses its importance as a symbol, will the nations of Latin America be prepared to expand their agency? Do they want to? Will they pay the price?

Notes

1. Quoted in the *New York Times*, February 6, 2015, A7. Robert Litwak explores the policy of engaging outlier states in *Outlier States: American Strategies to Contain, Engage, or Change Regimes* (Baltimore: Johns Hopkins University Press, 2012). The entire document is at http://www.whitehouse.gov/sites/default/files/docs/2015 _national_security_strategy.pdf.

2. Joseph S. Nye Jr., *Bound to Lead* (New York: Basic Books, 1990).

3. Speech by Muñoz, "Diálogo sobre integración regional: Alianza del Pacífico y Mercosur," November 24, 2014. This and other documents are at http://www.minrel.gob.cl/site/politica_exterior.

4. An easy entrée to the vast literature on this phenomenon is Thomas L. Friedman, *The World Is Flat* (New York: Farrar, Straus and Giroux, 2005).

5. One significant example is the project conducted by Guadalupe González at CIDE in Mexico. See Guadalupe González González, Jorge A. Schiavon, David Crow,

and Gerardo Maldonado, *The Americas and the World, 2010–2011: Public Opinion and Foreign Policy in Brazil, Colombia, Ecuador, Mexico, and Peru* (Mexico: CIDE, 2011); and Guadalupe Gonzalez et al., *Mexico, Las Americas y el Mundo, 2012–2013* (Mexico: CIDE, 2013). This project can be followed online at http://mexicoyelmundo.cide.edu. On the growing theoretical debate, see Juan Gabriel Tokatlián and Leonardo Carvajal, "Autonomía y política exterior en América Latina: Un debate abierto, un futuro incierto," *Revista CIDOB d'afers internacionals* 28 (1995): 7–31; Juan Gabriel Tokatlián and Roberto Russell, "From Antagonistic Autonomy to Relational Autonomy: A Theoretical Reflection from the Southern Cone," *Latin American Politics and Society*, 45.1 (2003): 1–24.

6. Argentina showed itself adept at playing off one community against another when at the World Bank/IMF meeting in Lima in October 2015, it got the final declaration to include a recommendation that all bond contracts should include a phrase ruling out the possibility of holdouts blocking efforts by sovereign states to refinance defaulted bonds and ending the observance of pari passu. See La Politica Online, October 10, 2015, www.lapoliticaonline.com.

7. The Argentine embassy in Washington sponsored a competition for the best essay on "International Reform of Sovereign Debt Restructuring."

8. Joseph Stiglitz, *Globalization and Its Discontents* (New York: Norton, 2003); Mario Rapoport and Neomi Brenta, *Las grandes crises del capitalismo contemporáneo* (Buenos Aires: Le Monde Diplomatique, 2012); José Luis Fiori, Carlos Medeiros, and Franklin Serrano, *The Myth of the Collapse of American Power* (Rio de Janeiro: Editora Record, 2008); Thomas Muhr, ed., *Counter-Globalization and Socialism in the 21st Century* (London: Routledge, 2013); Roger Burbach, Michael Fox, and Federico Fuentes, *Latin America's Turbulent Transitions—The Future of Twenty-First-Century Socialism* (New York: Zed Books, 2013).

9. For an analysis of geopolitical thinking in China, see Edward Friedman, "Succeeding in the Third World, Except Asia," in Lowell Dittmer and Maochun Yu, eds., *Routledge Handbook of Chinese Security* (New York: Routledge, 2015). On China's new role, see Ariel Armony, "China in Latin America," University of Miami, online, 2013; and the UNAM project, http://www.economia.unam.mx /cechimex/index.php.

10. Federico de la Balze, "En la fase menguante de la globalización," *Clarín*, October 4, 2014, sees centrifugal forces threatening globalization and says that it requires "a political architecture that supports it: a hegemonic nation or a concert of great powers that define and administer the rules of the game." Moisés Naím, "El fin de poder," *El país*, July 29, 2012, sees in these forces a declining ability to exercise power but a rise in the ability to thwart or stop the exercise of power. Both de la Balze and Naím wonder who will enforce the sanctions that the United States and European nations call for to chasten the countries that break the rules of the international community.

11. The results of the summits are at http://www.brics6.itamaraty.br. Also see Fatima Mello, "¿Hacia dondé van los BRICS?" *Nueva sociedad*, August 2014, http://nuso.org/articulo/hacia-donde-van-los-brics; Simon Romero, "Emerging Nations Bloc to Open Development Bank," *New York Times*, July 16, 2014, A9; Francis A. Kornegay, Jr., and Narnia Bohler-Muller, eds., *Laying the BRICS of a New Global Order: A Conceptual Scenario* (Pretoria: Africa Institute of South Africa, 2013); Marcos Degaut, "Do the BRICS Still Matter?" *A Report of the CSIS Americas Program* (October 2015). In what may have been a symbolic gesture, in November 2015 Goldman Sachs closed the fund set up to invest in the BRIC countries. See www.folha.uol.com.br /mercado/2015/11/170433.

12. The editorial board of the *New York Times* was unhappy with Obama's handling of the new bank, asserting that the president had no plan to counter the Chinese move. "US Allies, Lured by China's Bank," *New York Times*, March 22, 2015, A26; and

the news article, "Rush to Join China's New Asian Bank Surprises All, Even the Chinese," *New York Times*, April 3, 2015, A8; and "New China-Led Bank Pledges to Fend Off Graft," *New York Times*, Apr 12, 2015, A10. Although it is too early to know with confidence, it is just as plausible that by bringing China into an institution in which rules are set by the collective membership, in the long run, the United States will have enhanced its security by making China a more stable member of the international community. This new Asian bank would appear to render the BRICS bank redundant.

13. For example, the article by Sergio Bitar and Jorge Heine, "Chile y lo que está en juego en Siria," *El Mercurio*, September 13, 2013; Olga Pellicer, "Lo que no se informa," *Proceso*, September 15, 2014. For criticism of Latin American reticence, see Carl Meacham, "Where Is Latin America in the Fight Against ISIL?," Center for Strategic and International Studies, October 21, 2014, http://csis.org/publication/where-latin-america-fight-against-isil.

14. Nicco Mele, *The End of Big* (New York: St. Martin's, 2013). This is similar to Moisés Naím's notion of the end of power. Litwak, *Outlier States*, deals with the issue of enforcement.

15. Friedman modified his views over time. He began by seeing in the popular demonstrations a strong push for freedom he called the Arab Spring. By 2014, he had come to accept the fact that popular uprisings by themselves could not achieve democratic government. He came to see the world divided into forces of order and disorder: Thomas L. Friedman, "Order vs. Disorder, Part 2," *New York Times*, July 16, 2014, A23. The classic statement of the belief in the inexorable drive for human freedom and decency is Albert Camus, *The Rebel* (New York: Doubleday, 1965).

16. Friedman touted the "sharing economy" in noting that Airbnb booked over 120,000 people from 150 different countries in Brazil during the World Cup 2014, and that Brazilian Airbnb hosts earned an average of $4,000 for their rooms. "And Now for a Bit of Good News . . ." *New York Times*, July 20, 2014, SR1,11. A year later, just after President Obama announced the intention to resume normal relations with Cuba, Airbnb announced it had 100,000 listings in Cuba waiting for US tourists. Friedman also admires Uber, the ride-sharing service that by 2014 was operating in 20 countries. Moisés Naím, "Una visita al futuro," *El país*, November 2, 2014, shares Friedman's optimism about the power of innovation and the ability of new technology companies to change the lives of millions of people throughout the world.

17. As an example, see Thierry Cruvellier, "The Flaw in Human Rights Trials," *New York Times*, July 28, 2015, A21.

18. "Laos, Destination in Illegal Ivory Trade, So Far Eludes Global Crackdown," *New York Times*, August 2, 2015, A10.

19. Evan Osnos, "In the Land of the Possible," *New Yorker*, December 22, 2014, p. 90 et seq.

20. *New York Times*, March 13, 2015, A4.

21. Press statement by Secretary of State John Kerry, April 24, 2015, "The United States welcomes Guatemalan President Otto Pérez Molina's decision to renew the mandate of the International Commission Against Impunity in Guatemala for two years. This is a major step forward in the fight against organized crime. CICIG is an important partner of the government and people of Guatemala. It helps in their efforts to promote the rule of law, accountability, and the integrity of the institutions of justice and public order. CICIG's continuing role in Guatemala will advance the goals of Guatemala and the United States as articulated in the plan of the Alliance for Prosperity in the Northern Triangle. The US government has contributed more than $25 million in support for CICIG since it began operations in January 2008. . . . Through this commission, Guatemala can send an unequivocal message that no one stands above the law."

22. "Is Democracy in Decline?" special issue, *Journal of Democracy*, 26.1 (2015).

23. Joseph Nye urged the US government to take a more aggressive but constructive posture toward China; see his article "Work with China, Don't Contain It," *New York Times*, January 26, 2013, A19. Anne-Marie Slaughter thought his policy toward Syria was feckless, "Don't Fight in Iran and Ignore Syria," *New York Times*, June 18, 2014, A25. She was insistent that the United States should act forcefully against Moammar Gaddafi, "Fiddling While Libya Burns," *New York Times*, March 14, 2011, A21. For a European view, Clemens Wergin, "Is Obama's Foreign Policy Too European?" *New York Times*, July 9, 2014, http://www.nytimes.com/2014/07/09/opinion/clemens-wergin-is-obamas-foreign-policy-too-european.html. But Nye continued in his belief that the United States still was the most powerful country in the world, in *Is the American Century Over?* (Cambridge, MA: Polity Press, 2015). Obama's use of sanctions against Iran and Russia, among others, has stirred a fierce debate—among scholars as well as politicians—as to whether such measures are effective. It appears that they are effective, just not the magic bullet some advocates promised. In both Iran and Russia it is clear that the sanctions caused changes in the negotiating position of the adversary.

24. Robert Kagan, "Superpowers Don't Get to Retire," *New Republic*, May 26, 2014, http://www.newrepublic.com/article/117859/allure-normalcy-what-america-still-owes-world.

25. Frank Bruni, "Obama's Messy Words," *New York Times*, September 2, 2014, A19; Nicholas Kristof, "Critique from an Obama Fan," *New York Times*, September 11, 2014; Gail Collins, "A Man with a Plan," *New York Times*, September 11, 2014, http://www.nytimes.com/2014/09/11/opinion/nicholas-kristof-critique-from-an-obama-fan.html?_r=0. Some in Latin America saw these statements as evidence that the United States had lost influence in Latin America; Patricio D. Navia, "Vanishing US Influence in Latin America," *Buenos Aires Herald*, June 10, 2014. Others warned against mistaking policy diffidence for declining US power; Josef Joffe, *The Myth of America's Decline: Politics, Economics and a Half Century of False Prophecies* (New York: Liveright/Norton, 2013).

26. Thomas L. Friedman, "The Obama Doctrine and Iran," *New York Times*, April 6, 2015, A19; Joseph R. Biden Jr., "A Plan for Central America," *New York Times*, January 30, 2015, A21; more generally, Richard Feinberg, Emily Miller, and Harold Trinkunas, "Better than You Think: Reframing Inter-American Relations," Brookings Policy Brief, Washington, DC, March 2015.

27. Ricardo Lagos, "Cuba-Estados Unidos y nuestra generación," *El país*, January 5, 2015.

28. Gian Luca Gardini and Peter Lambert, *Latin American Foreign Policies: Between Ideology and Pragmatism* (London: Palgrave, 2011); Gerhard Drekonja, "Autonomía periférica redefinida: América Latina en la década de los noventa," in María Mercedes Gómez, Gerhard Drekonja, Juan Gabriel Tokatlián, and Leonardo Carvajal, "Redefiniendo la autonomía en política internacional," *Documentos ocasionales, CEI* [Colombia] 31 (1993); Roberto Russell and Juan Gabriel Tokatlián, "From Antagonistic Autonomy to Relational Autonomy," *Latin American Politics and Society* 45.1 (2003); Adalberto Rodriguez Giavarini, "Oportunidad para América Latina," *Agenda internacional* 1.1 (2004): 67–69.

29. Lagos, "Cuba-Estados Unidos y nuestra generación."

30. Diana Tussie, with Sanoussi Bilal and Philippe de Lambaerle, *Asymmetric Commercial Negotiations* (London: Ashgate, 2011); and Pia Riggirozzi and Diana Tussie, eds., *The Rise of Post-Hegemonic Regionalism,* United National University Series on Regionalism (London: Springer, 2012); Marcelo Saguier with Diana Tussie, "Emerging Trade Politics: The Continuous Pendulum from Multilateralism to Asymmetric Trade Negotiations," *Estudios internacionais* 2.1 (2014); Marcelo Saguier,

"Minería para el desarrollo integral en la estrategia de UNASUR," *Revista conjuntura austral*, 5.21–22 (2013–14): 39–65. Saguier has identified a new regime, which is called social solidarity economy, in "Regional Policy Framework of Social Solidarity Economy in South America," Occasional Paper Series no. 6, UNRISD, Geneva, 2011.

31. Tokatlián and Russell, "From Antagonistic Autonomy to Relational Autonomy." The same point was made a decade earlier in Joseph S. Tulchin and Ralph Espach. eds., *América Latina en el nuevo sistema internacional* (Barcelona: Bellaterra, 2004).

32. Andrés Serbin et al., eds., *El regionalism "post-liberal" en América Latina y el Caribe: Nuevos actores, nuevos temas, nuevos desafíos. Anuario de la Integración Regional de América Latina y el Gran Caribe 2012* (Buenos Aires: CRIES, 2012). CRIES and its journal *Pensamiento proprio* are important outlets for this perspective. The anuario includes several articles by Cubans. Including Cuba is the code embedded in the notion of the Gran Caribe. A similar view is Adrian Bonilla, "La CELAC y su III Cumbre: Identidad estrategica y diferencias con la OEA," *Novedades FLACSO*, January 26, 2014. The two best summaries of the recent history of regionalism in Latin America are Juan Gabriel Tokatlián, "Latinoamerica y el complejo integracionista: Un concepto a debate," *Desarrollo económico* 51.204 (2012); and Carlos Portales, "A dónde va el multilateralismo en las Américas? Proyectos superpuestos en un periodo de cambios globales," *Pensamiento propio* 39 (2014).

33. A summary of these difficulties can be found in the Workshop Reports, 1 and 2 of "Latin America: New Security Configurations in a Strategic Emerging Region," University of Aberdeen, directed by Andrea Oelsner, Rut Diamint, and Monica Herz; http://www.abdn.ac.uk/global-security/news/8347. On the new regionalism, see Marcial A. Garcia Suarez, Rafael A. D. Villa, and Brigitte Weiffen, eds., *Power Dynamics and Regional Security in Latin America* (London: Palgrave, 2016).

34. See http://www.LaPoliticaOnline, July 19, 2014. On China's role in Latin America, see http://www.universityofmiami/latinamericancenter/china and http://www.economia.unam.mx/cechimex.

35. Rodrigo Tavares, *Security in South America: The Roles of States and Regional Organizations* (Boulder, CO: Lynne Rienner, 2013); Daniel C. Thomas, "Boomerangs and Superpowers: International Norms, Transitional Networks and US Foreign Policy," *Cambridge Review of International Affairs* 15.1 (2002): 24–44; Brigitte Weiffen, Leslie Wehner, and Detlef Nolte, "Overlapping Security Institutions in South America: The Case of UNASUR and OAS," *International Area Studies Review* 16.4 (2013): 370–389; the interview with the president of Costa Rica, Luis Guillermo Solís, on CELAC as the "Future of Latin America," http://actualidad.rt.com/actualidad/view/124649-entrevista. On the slow development of norms or regimes in sectoral matters, see José Barbero and Rodrigo Rodriguez Tornquist, "Transporte y cambio climático: Hacia un desarrollo sostenible y de bajo carbono," *Revista transporte y territorio* 6 (2012): 8–26, http://www.rtt.filo.uba.ar/RTT00602008. The authors describe new modes of cooperation on a regional level that ignores or bypasses political conflicts.

36. All of Muñoz's speeches as foreign minister can be found at http://www.minrel.gob.cl.

37. Interview with Solís is at http://www.WorldReview.info/content/costa-rica-latin-america-important-voice-international-community.

38. As of this writing, Costa Rica had entered formal negotiations to become a member of the alliance, and Panama had become an official observer.

39. Ethan Ellis, "The TPP is Foundational. . . ." www.LatinAmericaGoesGlobal, October 9, 2015.

40. In her volume of memoirs, *Hard Choices* (New York: Simon and Schuster, 2014), Hillary Clinton follows this narrative of Brazilian meddling. Brazilian foreign

minister at the time, Celso Amorim, has published his own memoirs, in which he states that Clinton knew of the Brazilian plan in advance and did nothing to alter the timing of Lula's visit (*Breves narrativas diplomáticas* [Rio de Janeiro: TAEDA, 2014]).

41. The Brazilian literature on foreign policy has become enormous. There are several journals dedicated to international affairs and a burgeoning production of books and articles chronicling the ongoing debate. See, for example, Gelson Fonseca Jr., "Notes on the Evolution of Brazil's Multilateral Diplomacy," *Global Governance*, 17.3 (2011): 374–397; Luis L. Schenoni, "Brasil en América del Sur," *Nueva sociedad*, 250 (2014): 138–149 denies that Brazil is a true hegemon; José Augusto Guilhon Albuquerque, "A liderança do Brasil na America do Sul—2002/2012," in Bernardo Sorj and Sergio Fausto, eds., *O Brasil e a Governança da América Latina: Que tipo de liderança e possivel?* (São Paulo: Fundação iFHC and Centro Edelstein, 2013) argues that the scheme to use regional influence as a springboard to global agency is confused. Also see the online publications of Sobreet; Rubens Barbosa, *The Washington Dissensus: A Privileged Observer's Perspective on US-Brazilian Relations* (Nashville, TN: Vanderbilt University Press, 2014). For more than a decade, Guilhon Albuquerque, a critical figure in the hemispheric epistemological community, edited a seminal newsletter on foreign affairs, *Carta Internacional*, as part of the graduate program in international relations at the University of São Paulo. *The Carta* has been resurrected by the Brazilian International Relations Association and is available on the website for SciELO (http://www.scielo.br).

42. Luis Leandro Schenoni, "The Brazilian Rise and the Elusive South American Balance," GIGA Working Papers no. 269, March 2015. In an interview during his stay at Harvard, former minister Celso Amorim, in referring to Brazil's role in South America, said that "[Brazil] is a gentle hegemon," suggesting that the United States was not gentle. "Celso Amorim discusses Brazil's role in the world and US-Brazil ties," July 8, 2011. Unpublished text in possession of the author. A gentle Argentine summary of Brazil's difficulties in achieving its global pretensions is Federico Merke, "Brasil y tres lecciones para los emergentes," *La Nación*, November 1, 2015, A5. A summary of Brazil's case for being a global player is Juan Bracy, "Brazil and UN Peacekeeping . . ." *Contexto international* 33.2 (2011).

43. Some analysts would call this strategic culture. The problem with this culture is that it seeks to minimize costs without necessarily maximizing benefits.

44. Sean Burges, "Consensual Hegemony: Theorizing Brazilian Foreign Policy," *International Relations* 22.1 (2008) and "Brazil's International Development Co-operation: Old and New Motivations," *Development Policy Review* 32.3 (2014): 355–374. The richness of the academic and media debate enhances Brazilian influence.

45. Joseph S. Tulchin, "New Peru-Chile Maritime Boundary Ends Century-Old-Dispute," *Geopolitical Information Service*, February 12, 2014, http://gisweb.rapidpublish.info/en/geopolitics/new-peru-chile-maritime-bondary-ends-century-old-dispute.

46. Muñoz had been successful in doing the same thing a decade earlier in forming MINUSTAH, the UN peacekeeping effort in Haiti.

47. The Chilean Ministry of Defense denies that it has a blue-water navy. They emphasize that their maritime force is suited for rescue missions, not the projection of power. The US Chief of Naval Operations lists Chile as one of two countries in the hemisphere with a blue-water navy.

48. It is fair to note that polarization and political dysfunction on occasion weakens US exercise of its agency as well.

49. The only other such funds in the hemisphere are Venezuela, which uses PDVSA as its bank, and Colombia, which has not yet put any money into the fund.

50. This disposition to play by the rules will be put to the test by the International Court's decision to recognize its competence to deal with the disagreement between Bolivia and Chile. On the other hand, having the court take up the dispute may be a

blessing in disguise for the government of Chile, which can hide behind the court in any settlement that involves the cession of territory to Bolivia. For Chilean government responses to the court's decision, see http://www.chileantelahaya.gob.cl.

51. The use of foreign policy as an instrument of domestic politics is detailed in the FIU study of strategic culture, Felix E. Martin and Marvin L. Astrada, *Argentine Strategic Culture*, Findings Report 9 (Miami: Florida International University Press, 2010).

52. The concept of pari passu, treat all the same, is precisely what Carlos Calvo worried about in the nineteenth century as an excuse for intervention by more powerful countries.

53. The supreme court of Ghana embargoed the Argentine training vessel *Libertad* at the request of the one of the funds. The federal court in Las Vegas is investigating bags of money the Kirchners may or may not be laundering.

54. Carlos Calvo would have enjoyed the wording of the resolution because it explicitly calls on the parties to ignore pari passu in dealing with creditors.

55. Two Mexicans, Carlos Rico and Arturo Sarukhán, deserve mention for their roles in formulating Mexican policy toward the United States and for the successes in dealing with the US Congress.

56. The CIDE public opinion project has already been cited. The changing debate on security is in Sergio Aguayo Quezada and Raúl Benítez Manaut, eds., *Atlas de la seguridad y de la defensa de México, 2012* (Mexico: CASEDE, 2012). On the current debate over foreign policy, Guadalupe González González and Olga Pellicer, eds., *La política exterior de México: Metas y obstaculos* (Mexico: ITAM and Siglo XXI, 2013); Humberto Garza Elizondo, Jorge A. Schiavon, and Rafael Vázquez Flores, eds., *Balance y perspectivas de la política exterior de México, 2006–2012* (Mexico: El Colegio de Mexico, 2014). As part of this resurgence, CIDE re-created its old center for the study of the United States and began a new series of publications; Luis Maira and Gustavo Vega, eds., *El segundo mandato de Obama* (Mexico: CIDE, 2013).

57. Andrew Selee, "¿Una estrategia hacia Centroamérica?," *El universal*, July 19, 2014, http://www.eluniversalmas.com.mx/editoriales/2014/07/71405.php; Randal C. Archibold, "Trying to Slow the Illegal Flow of Young Migrants," *New York Times*, July 21, 2014, A7.

58. See, for example, the statement by the new president of Honduras, Juan Orlando Hernández, "La guerra al narco es una guerra que no es nuestra" [The war on drugs is not our war], *El país*, October 4, 2014.

59. At this point, the discussion of fixing the Mexican problem of crime and violence does not appear to include the fact that the traffic in drugs depends on demand for the drugs in the United States, just as demand for cheap labor is a critical element in the illegal migration of Central Americans and Mexicans into the United States. On the question of impunity, the Argentine government suffers from this problem as well. It has been accused of covering up the terrorist bombings of the Israeli embassy and the Jewish Association Center (AMIA), which resulted in hundreds of deaths. The special prosecutor Alberto Nisman was found dead in his apartment in Buenos Aires in January 2015 and nothing has been done to clarify his death nor his accusations that president Fernández de Kirchner and her circle deliberately sabotaged the investigation in order to strike private deals with the government of Iran.

60. Cristina Eguizábal, "Central America," in Jorge Dominguez and Rafael Fernández de Castro, eds., *Contemporary US–Latin American Relations: Cooperation or Conflict in the 21st Century?* (New York: Routledge, 2010).

61. See http://www.Globalfirepower.com/countries-listing.asp. Uruguay ranks 109 out of the 126 countries on the list; Brazil, at 22, is the highest-ranking Latin American country, Mexico is 31, and Chile is 43.

62. Michael Shifter, "Hay menos lugar para la retórica antiimperialista en la

región," *El Deber*, April 25, 2015. For a very different view, expressing angry anti-Americanism, see *Voces en el Fenix* 44 (2015), http://www.vocesenelfenix.com /category/ediciones/n%C2%BA-44.

63. Joe Nocera, "A World without OPEC?," *New York Times*, October 21, 2014, A25; Edward Glab, "Changing Global Energy Markets and the Impact on the Americas," Perspectives on the Americas, University of Miami, Center for Hemispheric Policy, April 9, 2015, https://umshare.miami.edu/web/wda/hemisphericpolicy /Perspectives_on_the_Americas/Glab%20-%20Final%20Paper.pdf.

64. "China's Global Ambitions, Cash and Strings Attached," *New York Times*, July 26, 2015, A1, 10, 11, 12. The Inter-American Dialogue, Boston University, and UNAM (Mexico) all maintain active websites that track Chinese investment in Latin America.

65. *New York Times*, April 12, 2015, A10.

66. www.nytimes.com/2014/10/20/opinion/cubas-impressive-role-on -ebola.html; www.atlanticphilanthropies.org/news/how-cuba-leading-international-fight-against-ebola.html.

67. "Too Few Carry Efforts for Peace," *New York Times*, July 29, 2015, A7.

68. Moisés Naím, "Los autogoles de la superpotencia," *El país*, May 9, 2015.

69. The twelve nations signing the agreement are the United States, Canada, Mexico, Japan, Australia, New Zealand, Singapore, Vietnam, Malaysia, Brunei, Peru, and Chile. They comprise 40 percent of the world's GDP and represent nearly $28 trillion in GDP. President Obama made his strategic objectives clear in pursuing this agreement: "When more than 95 percent of our customers live outside our borders, we can't let countries like China write the rules of the global economy.... We should write those rules,... while setting high standards for protecting workers and preserving our environment." www.nytimes.com/2015/10.06.business/trans-pacific-partnership-trade-deal-is-reached.html.

70. The index of global presence most followed in Latin America does not include Cuba in its list of important countries. Perhaps it should. On that list, Mexico is the most "present" Latin American country at 20, followed by Brazil (25), Venezuela (38), Argentina (39), Chile (43), and Colombia (44). *Elcano Global Presence Index* (2011), http://www.realinstitutoelcano.org.

Bibliography

Abelson, Don. "Energy Policy in the Western Hemisphere." Latin American Program, Woodrow Wilson Center, Working Paper no. 195. Washington, DC: Woodrow Wilson Center, 1991.

Aggarwal, Vinod K. *Debt Games*. New York: Cambridge University Press, 1996.

Aggarwal, Vinod K. "International Debt Threat: Bargaining among Creditors and Debtors in the 1980s." *Policy Papers in International Affairs* 29 (1987).

Aggarwal, Vinod K. "Reconciling Multiple Institutions: Bargaining, Linkages, and Nesting." In Vinod K. Aggarwal, ed., *Institutional Designs for a Complex World: Bargaining, Linkages, and Nesting*. Ithaca, NY: Cornell University Press, 1998, 1–32.

Aggarwal, Vinod K., Ralph Espach, and Joseph S. Tulchin, eds. *The Strategic Dynamics of Latin American Trade*. Stanford, CA: Stanford University Press, 2004.

Aguayo Quezada, Sergio, and Raúl Benítez Manaut, eds. *Atlas de la seguridad y de la defensa de México, 2012*. Mexico: CASEDE, 2012.

Aguirre, Mariano, and Ana Montes, eds. *De Bolívar al frente sandinista: Antología del pensamiento anti-imperialista latinoamerica*. Madrid: Ediciones de la Torre, 1979.

Allison, Graham T. *The Essence of Decision*. New York: Little, Brown, 1971.

Amorim, Celso, *Breves narrativas diplomáticas*. Rio de Janeiro: TAEDA, 2014.

Andrade, Oswald de. "Manifesto antropófago." *Revista de antropófago* 1 (1928).

Archibold, Randal C. "Trying to Slow the Illegal Flow of Young Migrants." *New York Times*, July 21, 2014, A7.

Arias, Óscar. "The Quest for a New World Leadership." Latin American Program, Woodrow Wilson Center, Working Paper no. 199. Washington, DC: Woodrow Wilson Center, 1992

Armony, Ariel C. "China in Latin America." University of Miami, 2013.

Armony, Ariel C. *The Dubious Link: Civic Engagement and Democratization*. Stanford, CA: Stanford University Press, 2004.

Armony, Ariel C., and Hector E. Schamis. "Babel in Democratization Studies." *Journal of Democracy* 16.4 (2005): 113–128.

Armony, Ariel C., Hector Schamis, and Giselle Cohen. *Repensando la Argentina: Antes de diciembre de 2001 y más allá de mayo de 2003*. Wilson Center Reports on the Americas 7. Washington, DC: Woodrow Wilson Center, 2003.

Arnson, Cynthia J., ed. *Comparative Peace Processes in Latin America*. Washington, DC: Wilson Center Press, 1999.

Arnson, Cynthia J., and Tamara Taraciuk, eds. *Argentina–United States Bilateral Relations*. Wilson Center Reports on the Americas 8. Washington, DC: Woodrow Wilson Center, 2003.

Azcárate, Pablo de. *La Guerra del 98*. Madrid: Alianza Editorial, 1968.

Bailey, Norman A. "The Inter-American System for the Maintenance of Peace and Security in the Western Hemisphere." Ph.D. dissertation. Columbia University, 1962.

Bailey, Norman A. *Latin America in World Politics*. New York: Walker, 1967.

Balze, Federico de la. "En la fase menguante de la globalización." *Clarín*, October 4, 2014, http://www.clarin.com/opinion/fase-menguanteglobalizacion_0_1222678042.html (accessed January 9, 2015).

Baran, Paul A. *The Political Economy of Growth*. New York: Monthly Review, 1957.

Barbero, José A., and Rodrigo Rodriguez Tornquist. "Transporte y cambio climático: Hacia un desarrollo sostenible y de bajo carbono." *Revista transporte y territorio* 6 (2012): 8–26.

Barbosa, Rubens. *The Washington Dissensus: A Privileged Observer's Perspective on US-Brazilian Relations*. Nashville, TN: Vanderbilt University Press, 2014.

Bastert, Russell H. "A New Approach to the Origins of Blaine's Pan American Policy." *Hispanic American Historical Review*, 39 (1959).

Bautista de Lavalle, Juan. *El Perú y la Gran Guerra*. Lima: Imprenta Americana, 1919.

Beelen, George D. "The Harding Administration and Mexico: Diplomacy by Economic Persuasion." *The Americas* 41.2 (1984): 177–189.

Bemis, Samuel F. *The Latin American Policy of the United States*. New York: Harcourt, Brace, 1943.

Benítez Manaut, Raúl. *Mexican Security and Defense Doctrines: From the 19th to the 21st Centuries*. Woodrow Wilson Center Update on the Americas: Creating Community 9. Washington, DC: WWICS, 2002.

Benítez Manaut, Raúl. *Seguridad hemisférica: Debates a inicios del siglo XXI*. Woodrow Wilson Center Update on the Americas: Creating Community 11. Washington, DC: WWICS, 2003.

Beruff, Jorge Rodriguez. *Los militares y el poder*. Lima: Mosca Azul, 1983.

Bethell, Leslie. *The Abolition of the Brazilian Slave Trade*. Cambridge: Cambridge University Press, 1970.

Bethell, Leslie. "Brazil and 'Latin America.'" *Journal of Latin American Studies* 42 (2010): 457–485.

Bethell, Leslie. "O Brasil entre a Europa, os Estados Unidos e a América Latina no pensamento de Joaquim Nabuco." *Novos estudos* 88 (2010): 73–87.

Bethell, Leslie, and Ian Roxborough, eds. *Latin America between the Second World War and the Cold War, 1944–1948*. Cambridge: Cambridge University Press, 1992.

Billington, R. A. *Western Expansion*. New York: Macmillan, 1949.

Bitar, Sergio. *Un futuro común Chile, Bolivia, Perú*. Santiago: Aguilar, 2011.

Bitar, Sergio, and Jorge Heine. "Chile y lo que está en juego en Siria." *El Mercurio*, September 13, 2013.

Bitencourt, Luis. *Defining Brazil's Security Agenda: From Favelas to the United Nations*. Woodrow Wilson Center Update on the Americas: Creating Community 23. Washington, DC: WWICS, 2006.

Bobea, Lilian. *La construcción de la seguridad democrática en el Caribe*. Woodrow Wilson Center Update on the Americas: Creating Community 25. Washington, DC: WWICS, 2006.

Bobea, Lilian. *Gobernabilidad de la seguridad en el Caribe.* Woodrow Wilson Center Update on the Americas: Creating Community 17. Washington, DC: WWICS, 2005.

Bonilla, Adrian. "La CELAC y su III Cumbre: Identidad estratégica y diferencias con la OEA." *Novedades FLACSO,* January 26, 2014.

Bowles, Samuel, et al. "Estimates of the Impact of the Free Trade Agreement on Direct US Investment in Mexico." Trade Policy Staff Committee Public Hearings. Boston, MA. September 11, 1991. Public testimony.

Box, Pelham H. *The Origins of the Paraguayan War.* Champaign: University of Illinois Press, 1930.

Brands, Hal, *Latin America's Cold War.* Cambridge, MA: Harvard University Press, 2012.

Bresser Pereira, Luiz Carlos, José María Maravall, and Adam Przeworski. *Economic Reforms in New Democracies: A Social-Democratic Approach.* Cambridge: Cambridge University Press, 1993.

Brockett, Charles D. *Political Movements and Violence in Central America.* New York: Cambridge University Press, 2005.

Brum, Baltasar. *American Solidarity.* Montevideo: Imprenta Nacional, 1920.

Bruni, Frank. "Obama's Messy Words." *New York Times,* September 1, 2014, A19.

Bryan, Elizabeth, ed. *Understanding Cuba.* Woodrow Wilson Center Update on the Americas: Creating Community 26. Washington, DC: WWICS, 2007.

Bryan, Elizabeth, Cynthia J. Arnson, José Raúl Perales, and Johanna Mendelson Forman. *Governance and Security in Haiti: Can the International Community Make a Difference?* Woodrow Wilson Center Update on the Americas: Creating Community 27. Washington, DC: WWICS, 2007.

Bull, Hedley. *The Anarchical Society: A Study of Order in World Politics.* New York: Columbia University Press, 1977.

Bunge, Alejandro. *El desarrollo en la Argentina.* Buenos Aires: Banco de la nación, 1924.

Burbach, Roger, Michael Fox, and Federico Fuentes, *Latin America's Turbulent Transitions—The Future of Twenty-First-Century Socialism.* New York: Zed, 2013.

Burges, Sean. "Brazil's International Development Co-operation: Old and New Motivations." *Development Policy Review* 32.3 (2014): 355–374.

Burges, Sean. "Consensual Hegemony: Theorizing Brazilian Foreign Policy," *International Relations* 22.1 (2008).

Burr, Robert N. *By Reason or Force.* Berkeley: University of California Press, 1965.

Calleo, David P. *Beyond American Hegemony.* New York: Basic Books, 1987.

Camus, Albert. *The Rebel.* New York: Doubleday, 1965.

Cancino, Francisco Cuevas. *Bolívar el ideal panamericano del libertador.* Mexico: Fondo de Cultura, 1951.

Cardona, Diego, Carlo Nasi, Liliana Obregón, Arlene B. Tickner, and Juan Gabriel Tokatlián. *Colombia-Venezuela: Crisis o negociacion?* Bogota: FESCOL, 1992.

Cardoso, Fernando Henrique. *Charting a New Course: The Politics of Globalization and Social Transformation.* New York: Rowman and Littlefield, 2001.

Cardoso, Fernando Henrique, and Enzo Faletto. *Dependencia y desarrollo.* Mexico: Siglo XXI, 1969.

Cardozo, Efraím. *El imperio del Brasil y el Rio de la Plata.* Buenos Aires: Librería del Plata, 1961.

Carothers, Thomas. *In the Name of Democracy.* Berkeley: University of California Press, 1991.

Chambers, Sarah. *From Subjects to Citizens: Honor, Gender and Politics in Arequipa, Peru, 1780–1854.* State College: Pennsylvania State University Press, 1999.

Chase, Robert, Emily Hill, and Paul Kennedy, eds. *The Pivotal States.* New York: Norton, 1999.

Chasteen, John C. *Americanos.* New York: Oxford University Press, 2008.

Chasteen, John C. *Heroes on Horseback.* Albuquerque: University of New Mexico Press, 1995.

Chasteen, John C., and Sara Castro-Klaren, eds. *Beyond Imagined Communities: Reading and Writing the Nation in Nineteenth-Century Latin America.* Washington, DC: Woodrow Wilson Center Press, 2003.

Child, Jack. *The Central American Peace Process, 1983–1991.* Boulder, CO: Lynne Rienner, 1992.

"China en el Congreso." *La política online,* July 19, 2014, http://www.lapoliticaonline.com/nota/82066 (accessed January 9, 2015).

Christensen, Thomas J. *The China Challenge Shaping the Choices of a Rising Power.* New York: Norton, 2015.

Cid, Gabriel. "En defensa de la 'Patria Grande': Guerra e imaginario en el Chile de los 1860s." Paper presented at the seminar Arma Virumque: Estado, nación y guerra en América Latina, 1810–1895, Centro de Estudios Bicentenario-Perú/Cooperación Regional Francesa para los Países Andinos. Lima, July 4, 2012.

Cid, Gabriel. *La Guerra contra la Confederación. Imaginario nacionalista y memoria colectiva en el siglo XIX chilena.* Santiago: Ediciones Universidad Diego Portales, 2011.

Cisneros, Andrés, and Carlos Escudé. *Historia general de las relaciones exteriores de la república Argentina.* 20 vols. Buenos Aires: Grupo Editor, 2000.

Clinton, Hillary. *Hard Choices.* New York: Simon and Schuster, 2014.

Clinton, Richard L., "The Modernizing Military: The Case of Peru." *Inter-American Economic Affairs* 24.4 (1971).

Coates, Benjamin A. "The Pan-American Lobbyist: William Elroy Curtis and U.S. Empire, 1884–1899." *Diplomatic History* 38.1 (2014).

Coatsworth, John H. *Central America and the United States: The Clients and the Colossus.* New York: Twayne, 1994.

Coatsworth, John H. "Inequality, Institutions, and Economic Growth." *Journal of Latin American Studies,* 40 (2008).

Coatsworth, John H. "Structures, Endowments, Institutions and Growth in Latin American Economic History." *Latin American Research Review* 40.3 (2005).

Cohen, Benjamin J. *Building Bridges: The Construction of International Political Economy.* Princeton, NJ: Princeton University Press, 2008.

Cohen, Benjamin J. *International Political Economy: An Intellectual History.* Princeton, NJ: Princeton University Press, 2008.

Cohen, Giselle, and Rut Diamint. *La seguridad hemisférica: Una mirada desde el sur de las Américas.* Woodrow Wilson Center Update on the Americas: Creating Community 15. Washington, DC: WWICS, 2003.

Collier, Simon. *Chile: The Making of a Republic, 1830–1865.* New York: Cambridge University Press, 2003.

Collins, Gail. "A Man with a Plan." *New York Times,* September 11, 2014, A27.

Conn, Stetson, and Byron Fairchild. *The Western Hemisphere: The Framework of Hemispheric Defense.* 2 vols. Washington, DC: Office of the Chief of Military History, Department of the Army, 1960.

Conway, Ed. *The Summit: Bretton Woods, 1944: J. M. Keynes and the Reshaping of the Global Economy.* New York: Pegasus Books, 2015.

Coolidge, Archibald C. *The United States as a World Power.* New York: Macmillan, 1908.

Cooper, Andrew F., and Thomas Legler. *Intervention without Intervening?* New York: Palgrave Macmillan, 2006.

Corrales, Javier, and Richard E. Feinberg. "Regimes of Cooperation in the Western

Hemisphere: Power, Interests, and Intellectual Traditions." *International Studies Quarterly* 43.1 (1999): 1–36.

Cotler, Julio, and Richard R. Fagen. *Latin America and the United States: The Changing Political Realities.* Stanford, CA: Stanford University Press, 1974.

Couto e Silva, Golbery do. *Geopolitico do Brasil.* Rio de Janeiro: Jose Olympio, 1967.

Couto e Silva, Golbery do. *Planejamento estratégico.* Rio de Janeiro: Biblioteca de Exercito, Rio, 1955.

Crahan, Margaret E. *Whither Cuba? The Role of Religion.* Woodrow Wilson Center Update on the Americas: Creating Community 14. Washington, DC: WWICS, 2003.

Danelski, David J., and Joseph S. Tulchin, eds. *The Autobiographical Notes of Charles Evans Hughes.* Cambridge, MA: Harvard University Press, 1973.

Darnton, Christopher. "After Decentering: The Politics of Agency and Hegemony in Hemispheric Relations," *Latin American Research Review* 48.3 (2013).

de la Reza, German A. "The Formative Platform of the Congress of Panama (1810–1826): The Pan-American Conjecture Revisited." *Revista brasileira de política internacional* 56.1 (2013).

Deustua, Alejandro. "La política exterior peruana." *La república,* January 26, 2001.

Diamint, Rut. "América Latina en la agenda global." In José Antonio Sanahuja and Celestino del Arenal, eds., *América Latina y los bicentenarios: Una agenda de futuro tras 200 años de independencia.* Madrid: Siglo XXI, 2010.

Diamint, Rut. "Amérique latine: Une course aux armements?" *Cahiers d'Amérique Latine* 63 (2010): 117–131.

Diamint, Rut. "Conducción civil de las políticas de defensa." In Marcela Donadío, ed., *La reconstrucción de la seguridad nacional: Defensa, democracia y cuestión militar en América Latina.* Buenos Aires: Prometeo, 2010.

Diamint, Rut. "Confianza y conflicto en América Latina." In Julio César Theiler, Claudio Maíz, and Luis Felipe Agramunt, eds., *Los desafíos de la integración en el siglo XXI.* Santa Fé, Argentina: Universidad Nacional del Litoral, 2011, 145–154.

Diamint, Rut. "La historia sin fin: El control civil de los militares en Argentina." *Nueva Sociedad* 213 (2008): 95–111.

Diamint, Rut. "Latin America and the Military Subject Reexamined." In David Mares, ed., *Debating Civil-Military Relations in Latin America.* Sussex: Academic Press, 2014.

Diamint, Rut. "A More Secure Hemisphere?" In Gordon Mace, Andrew F. Cooper, and Timothy M. Shaw, eds., *Inter-American Cooperation at a Crossroads: 2010 Onwards.* Basingstoke, UK: Palgrave, 2011.

Diamint, Rut. "Nouveaux profils de pouvoir militaire." In David Mares, ed., *Armees et pouvoirs en Amerique Latine.* Paris: IHEAL, 2004.

Diamint, Rut. "Regionalismo y posicionamiento suramericano. El papel de UNASUR y ALBA." *Revista CIDOB d'afers internacionals* 101 (2013): 55–79.

Diamint, Rut. "Security Communities, Defence Policy Integration and Peace Operations in the Southern Cone: An Argentine Perspective." *International Peacekeeping* 17.5 (2010): 662–667.

Diamint, Rut. *Sin gloria.* Buenos Aires: EUDEBA, 2015.

Diamint, Rut, ed. *Control civil y fuerzas armadas en las nuevas democracias latinoamericana.* Buenos Aires: University Torcuato di Tella, 1999.

Diamint, Rut, and Arlene B. Tickner. *Percepciones hemisféricas sobre la crisis colombiana.* Woodrow Wilson Center Update on the Americas: Creating Community 16. Washington, DC: WWICS, 2005.

Domínguez, Jorge I. *Cuba: Order and Revolution.* Cambridge, MA: Harvard University Press, 2009.

Domínguez, Jorge I. *To Make a World Safe for Revolution: Cuba's Foreign Policy.* Cambridge, MA: Harvard University Press, 1987.

Domínguez, Jorge I., and Ana Covarrubias, eds. *Routledge Handbook of Latin America in the World*. New York: Routledge, 2015.

Domínguez, Jorge I., and Rafael Fernández de Castro, eds. *Contemporary US-Latin American Relations*. New York: Routledge, 2010.

Dornbusch, Rudiger, and Sebastian Edwards, eds. *Macroeconomía del populismo en la América Latina*. Mexico: Fondo de Cultura Económica, 1992.

Draibe, Sônia M. "Social Policy Reform." In Mauricio Font and Anthony Peter Spanakos, eds., *Reforming Brazil*. Lanham, MD: Lexington Books, 2004.

Drake, Paul. *The Money Doctors in the Andes*. Durham, NC: Duke University Press, 1989.

Drekonja, Gerhard. "Autonomía periférica redefinida: América Latina en la década de los noventa." In María Mercedes Gómez, Gerhard Drekonja, Juan Gabriel Tokatlián, and Leonardo Carvajal, "Redefiniendo la autonomía en política internacional," *Documentos ocasionales*, CEI [Colombia] 31 (1993).

Eguizábal, Cristina. *Armies in Times of Peace: The Division of Labor Between the Armed Forces and Police*. Woodrow Wilson Center Update on the Americas: Creating Community 8. Washington, DC: WWICS, 2002.

Eguizábal, Cristina. "Central America." In Jorge Dominguez and Rafael Fernández de Castro, eds., *Contemporary US–Latin American Relations: Cooperation or Conflict in the 21st Century?* New York: Routledge, 2010.

Eguizábal, Cristina, ed., *America Latina y la crisis centro-americana: En busca de una solución regional*. Buenos Aires: GEL, 1989.

Einaudi, Luigi. "Revolution from Within? Military Rule in Peru since 1968." *Studies in Comparative Development*, 8.1 (1973).

Ellis, L. Ethan. *Frank B. Kellogg and American Foreign Policy*. New Brunswick, NJ: Rutgers University Press, 1961.

Escudé, Carlos. *La Argentina: ¿Paria internacional?* Buenos Aires: Belgrano, 1984.

Etchepareborda, Roberto. "Zeballos y la política exterior argentina," *Estrategia y Política* (Buenos Aires: Pleamar, 1980).

Fagen, Richard R., ed. *Capitalism and the State in US–Latin American Relations*. Stanford, CA: Stanford University Press, 1979.

Feinberg, Richard, Emily Miller, and Harold Trinkunas. "Better than You Think: Reframing Inter-American Relations." Brookings Policy Brief, March 2015.

Ferrell, Robert H. *Peace in Their Time*. New Haven, CT: Yale University Press, 1952.

Finchelstein, Federico. *Transatlantic Fascism*. Durham, NC: Duke University Press, 2010.

Fiori, José Luis, Carlos Medeiros, and Franklin Serrano. *The Myth of the Collapse of American Power*. Rio de Janeiro: Editora Record, 2008.

Fitch, J. Samuel. *Bridging the Conceptual Gap: Latin American Views of Democracy, Politics, and Policy*. Woodrow Wilson Center Update on the Americas: Creating Community 2. Washington, DC: WWICS, 2002.

Fonseca, Gelson, Jr. "Notes on the Evolution of Brazil's Multilateral Diplomacy." *Global Governance* 17.3 (2011): 375–397.

Frechette, Myles. "United States–Latin American Relations." American University, Washington, DC, June 1992.

Freyre, Gilberto, *New World in the Tropics The Culture of Modern Brazil* New York: Knopf, 1959

Friedman, Edward. "Succeeding in the Third World, Except Asia." In Lowell Dittmer and Maochun Yu, eds., *Routledge Handbook of Chinese Security*. New York: Routledge, 2015.

Friedman, Max Paul. *Nazis and the Good Neighbor: The United States Campaign Against the Germans of Latin America in World War II*. New York: Cambridge University Press, 2003.

Friedman, Max Paul. *Rethinking Anti-Americanism: The History of an Exceptional Concept in American Foreign Relations.* New York: Cambridge University Press, 2013.

Friedman, Max Paul, and Tom Long, "Soft Balancing in the Americas: Latin American Opposition to U.S. Intervention, 1898–1936." *International Security* Summer 2015

Friedman, Thomas L. "And Now for a Bit of Good News...." *New York Times,* July 20, 2014, SR1, 11.

Friedman, Thomas L. *The Lexus and the Olive Tree.* New York: Farrar, Straus and Giroux, 1999.

Friedman, Thomas L. "Order vs. Disorder, Part 2." *New York Times,* July 16, 2014, A23.

Friedman, Thomas L. *The World Is Flat.* New York: Farrar, Straus and Giroux, 2005.

Fuentes, Claudio, ed. *Bajo la mirada del halcón.* Santiago: FLACSO, 2004.

Fukuyama, Francis. "The End of History?" *National Interest* 16 (1989): 3–18.

Fukuyama, Francis. *The End of History and the Last Man.* New York: Free Press, 1992.

Galeano, Eduardo. *Las venas abiertas de America Latina.* Buenos Aires: Siglo XXI, 1971.

Garcia-Suarez, Marcial A., Rafael A. D. Villa and Brigitte Weiffen, eds., *Power Dynamics and Regional Security in Latin America.* London: Palgrave, 2016.

Gardini, Gian Luca, and Peter Lambert. *Latin American Foreign Policies: Between Ideology and Pragmatism.* London: Palgrave, 2011.

Gardner, Lloyd. *Safe for Democracy: The Anglo-American Response to Revolution, 1913–1923.* New York: Oxford University Press, 1984.

Garretón, Manuel Antonio, Marcelo Cavarozzi, Peter S. Cleaves, Gary Gereffi, and Jonathan Hartlyn. *Latin America in the 21st Century.* Miami: North-South Center, 2003.

Garza Elizondo, Humberto, Jorge A. Schiavon, and Rafael Vázquez Flores, eds. *Balance y perspectivas de la política exterior de México, 2006–2012.* Mexico: El Colegio de Mexico, 2014.

Gil, Federico G. *Latin American United States Relations.* New York: Harcourt Brace, 1971.

Gilbert, Felix. *To the Farewell Address: Ideas of Early American Foreign Policy.* Princeton, NJ: Princeton University Press, 1961.

Ginzparg, Melina. *Diplomacia subregional: Cooperación y seguridad en América del Sur.* Woodrow Wilson Center Update on the Americas: Creating Community 18. Washington, DC: WWICS, 2005.

Ginzparg, Melina. *Taller de reflexión: "Diplomacia subregional: Cooperación y seguridad en América del Sur."* Woodrow Wilson Center Update on the Americas: Creating Community 19. Washington, DC: WWICS, 2005.

Glab, Edward. "Changing Global Energy Markets and the Impact on the Americas." Perspectives on the Americas, University of Miami, Center for Hemispheric Policy, April 9, 2015, https://umshare.miami.edu/web/wda/hemisphericpolicy/Perspectives_on_the_Americas/Glab%20-%20Final%20Paper.pdf.

Gleijeses, Piero. *Shattered Hope: The Guatemalan Revolution and the United States, 1944–1954.* Princeton, NJ: Princeton University Press, 1991.

Gobat, Michel. *Confronting the American Dream: Nicaragua under U.S. Imperial Rule.* Durham, NC: Duke University Press, 2005.

Golding, Heather A. *Challenges to Creating Community in the Americas.* Woodrow Wilson Center Update on the Americas: Creating Community 3. Washington, DC: WWICS, 2002.

Golding, Heather A. *Terrorism and the Triple Frontier.* Woodrow Wilson Center Update on the Americas: Creating Community 4. Washington, DC: WWICS, 2002.

Golding, Heather A. *US Drug Certification and the Search for a Multilateral Alternative.* Woodrow Wilson Center Update on the Americas: Creating Community 1. Washington, DC: WWICS, 2001.

Gomez-Mera, Laura. "The Diffusion of Global Prohibition Norms: Sex, Labor, and Organ Trafficking." Paper presented at the Annual Meeting of the Internaitonal Studies Association, San Francisco, 2013.

Gomez-Mera, Laura. "The Impact of International Agreements against Human Trafficking: Evidence from Latin America." Paper presented at the annual meeting of the Latin American Studies Association, San Francisco, May 23–26, 2012.

Gomez-Mera, Laura. *Power and Regionalism in Latin America: The Politics of Mercosur.* South Bend, IN: University of Notre Dame Press, 2013.

González, Guadalupe González. "México en América Latina: Entre el Norte y el Sur o el deficil juego del equilibrista." In Ricardo Lagos, ed., *America Latina: ¿Integracion o fragmentacion?* Buenos Aires: Edhasa, 2008.

González, Guadalupe González. "Un siglo de política exterior mexicana (1910–2010): Del nacionalismo revolucionario a la intemperie global." In Maria Amparo Casar and Guadalupe González González, eds., *México 2010: El juicio del siglo.* Mexico: Editorial Taurus, 2010.

González, Guadalupe González, and Olga Pellicer, eds. *La política exterior de México: Metas y obstaculos.* Mexico: ITAM and Siglo XXI, 2013.

González, Guadalupe González, Jorge A. Schiavon, David Crow, and Gerardo Maldonado. *The Americas and the World, 2010–2011: Public Opinion and Foreign Policy in Brazil, Colombia, Ecuador, Mexico, and Peru.* Mexico: CIDE, 2011.

González, Guadalupe González, Jorge A. Schiavon, Gerardo Maldonado, Rodrigo Morales Castillo, and David Crow. *México, Las Américas y el mundo, 2012–2013.* Mexico: CIDE, 2013.

Graham, Otis L., Jr., "The Uses and Misuses of History: Roles in Policymaking." *Public Historian* 5.2 (1983).

Grandin, Greg. "Halfway In with Obama." *New York Times*, April 24, 2011, WK1, 5.

Grandin, Greg. "The Pentagon's New Monroe Doctrine." *The Nation*, February 8, 2010, 9–12.

Gray, C. S. "Strategic Culture as Context: The First Generation of Theory Strikes Back." *Review of International Studies* 25.1 (1999).

Green, Rosario. *Encuentros y desencuentros: Desafios iberoamericanos.* Madrid: SECIB, n.d.

Gregario-Cernadas, Maximiliano G. *Vestigios conceptuales del idealismo kantiano en las ideas e instituciones que confirguraron la política de seguridad eternal del gobierno de Alfonsin.* Collection of Joseph S. Tulchin, Brookline, MA, n.d.

Grinspun, Ricardo, and Maxwell A. Cameron, eds. *The Political Economy of North American Free Trade.* New York: St. Martin's, 1993.

Guardino, Peter. *Peasants, Politics, and the Formation of Mexico's National State: Guerrero, 1800–1857.* Stanford, CA: Stanford University Press, 1996.

Guardino, Peter. *The Time of Liberty: Popular Political Culture in Oaxaca, 1750–1850.* Durham, NC: Duke University Press, 2005.

Guilhon Albuquerque, Jose Augusto. "A liderança do Brasil na America do Sul— 2002/2012." In Bernardo Sorj and Sergio Fausto, eds., *O Brasil e a governancada América Latina: Que tipo de lieranca e posssivel?* São Paulo: Fundacao iFHC and Centro Edelstein, 2013.

Guzmán, German, Orlando Fals Borda, and Eduardo Umaña Luna. *La violencia en Colombia.* 2 vols. Bogotá: Tercer Mundo, 1962.

Hakim, Peter. "The Enterprise for the Americas Initiative: What Washington Wants." *Brookings Review* 10.4 (1992): 42–45.

Hakim, Peter. "President Bush's Southern Strategy: The Enterprise for the Americas Initiative." *Washington Quarterly*, 15.2 (1992): 93–106.

Halperin Donghi, Tulio, Ivan Jaksic, Gwen Kirkpatrick, et. al. *Sarmiento: Author of a Nation?* Berkeley: University of California Press, 1994.

Hardy, Clarisa. *A New Generation of Social Reforms.* Woodrow Wilson Center Update on the Americas: Creating Community 6. Washington, DC: WWICS, 2002.

Harrison, Benjamin T. *Dollar Diplomat: Chandler Anderson and American Diplomacy in Mexico and Nicaragua, 1913–1928.* Pullman: Washington State University Press, 1988.

Hart, Alberto B. *The Monroe Doctrine: An Interpretation.* Boston: Little, Brown, 1916.

Haseler, Stephen. *The Varieties of Anti-Americanism: Reflex and Response.* Washington, DC: Ethics and Public Policy Center, 1985.

Hernández, Juan Orlando. "La guerra al narco es una guerra que no es nuestra." *El país*, October 4, 2014, http://internacional.elpais.com/internacional/2014/10/01 /actualidad/1412199282_188307.html (accessed January 9, 2015).

Herrera, Octavio, and Arturo Santa Cruz. *América del Norte.* Historia de las relaciones internacionales de México, 1821–2010, 1. Mexico: Secretaría de Relaciones Exteriores, Dirección General del Archivo Histórico Diplomático, 2011.

Herz, Monica. *The Organization of American States.* New York: Routledge, 2011.

Hilton, Stanley. *Brazil and the Great Powers.* Austin: University of Texas Press, 1976.

Hilton, Stanley. *German Military Espionage and Allied Counter Espionage in Brazil.* Baton Rouge: Louisiana State University Press, 1981.

Hixson, Walter L. *The Myth of American Diplomacy: National Identity and US Foreign Policy.* New Haven, CT: Yale University Press, 2008.

Hoetink, Harry. *The Two Variants in Caribbean Race Relations.* New York: Oxford University Press, 1967.

Hogan, Michael, and Thomas Paterson, eds. *Explaining the History of American Foreign Relations.* 2nd ed. New York: Cambridge University Press, 2004.

Homeland Security and the Bilateral Relationship between the United States and Argentina. Woodrow Wilson Center Update on the Americas: Creating Community 24. Washington, DC: WWICS, 2006.

Hunt, Michael H. *The American Ascendancy: How the United States Gained and Wielded Global Dominance.* Chapel Hill: University of North Carolina Press, 2007.

Hunt, Michael H. *Ideology and US Foreign Policy.* 2nd ed. New Haven, CT: Yale University Press, 2009.

Ikenberry, John. *New Thinking in International Relations.* Boulder, CO: Westview, 1997.

Ikenberry, John, Anne-Marie Slaughter, Thomas J. Knok, and Tony Smith. *The Crisis of American Foreign Policy: Wilsonianism in the Twenty-First Century.* Princeton, NJ: Princeton University Press, 2008.

Irizarry y Puente, J. "The Doctrines of Recognition and Intervention in Latin America." *Tulane Law Review* 28.3 (1954): 313–342.

Joffe, Josef. *The Limited Partnership.* Cambridge, MA: Ballinger, 1987.

Joffe, Josef. *The Myth of America's Decline: Politics, Economics and a Half Century of False Prophecies.* New York: Liveright/Norton, 2013.

Kagan, Robert. "Superpowers Don't Get to Retire." *New Republic*, May 26, 2014. http://www.newrepublic.com/article/117859/allure-normalcy-what-america-still -owes-world (accessed January 9, 2015).

Kaltenthaler, Karl, and Frank O. Mora. "Explaining Latin American Economic Integration: The Case of Mercosur." *Review of International Political Economy* 9.1 (2002).

Kamman, William. *A Search for Stability: United States Diplomacy toward Nicaragua 1925–1933.* South Bend, IN: University of Notre Dame Press, 1968.

Katz, Julius. Congressional testimony. Hearing Before the United States Senate Finance Committee, 102nd Congress, 1st Session. Dirksen Senate Office Building, Washington, DC, April 24, 1991.

Kaufman, Robert R., and Joan Nelson. *The Politics of Education Sector Reform: Cross-National Comparisons.* Woodrow Wilson Center Update on the Americas: Creating Community 13. Washington, DC: WWICS, 2003.

Keck, Margaret. *Activists Beyond Borders: Advocacy Networks in International Politics.* Ithaca, NY: Cornell University Press, 1998.

Kennedy, Paul. *The Rise and Fall of the Great Powers.* New York: Random House, 1987.

Kenworthy, Eldon. *America/Americas: Myth in the Making of US Policy Towards Latin America.* State College: Pennsylvania State University Press, 1995.

Kiernan, V. G. "Foreign Intervention in the War of the Pacific." *Hispanic American Historical Review* 35 (1955).

Kissinger, Henry. "Unsolved Problems." In *Lisbon 1992: The Annual Meeting of the Trilateral Commission.* Paris: Trilateral Commission, 1992.

Klepak, Hal. *Confidence Building Sidestepped: The Peru-Ecuador Conflict of 1995.* Ottawa: FOCAL/York University Press, 1998.

Knorr, Klaus, and James N. Rosenau, eds. *Contending Approaches to International Politics.* Princeton, NJ: Princeton University Press, 1967.

Kornegay, Francis A., Jr., and Narnia Bohler-Muller, eds. *Laying the BRICS of a New Global Order.* Pretoria: Africa Institute of South Africa, 2013.

Kramer, Paul A. *The Blood of Government: Race, Empire, the United States and the Philippines.* Chapel Hill: University of North Carolina Press, 2006.

Krautheimer, Charles. *Democratic Realism: An American Foreign Policy for a Unipolar World.* Washington, DC: American Enterprise Institute, 2004.

Krieger, Joel. *Reagan, Thatcher and the Politics of Decline.* New York: Oxford University Press, 1987.

Kristof, Nicholas. "Critique from an Obama Fan." *New York Times*, September 11, 2014, http://www.nytimes.com/2014/09/11/opinion/nicholas-kristof-critique-from-an-obama-fan.html?_r=0 (accessed January 9, 2015).

Lafer, Celso. Mudam-se Os Tempos. São Paulo: Fundação Alijandre de Gusmão, 2001.

Lahitte, Emilio. *Informes y estudios I.* Buenos Aires: Sociedad Rural Argentina, 1914.

Lamounier, Bolivar, ed., *A Era FHC: Um balanço.* (São Paulo: Cultura Editores, 2002).

Lantis, J. S. "Strategic Culture and National Security Policy." *International Studies Review*, 4.3 (2003).

Lanús, Archibaldo. "Una perspectiva desde Genebra." Relaciones Argentina-EEUU, FLACSO. Buenos Aires, March 6, 1992.

Lapid, Yosef, and F. V. Kratochwil, eds. *The Return of Culture and Identity to IR Theory.* Boulder, CO: Lynne Rienner, 1996.

Leiva Lavalle, Patricio, ed. *Analisis del fallo de la haya y perspectivas para las relaciones entre Chile y Perú.* Santiago: Universidad Miguel de Cervantes, 2014.

Levitsky, Steven, and Lucan A. Way. *Competitive Authoritarianism.* New York: Cambridge University Press, 2010.

Levitsky, Steven, and Lucan A. Way. "International Linkage and Democratization." *Journal of Democracy* 16.3 (2005).

Levitsky, Steven, and Lucan A. Way. "Linkage versus Leverage." *Comparative Politics* 38.4 (2006).

Link, Arthur. *Wilson: The Struggle for Neutrality, 1914–1915.* Princeton, NJ: Princeton University Press, 1960.

Lins da Silva, Carlos Eduardo. "Futbol, paz e riscos paro o Brasil no Haiti," *Política Externa* 13.2 (2004).

Litwak, Robert. *Outlier States: American Strategies to Contain, Engage, or Change Regimes*. Baltimore, MD: Johns Hopkins University Press, 2012.

Litwak, Robert. *Regime Change: US Strategies Through the Prism of 9/11*. Baltimore, MD: Johns Hopkins University Press, 2007.

Litwak, Robert. *Rogue States*. Baltimore, MD: Johns Hopkins University Press, 1996.

Longley, Kyle. *The Sparrow and the Hawk: Costa Rica and the United States during the Rise of José Figueres*. Tuscaloosa: University of Alabama Press, 1997.

Lopez Muñoz, Ricardo. "El americanismo en Chile ante la expansión política y militar europea sobre Hispanoamérica (1861–1871)." Ph.D dissertation. University of Chile, 2011.

Love, Eric T. L. *Race Over Empire: Racism and US Imperialism, 1865–1900*. Chapel Hill: University of North Carolina Press, 2004.

Loveman, Brian. *No Higher Law: American Foreign Policy and the Western Hemisphere since 1776*. Chapel Hill: University of North Carolina Press, 2011.

Lowenthal, Abraham F. "Obama and the Americas." *Foreign Affairs* 89.4 (2010): 110–124.

Luna, Juan Pablo. "Representación política en América Latina: Hacia una nueva agenda de investigación." *Política y gobierno* 14.2 (2007).

Mahan, Alfred Thayer. *The Influence of Sea Power upon History, 1660–1783*. New York: Little, Brown, 1890.

Mahoney, James. *The Legacies of Liberalism: Path Dependence and Political Regimes in Central America*. Baltimore, MD: Johns Hopkins University Press, 2001.

Maira, Luis, et al. *Centroamérica, crisis y política internacional*. Mexico: Siglo XXI, 1982.

Maira, Luis, and Gustavo Vega, eds. *El segundo mandato de Obama*. Mexico: CIDE, 2013.

Mallon, Florencia. "Indigenous Peoples and Nation-States in Spanish America, 1780–2000." In Jose C. Moya, ed., *The Oxford Handbook of Latin American History*. New York: Oxford University Press, 2011.

Mallon, Florencia. *Peasant and Nation: The Making of Postcolonial Mexico and Peru*. Berkeley: University of California Press, 1994.

Malosetti Costa, Laura. *Los primeros modernos: Arte y sociedad en Buenos Aires* (Buenos Aires: Fondo de Cultura, 2001).

Malpass, David R. Testimony before the International Trade Commission. 1990.

Marcella, Gabriel, and Richard Downes, eds. *Security Cooperation in the Western Hemisphere: Resolving the Ecuador-Peru Conflict*. Miami: University of Miami Press, 1999.

Mares, David R. *Violent Peace: Militarized Interstate Bargaining in Latin America*. New York: Columbia University Press, 2001.

Mariátegui, José Carlos. *Siete ensayos de interpretación de la realidad peruana*. Lima: Biblioteca Amauta, 1928.

Marichal, Carlos, ed. *México y las conferencias panamericanas, 1889–1938*. Mexico: SRE, 2002.

Martin, Felix E. *Chilean Strategic Culture*. Findings Report 10. Miami: Florida International University Press, 2010.

Martin, Felix E., and Marvin L. Astrada. *Argentine Strategic Culture*. Findings Report 9. Miami: Florida International University Press, 2010.

Martin, Percy Allen. *Latin America and the War*. Baltimore, MD: Johns Hopkins University Press, 1925.

Martz, John D. "Justo Rufino Barrios and Central American Union." University of Florida Monographs no. 21. September 1962.

Mathews, Jessica T. "Power Shift." *Foreign Affairs* 76.1 (1997): 50–66.

Mauceri, Philip. *State Under Siege: Development and Policy Making in Peru*. Boulder, CO: Westview, 1998.

Maurer, Noel, and Carlos Yu. *The Big Ditch: How America Took, Built, Ran, and Ultimately Gave Away the Panama Canal.* Princeton, NJ: Princeton University Press, 2011.

May, Ernest R. *American Imperialism: A Speculative Essay.* New York: Atheneum, 1968.

May, Ernest R. *Imperial Democracy.* New York: Harcourt, Brace & World, 1961.

May, Ernest R. *"Lessons" of the Past: The Use and Misuse of History in American Foreign Policy.* London: Oxford University Press, 1973.

May, Ernest R. *The Monroe Doctrine.* Cambridge, MA: Harvard University Press, 1975.

May, Ernest R. "The Nature of Foreign Policy: The Calculated versus the Axiomatic." *Daedalus* 91.4 (1992): 653–68.

May, Ernest R. *The Ultimate Decision.* New York: Braziller, 1960.

McCann, Frank D., Jr. *The Brazilian-American Alliance, 1937–1945.* Princeton, NJ: Princeton University Press, 1973.

McClintock, Cynthia. *Self-Management and Policy Participation in Peru, 1969–1975: The Corporatist Illusion.* London: Sage, 1977.

McEvoy, Carmen. *Guerreros civilizadores: Política, sociedad y cultura en Chile durante la Guerra del Pacífico.* Santiago: Ediciones Universidad Diego Portales, 2011.

McGann, Thomas F. *Argentina, the United States and the Inter-American System, 1880–1914.* Cambridge, MA: Harvard University Press, 1957.

McPherson, Alan. *Yankee No! Anti-Americanism in US–Latin American Relations.* Cambridge, MA: Harvard University Press, 2003.

Meacham, Carl. "Where Is Latin America in the Fight Against ISIL?" Center for Strategic and International Studies, October 21, 2014, http://csis.org/publication/where -latin-america-fight-against-isil (accessed January 9, 2015).

Mearsheimer, John. "The False Promise of International Institutions." *International Security*, 19.3 (1994/1995).

Mearsheimer, John. "Realists and Idealists." *Security Studies* 20.3 (2011).

Mearsheimer, John. "A Realist's Reply." *International Security* 20.1 (1995).

Mele, Nicco. *The End of Big.* New York: St. Martin's, 2013.

Mello, Fatima. "¿Hacia dónde van los BRICS?" *Nueva sociedad*, August 2014, http://nuso.org/articulo/hacia-donde-van-los-brics (accessed January 9, 2015).

Meseguer, Covadonga, and Abel Escriba-Folch. "Learning, Political Regimes and the Liberalization of Trade." *European Journal of Political Research* 50.6 (2011): 775–810.

Middlekauff, Robert. *Washington's Revolution: The Making of America's First Leader.* New York: Knopf, 2015.

Millington, Herbert. *American Diplomacy in the War of the Pacific.* New York: Columbia University Press, 1948.

Monaldi, Francisco J. "Politics Hampers Latin America's Exploitation of Its Untapped Oil Potential." *Geopolitical Information Service*, July 26, 2013, http://www.geopolitical-info.com/en/article/politics-hampers-latin-americas -exploitation-of-its-untapped-oil-potential (accessed January 9, 2015).

Moon, Parker T. *Imperialism and World Politics.* New York: Macmillan, 1926.

Moore, John Bassett. *Collected Papers of John Bassett Moore.* New Haven, CT: Yale University Press, 1944.

Moreno Quintana, L. M. *Política americana.* Buenos Aires: Menéndez, 1922.

Morison, Elting E. *Turmoil and Tradition.* Boston: Houghton Mifflin, 1960.

Morison, Elting E., ed. *The Letters of Theodore Roosevelt.* Cambridge, MA: Harvard University Press, 1951.

Morley, Samuel J., ed. *Poverty and Income Distribution in Latin America.* Washington, DC: World Bank, 1997.

Muhr, Thomas, ed. *Counter-Globalization and Socialism in the 21st Century*. London: Routledge, 2013.

Muñoz, Heraldo. "Cambio y continuidad en el debate sobre dependencia." *Estudios internacionales* 11.44 (1978): 88–138.

Muñoz, Heraldo. *The Dictator's Shadow: Life Under Augusto Pinochet*. New York: Basic Books, 2008.

Muñoz, Heraldo. "The OAS and Democratic Governance." *Journal of Democracy* 4.3 (1993).

Muñoz, Heraldo. "The Strategic Dependency of the Centers and the Economic Importance of the Latin American Periphery." *Latin American Research Review* 16.3 (1981): 3–29.

Muñoz, Heraldo, and Joseph S. Tulchin, eds. *Latin American Nations in World Politics*. Boulder, CO: Westview, 1984.

Munro, Dana G. *Intervention and Dollar Diplomacy in the Caribbean, 1900–1921*. Princeton, NJ: Princeton University Press, 1964.

Munro, Dana G. *The United States and the Caribbean Republics, 1921–1933*. Princeton, NJ: Princeton University Press, 1974.

Murilo de Carvalho, Jose. "Political Elites and State Building: The Case of Nineteenth Century Brazil." *Comparative Studies in Society and History* 24.3 (1982): 378–399.

Naím, Moisés. "El fin de poder." *El país*, July 29, 2012 (accessed January 9, 2015).

Naím, Moisés. *Illicit*. New York: Doubleday, 2005.

Naím, Moisés. "Una visita al futuro." *El país*, November 2, 2014, http://internacional.elpais.com/internacional/2014/11/01/actualidad/1414874393_202407.html (accessed January 9, 2015).

Naón, Rómulo S. "The European War and Pan Americanism." *Columbia University Quarterly*, 20 (1919).

Nau, Henry R. *The Myth of America's Decline*. New York: Oxford University Press, 1990.

Navia, Patricio D. "Vanishing US Influence in Latin America." *Buenos Aires Herald*, June 10, 2014, http://www.buenosairesherald.com/article/161679/vanishing-us-influence-in-latam (accessed January 9, 2015).

Nelson, Joan, and Robert R. Kaufman. *The Politics of Health Sector Reforms: Cross-National Comparisons*. Woodrow Wilson Center Update on the Americas: Creating Community 12. Washington, DC: WWICS, 2003.

Neustadt, Richard E., and Ernest R. May. *Thinking in Time: The Uses of History for Decision Makers*. New York: Free Press, 1986.

Nicholls, Daniel H. "Relational Structures: Counterhegemony and Material Power: A Network Approach to Hierarchy and US Power Projection in the Americas," Ph.D. dissertation. University of London, 2015.

Nocera, Joe. "A World without OPEC?" *New York Times*, October 21, 2014, A25.

North, Douglass, William Summerhill, and Barry R. Weingast. "Order, Disorder and Economic Change: Latin America versus North America." In Bruce Bueno de Mesquita and Hilton L. Root, eds., *Governing for Prosperity*. New Haven, CT: Yale University Press, 2000.

Nye, Joseph S., Jr. *Bound to Lead*. New York: Basic Books, 1990.

Nye, Joseph S., Jr. *Is the American Century Over?* Cambridge, MA: Polity Press, 2015.

Nye, Joseph S., Jr. *Soft Power: The Means to Success in World Politics*. New York: Public Affairs, 2004.

Nye, Joseph S., Jr. "Work with China, Don't Contain It." *New York Times*, January 26, 2013, A19.

Nye, Joseph S., Jr., and Robert O. Keohane, *World Politics in Transition*. New York: Little, Brown, 1977.

Obregón, Liliana. "Should There Be an American International Law?" In Rene Uruena, ed., *Derecho Internacional*. Bogotá: Universidad de los Andes, 2012.

O'Donnell, Guillermo. "Reflections on the Patterns of Change in the Bureaucratic-Authoritarian State." *Latin American Research Review* 12.1 (1978): 3–38.

Oelsner, Andrea, Rut Diamint, and Monica Herz. Workshop Reports 1 and 2, in New Security Configurations in a Strategic Emerging Region. Aberdeen, Scotland: University of Aberdeen, 2015. http://www.abdn.ac.uk/global-security/news/8347.

Olarte, Efraín Gonzales de. *El neoliberalismo a la Peruana*. Lima: Instituto de Estudio Peruanos, 1998.

Olarte, Efraín Gonzales de, ed. *Nuevos rumbos para el desarrollo del Perú y América Latina*. Lima: IEP, 1991.

O'Neil, Shannon. *Two Nations Indivisible: Mexico, The United States and the Road Ahead*. New York: Oxford, 2013.

Osnos, Evan. "In the Land of the Possible." *New Yorker*, December 22, 2014, p. 90.

Paige, Jeffrey. *Coffee and Power: Revolution and the Rise of Democracy in Central America*. Cambridge, MA: Harvard University Press, 1997.

Palmer, David Scott. *Peru: The Authoritarian Tradition*. New York: Praeger, 1980.

Patrick, Stewart, and Shepard Forman, eds. *Multilateralism and U. S. Foreign Policy*. Boulder, CO: Lynne Rienner, 2002.

Pellicer, Olga. "Lo que no se informa." *Proceso*, September 15, 2014, http://www .proceso.com.mx/?p=382136 (accessed January 9, 2015).

Peña, Felix. *Competitividad, democracia e integración en las Américas*. Rio de Janeiro: Getulio Vargas, 1992.

Pérez, Orlando J. *La agenda de seguridad en Centroamérica*. Woodrow Wilson Center Update on the Americas: Creating Community 20. Washington, DC: WWICS, 2006.

Pérez Alfonso, Juan Pablo. *Petróleo: Jugo de la tierra*. Caracas: Editorial Arte, 1961.

Perkins, Dexter. *The American Approach to Foreign Policy*. Cambridge, MA: Harvard University Press, 1952.

Perkins, Dexter. *Hands Off! A History of the Monroe Doctrine*. Cambridge, MA: Harvard University Press, 1927.

Perkins, Dexter. *A History of the Monroe Doctrine*. Boston: Little, Brown, 1963.

Pietri, Arturo Uslar. *De una a otra Veneuela*. Caracas: Monte Avila, 1949.

Pore, S. "What Is the Context?" *Review of International Studies* 29.2 (2003).

Portales, Carlos. "A dónde va el multilateralismo en las Américas? Proyectos superpuestos en un período de cambios globales." *Pensamiento propio* 39 (2014).

Porter, Roger B. "The Enterprise for the Americas Initiative: A New Approach to Economic Growth." *Journal of Interamerican Studies*, 32.4 (1990): 1–12.

Posner, Eric. *The Perils of Global Legalism*. Chicago: University of Chicago Press, 2009.

Prado, Eduardo. *A Ilusão Americana*. São Paulo: Brasiliense, 1958.

Prebisch, Raúl. *The Economic Development of Latin America and Its Principal Problems*. Lake Success, NY: United Nations Department of Economic Affairs, 1950.

Preston, Andrew. *Sword of the Spirit, Shield of Faith: Religion in American War and Diplomacy*. New York: Anchor, 2012.

Rabe, Stephen G. *Eisenhower and Latin America: The Foreign Policy of Anticommunism*. Chapel Hill: University of North Carolina Press, 1988.

Rabe, Stephen G. *The Most Dangerous Area in the World: John F. Kennedy Confronts the Communist Revolution in Latin America*. Chapel Hill: University of North Carolina Press, 1999.

Rapoport, Mario, and Neomi Brenta. *Las grandes crises del capitalismo contemporáneo*. Buenos Aires: Le Monde Diplomatique, 2012.

Recuant y Figueroa, Enrique. *The Neutrality of Chile*. Valparaiso: n.p., 1919.

Reform of the United Nations Security Council and the Role of Latin America. Woodrow Wilson Center Update on the Americas: Creating Community 21. Washington, DC: WWICS, 2006.

Reid, Michael. *Brazil: The Troubled Rise of a Global Power*. New Haven, CT: Yale University Press, 2004.

Reid, Michael. *Forgotten Continent: The Battle for Latin America's Soul*. New Haven, CT: Yale University Press, 2007.

Reuters. "US Attends Ebola Meeting in Cuba Called by Leftist Bloc." *New York Times*, October 29, 2014, http://in.reuters.com/article/2014/10/30/health-ebola-cuba-idINKBN0II2M920141030 (accessed January 9, 2015).

Riche, Martha F. "The American Institute for Free Labor Development." *Monthly Labor Review* 88.9 (1975).

Ricupero, Rubens. *Trans Atlantic Futures*. Washington, DC: n.p., 1992.

Riggirozzi, Pia, and Diana Tussie, eds. *The Rise of Post-Hegemonic Regionalism*. United Nations University Series on Regionalism 4. London and New York: Springer, 2012.

Rock, David, ed. *Latin America in the 1940s*. Berkeley: University of California Press, 1994.

Rodriguez Giavarini, Adalberto. "Oportunidad para América Latina." *Agenda internacional* 1.1 (2004): 67–69.

Rojas Aravena, Francisco. *Arms Control and Limitation in Latin America: An Elusive Goal*. Woodrow Wilson Center Update on the Americas: Creating Community 5. Washington, DC: WWICS, 2002.

Rojas Aravena, Francisco, ed. *Cooperación y seguridad internacional en las Américas*. Caracas: Nueva Sociedad, 1999.

Rojas Aravena, Francisco, and Luis Guillermo Solís. *¿Súbditos o aliados?* San José, Costa Rica: FLACSO, 1998.

Romero, Simon. "Emerging Nations Bloc to Open Development Bank." *New York Times*, July 16, 2014, A9.

Rose-Ackerman, Susan. *Rethinking the Progressive Agenda*. New York: Free Press, 1992.

Rosenberg, Emily S. *Spreading the American Dream*. New York: Hill, 1982.

Rosenberg, Jonathan. *How Far the Promised Land? World Affairs and the American Civil Rights Movement from the First World war to Vietnam*. Princeton, NJ: Princeton University Press, 2005.

Russell, Roberto, and Juan Gabriel Tokatlián. "From Antagonistic Autonomy to Relational Autonomy." *Latin American Politics and Society* 45.1 (2003): 1–41.

Sabato, Hilda. *The Many and the Few: Political Participation in Republican Buenos Aires*. Stanford, CA: Stanford University Press, 2001.

Sabato, Hilda. "On Political Citizenship in Nineteenth-Century Latin America." *American Historical Review* 106.4 (2001): 1290–1315.

Sabato, Hilda, ed. *Ciudadanía política y formación de las naciones*. Mexico: Fondo de Cultura Económica, 2002.

Saguier, Marcelo. "Minería para el desarrollo integral en la estrategia de UNASUR." *Revista conjuntura austral* 5.21–22 (2013–2014): 39–65.

Saguier, Marcelo. "Regional Policy Framework of Social Solidarity Economy in South America." Occasional Paper Series no. 6. Geneva: UNRISD, 2014.

Saguier, Marcelo, and Diana Tussie. "Emerging trade politics: The continuous pendulum from multilateralism to asymmetric trade negotiations." *Estudios internacionales* 2.1 (2014): 9–26.

Salisbury, Richard V. *Anti-Imperialism and International Competition in Central America, 1920–1929.* Wilmington, DE: Scholarly Resources, 1989.

Sanchez, Luis E., and Peter Croal. "Environmental Impact Assessment, from Rio-92 to Rio+20 and Beyond." *Ambiente y sociedade* 15.3 (2012): 19–39.

Sarmiento, Domingo F., *Facundo: Civilization and Barbarism.* Berkeley: University of California Press, 2003.

Scheman, L. Ronald, ed. *The Alliance for Progress: A Retrospective.* New York, Westport, and London: Praeger, 1988.

Schenoni, Luis L. "Brasil en América del Sur." *Nueva sociedad* 250 (2014): 138–149.

Schenoni, Luis L. "The Brazilian Rise and the Elusive South American Balance." GIGA Working Paper no. 269, March 2015.

Schlesinger, Stephen, and Stephen Kinzer. *Bitter Fruit.* New York: Doubleday, 1982.

Schoultz, Lars. *Beneath the United States: A History of US Policy Towards Latin America.* Cambridge, MA: Harvard University Press, 1998.

Schoultz, Lars. *Human Rights and United States Policy Towards Latin America.* Princeton, NJ: Princeton University Press, 1981.

Schoultz, Lars. "Latin America in the United States." In Eric Hershberg and Fred Rosen, eds., *Latin America After Neo-Liberalism: Turning the Tide in the 21st Century.* New York: Norton, 2006.

Schoultz, Lars. *National Security and United States Policy toward Latin America.* Princeton, NJ: Princeton University Press, 1987.

Schuler, Friedrich. *Mexico between Hitler and Roosevelt.* Albuquerque: University of New Mexico Press, 1998.

La seguridad hemisférica: Perspectivos y realidades. Woodrow Wilson Center Update on the Americas: Creating Community 22. Washington, DC: WWICS, 2006.

Selee, Andrew. "¿Una estrategia hacia Centroamérica?" *El universal,* July 19, 2014, http://www.eluniversalmas.com.mx/editoriales/2014/07/71405.php (accessed January 9, 2015).

Sennes, Ricardo. *As mudanças da política externa brasileira nos anos 80.* Porto Alegre: UFRG, 2003.

Sennes, Ricardo, ed. *Brasil e a política internacional.* São Paulo: IDESP, 1999.

Serbin, Andrés, Laneydi Martínez, and Haroldo Ramanzini Júnior, eds. *El regionalism "post-liberal" en America Latina y el Caribe: Nuevos actores, nuevos temas, nuevos desafíos.* Buenos Aires: CRIES, 2012.

Serra, Narcís. *Controlling the Armed Forces in Democratic Transitions: Cases from Latin America.* Woodrow Wilson Center Update on the Americas: Creating Community 10. Washington, DC: WWICS, 2002.

Shafer, Robert J. *The Economic Societies in the Spanish World, 1763–1825.* Syracuse, NY: Syracuse University Press, 1956.

Sherrill, Charles Hitchcock. *Modernizing the Monroe Doctrine.* Boston: Houghton Mifflin, 1916.

Shurbutt, T. Ray, ed. *United States–Latin American Relations, 1800-1850.* Tuscaloosa: University of Alabama Press, 1991.

Sigmund, Paul. *The United States and Democracy in Chile.* New York: Twentieth Century Fund, 1993.

Sikkink, Kathryn A. *The Justice Cascade: How Human Rights Prosecutions Are Changing World Politics.* New York: Norton, 2011.

Singer, Hans. "The Distribution of Gains between Investing and Borrowing Countries." *American Economic Review, Papers and Proceedings* 40.2 (1950): 473–485.

Slaughter, Anne-Marie. "Don't Fight in Iraq and Ignore Syria." *New York Times,* June 18, 2014, A25.

Slaughter, Anne-Marie. "Fiddling While Libya Burns." *New York Times,* March 14, 2011, A21.

Slaughter, Anne-Marie. "International Law and International Relations Theory: A Dual Agenda." *American Journal of International Law*, 87.205 (1993).

Slaughter, Anne-Marie. *A New World Order*. Princeton, NJ: Princeton University Press, 2004.

Slaughter, Anne-Marie. "The Real New World Order." *Foreign Affairs* 76.5 (1997): 183–197.

Smith, Gordon, and Moisés Naím. *Altered States*. Ottawa: IDRC, 2000.

Smith, James Morton, ed., *The Republic of Letters. The Correspondence between Thomas Jefferson and James Madison*. 3 vols New York: Norton, 1995

Smith, Peter H. *Talons of the Eagle*. New York: Oxford University Press, 1996.

Solari Yrigoyen, Hipólito. *La dignidad humana*. Buenos Aires: EUDEBA, 1998.

Solís, Luis Guillermo. "Versión completa de la entrevista de RT al presdente electo de Costa Rica Luis Guillermo Solís." *RT en Español—Noticias internacionales*, April 8, 2014, http://actualidad.rt.com/actualidad/view/124649-entrevista-rt-presidente-costa-rica-luis-guillermo-solis (accessed January 9, 2015).

Sotomayor, Arturo. *The Myth of the Democratic Peacekeeper: Civil-Military Relations and the United Nations*. Baltimore, MD: Johns Hopkins University Press, 2014.

Spalding, Hobart A., Jr. *Organized Labor in Latin America*. New York: Harper, 1979.

Spenser, Daniela. "Forjando una nación posrevolucionaria." In Jorge Schiavon, Daniela Spenser, and Mario Vasquez Olivera, eds., *En busca de una nación soberana*. Mexico: CIDE, 2006.

Stanley, William. *Enabling Peace in Guatemala: The Story of MINUSTAH*. Boulder, CO: Lynne Rienner Publishers, 2013.

Stepan, Alfred C. *The Military in Politics: Changing Patterns in Brazil*. Princeton, NJ: Princeton University Press, 1971.

Stepan, Alfred C. *The State and Society: Peru in Comparative Perspective*. Princeton, NJ: Princeton University Press, 1978.

Stiglitz, Joseph E. *Globalization and Its Discontents*. New York: Norton, 2002.

Tavares, Rodrigo. *Security in South America: The Roles of States and Regional Organizations*. Boulder, CO: Lynne Rienner, 2013.

Thomas, Daniel C. "Boomerangs and Superpowers: International Norms, Transnational Networks and US Foreign Policy." *Cambridge Review of International Affairs* 15.1 (2002): 25–44.

Thorp, Rosemary. *Latin America in the 1930s: The Role of the Periphery in World Crisis*. London: St. Martin's, 1984.

Thurow, Lester. *Head to Head: The Coming Economic Battle among Japan, Europe, and America*. New York: William Morrow, 1992.

Tokatlián, Juan Gabriel, "Latinoamerica y el complejo integracionista: Un concepto a debate." *Desarrollo económico* 51.204 (2012).

Tokatlián, Juan Gabriel, and Leonardo Carvajal. "Autonomía y política exterior en América Latina: Un debate abierto, un futuro incierto." *Revista CIDOB d'afers internacionals* 28 (1995): 7–31.

Tokatlián, Juan Gabriel, and Roberto Russell. "From Antagonistic Autonomy to Relational Autonomy: A Theoretical Reflection from the Southern Cone." *Latin American Politics and Society* 45.1 (2003): 1–24.

Tramerye, Pierre de la. *The World Struggle for Oil*. New York: Knopf, 1924.

Trask, David F. *The War with Spain in 1898*. New York: Macmillan, 1981.

Tussie, Diana, with Sanoussi Bilal and Philippe de Lambaerle. *Asymmetric Commercial Negotiations*. London: Ashgate, 2011.

Tulchin, Joseph S. *The Aftermath of War*. New York: New York University Press, 1971.

Tulchin, Joseph S. *Argentina and the United States: A Conflicted Relationship*. Boston: Twayne, 1990.

Tulchin, Joseph S. "The Argentine Proposal for Non Belligerency, April 1940." *Journal of Interamerican Studies* 11.4 (1969): 671–704.

Tulchin, Joseph S. "Decolonizing an Informal Empire: Argentina, Great Britain and the United States, 1930–1943." *International Interactions* 1.3 (1974): 123–140.

Tulchin, Joseph S. "Edward Atkinson, the Reformer Who Would Not Succeed." *Essex Institute Historical Collections* 110.2 (1969): 1–21.

Tulchin, Joseph S. "The Malvinas War of 1982." *Latin American Research Review* 22.3 (1987): 123–41.

Tulchin, Joseph S. "New Peru-Chile Maritime Boundary Ends Century-Old Dispute." *Geopolitical Information Service*, February 12, 2014.

Tulchin, Joseph S. "The United States and Latin America in the 1960s." *Journal of Interamerican Studies* 30.1 (1988): 1–36.

Tulchin, Joseph S., Raúl Benítez Manaut, and Rut Diamint, eds. *El rompecabezas.* Buenos Aires: Prometeo, 2006.

Tulchin, Joseph S., and Gary Bland. *Getting Globalization Right.* Boulder, CO: Lynne Rienner, 2005.

Tulchin, Joseph S., and Ralph Espach, eds. *America Latina en el nuevo sistema internacional.* Barcelona: Bellaterra, 2004.

Tulchin, Joseph S., and Rafael Hernández, eds. *Cuba and the United States: Will the Cold War in the Caribbean End?* Boulder, CO: Lynne Rienner, 1991.

Tulchin, Joseph S., Jesús M. Rodés, and Salvador Martí Puig. *Hemispheric Collective Security in the Post–Cold War Era: Policy and Practice in Latin America.* Woodrow Wilson Center Update on the Americas: Creating Community 7. Washington, DC: WWICS, 2002.

Tulchin, Joseph S., and Francisco Rojas Aravena, eds., with Ralph Espach. *Strategic Balance and Confidence Building Measures in the Americas.* Stanford, CA: Stanford University Press, 1998.

Tulchin, Joseph S., Andrés Serbin, and Rafael Hernández, eds. *Cuba and the Caribbean.* Wilmington, DE: Scholarly Resources, 1997.

Turner, Mark, and Andres Guerrero, eds. *After Spanish Rule: Post Colonial Predicaments of the Americas.* Durham, NC: Duke University Press, 2004.

US Department of State. *US Statement on Support for Democracy in Chile.* Washington, DC: US Department of State, 1987.

Vaky, Viron P., and Heraldo Muñoz. *The Future of the Organization of American States.* New York: Twentieth Century Fund, 1993.

Van Young, Eric. *The Other Rebellion: Popular Violence and Ideology in Mexico, 1810–1821.* Stanford, CA: Stanford University Press, 2001.

Varas, Augusto, ed. *Hacia el Siglo XXI: La proyección estratégica de Chile.* Santiago: FLACSO, 1989.

Vasconcelos, José. *La raza cósmica.* Mexico: Espasa Calpe, 1925.

Veeser, Cyrus. *A World Safe for Capitalism: Dollar Diplomacy and America's Rise to Power.* New York: Columbia University Press, 2002.

Velasco, Jesús. *Neoconservatives in U.S. Foreign Policy under Ronald Reagan and George W. Bush.* Washington, DC: Wodrow Wilson Center Press, 2010.

Viñas, David. *De Sarmiento a Dios: Viajeros argentinos a los Estados Unidos.* Buenos Aires: Sudamericana, 1998.

Wagner, R. Harrison. *United States Policy toward Latin America.* Stanford, CA: Stanford University Press, 1970.

Walker, Vanessa, "At the End of Influence: The Letelier Assassination, Human Rights, and Rethinking Intervention in US–Latin American Relations." *Journal of Contemporary History* 46.1 (2011).

Walker, Vanessa, "Ambivalent Allies: Advocates, Diplomats, and the Struggle for an 'American' Human Rights Policy," Ph.D. dissertation, University of Wisconsin, 2011.

Walter, Knut. *The Regime of Anastasio Somoza.* Chapel Hill: University of North Carolina Press, 1993.

Walworth, Arthur. *Woodrow Wilson: American Prophet.* 2 vols. New York: Longmans, 1958.

Weiffen, Brigitte, Leslie Wehner, and Detlef Nolte. "Overlapping Security Institutions in South America: The Case of UNASUR and OAS." *International Area Studies Review* 16.4 (2013): 370–389.

Weintraub, Sidney. "The New US Economic Initiative toward Latin America." *Journal of Interamerican Studies* 33.1 (1991): 1–18.

Weisbrot, Mark. "Hard Choices: Hillary Clinton Admits Role in Honduras Coup Aftermath." *Al Jazeera America*, September 29, 2014, http://america .aljazeera.com/opinions/2014/9/hillary-clinton-honduraslatinamericaforeignpolicy.html (accessed January 9, 2015).

Weld, Kirsten. *Paper Cadavers: The Archives of Dictatorship in Guatemala.* Durham, NC: Duke University Press, 2014.

Welles, Sumner. *The Time for Decision.* New York: Harper, 1944.

Wells, Allen. *Tropical Zion.* Durham, NC: Duke University Press, 2009.

Wergin, Clemens. "Is Obama's Foreign Policy Too European?" *New York Times*, July 9, 2014, http://www.nytimes.com/2014/07/09/opinion/clemens-wergin-is -obamas-foreign-policy-too-european.html (accessed January 9, 2015).

Whitaker, Arthur P. *The Western Hemisphere Idea.* Ithaca, NY: Cornell University Press, 1954.

Williams, Mark Eric. *Understanding US-Latin American Relations.* New York: Routledge, 2012.

Williams, W. A. "Brooks Adams and American Expansion." *New England Quarterly*, 25 (1952): 225–228.

Williamson, John. "What Washington Means by Policy Reform." In John Williamson, ed., *Latin American Adjustment: How Much Has Happened?* Washington, DC: Institute for International Economics, 1990.

Wirth, John D. *The Politics of Brazilian Development, 1930–1954.* Stanford, CA: Stanford University Press, 1970.

Wolfsonian Foundation of Decorative and Propaganda Arts, ed. *The Journal of Decorative and Propaganda Arts* 18 (1992).

Wood, Bryce. *The Dismantling of the Good Neighbor Policy.* Austin: University of Texas Press, 1985.

Wood, Bryce. *The Making of the Good Neighbor Policy.* New York: Columbia University Press, 1961.

Wood, Bryce. *The United States and Latin American Wars, 1932–1943.* New York: Columbia University Press, 1966.

Wood, James A. *The Society of Equality: Popular Republicanism and Democracy in Santiago de Chile, 1818–1851.* Albuquerque: University of New Mexico Press, 2011.

Working Group on Development and the Environment in the Americas. *Foreign Investment and Sustainable Development: Lessons from the Americas.* Boston: GDAE, 2009.

Zeballos, Estanislao. *Las conferencias en Williamstown.* Buenos Aires: Talleres Gráficos de la Penitenciaría Nacional, 1927.

Zeballos, Estanislao. "Theodore Roosevelt y la política internacional americana." *Revista de derecho, historia y letras*, December 1913.

Zimmermann, Eduardo. "Translations of the 'American Model' in Nineteenth Century Argentina: Constitutional Culture as a Global Legal Entanglement." In Thomas Duve, ed., *Entanglements in Legal History: Conceptual Approaches to Legal History*. Frankfurt: Max Planck Institute, 2014.

Zook, David H. *The Conduct of the Chaco War.* New York: Bookman, 1960.

Index

Abrams, Elliott, 95

Academic community facilitating communication on the policy process, 10–11

Accountability in the policy process, 9–11, 161–162

Administrative reforms, 21

Afghanistan, US intervention in, 159, 166–167

African Americans, civil rights of, 25

Afro-Caribbean population: Costa Rica, 92

Agency, exercise of: as anti-bullying measure, 8–9; Argentina's period of growth, 42; Caribbean Basin and US hegemony, 58–59; Chile leveraging soft power, 143–145; Costa Rica's foreign policy, 91–92; Cuba, 190–191; democratic transition heightening the accessibility of, 9–14; early expressions of, 7–8, 33; existence of power in all nations, 6–7; global trade regime, 149; lack of democratic governance as obstacle to, 180; Mexico's increasing agency in global affairs, 178–180; obstacles to, 181–182; partial or perverted agency, 11–12; peacekeeeping missions, 146–147; post-Cold War agency in Latin America, 101–102, 112–113, 128–129; post-Cold War

global system, 138; post-independence lack of agency, 25–26; regionalism enhancing, 169–174; slow development of, 143; US relations and, 183–184

Aguilar Zinser, Adolfo, 140–141, 147, 155(n4)

Albany Plan, 22

Alberdi, Juan Bautista, 35–36

Alfonsín, Raúl, 95, 98–99, 104–105(n33), 123

Alianza Bolivariana para los Pueblos de Nuestra América (ALBA), 12, 14, 139–140, 149, 170–171, 188

Allende, Salvador, 90

Alliance for Progress, 86, 113–114

Allied Powers, 71–75, 93

Allison, Graham T., 16(n9)

Almagro Lemes, Luis, 183

Alvear, Marcelo T. de, 63

Amaral, Sergio, 115

American Popular Revolutionary Alliance (APRA), 64–65

Americanistas, 37–38

Amorim, Celso, 195(n40), 196(n42)

Amphictyonic Congress of Panama, 25, 27

Andean Pact, 117

Anderson, Chandler P., 57–58

Andrade, Oswald de, 65

Anti-Americanism: Bolívar's union of

About the Book

In recent years, the countries of Latin America have moved out from under the shadow of the United States to become active players in the international system. What changed? Why? And why did it take so long for that change to happen? To answer those questions, Joseph S. Tulchin explores the evolving role of Latin American states in world affairs from the early days of independence to the present.

Joseph S. Tulchin is former director of the Latin American Program at the Woodrow Wilson International Center for Scholars.